John Bailey is an Australian author with seven books to his credit. Bailey's approach to writing has been to create a strong narrative against the background of an exotic or remote location.

His first book, *The Wire Classroom* (1969), described colonial life in New Guinea. His second, *The Moon Baby* (1972), was set in the future in an unnamed metropolis. His third, *The White Divers of Broome* (2001), concerned pearl shell diving in the coastal town of Broome in the north of Western Australia. *The Lost German Slave Girl* (2003) related the true story of a slave woman in Louisiana who claimed to be a German immigrant who had been illegally taken into bondage when she was a child. *Mr Stuart's Track* (2006) revealed the forgotten life of John McDouall Stuart, the first explorer to cross Australia from coast to coast. *Into the Unknown* (2011), a biography of the explorer Ludwig Leichhardt, was released in October 2011.

Both *The Wire Classroom* and *The Moon Baby* were published 40 years ago. Although obtaining critical acclaim, they were not a commercial success and Bailey – then married with children – decided that it was time he earned some money. Over the next twenty-five years, Bailey enjoyed a varied career, as a public servant in New Guinea, a teacher in England and a barrister in Melbourne. During this time, although he did not write, he retained the hope that some day he would eventually follow his dream to become a fulltime writer. Finally in the year 1999 he took the plunge. He threw in the law and moved a thousand kilometres north to a small town close to the Queensland border in sub-tropical New South Wales where he lives with his wife Annie.

His risky decision to change careers at the age of fifty-five paid off. His books have been well received by the critics and the public alike. They have won, or been short-listed for, literary prizes and have been optioned for movies.

In 2003 he was awarded the Centenary Medal by the Australian Government for services to literature. John Bailey's writing has been described as 'a blend of Steinbeck, Hemingway.'

Also by John Bailey

Jefferson's Second Father

John Bailey

mom**entum**

This edition published in 2013 by Momentum
Pan Macmillan Australia Pty Ltd
1 Market Street, Sydney 2000

A CIP record for this book is available at the National Library of Australia

Jefferson's Second Father

EPUB format: 9781743342145
Mobi format: 9781743342152
Print on Demand format: 9781743342169

Cover design by XOU Creative
Edited by Sybil Nolan
Proofread by Thomasin Litchfield

Macmillan Digital Australia: www.macmillandigital.com.au

To report a typographical error, please visit momentumbooks.com.au/contact/

Visit www.momentumbooks.com.au to read more about all our books and to buy books online. You will also find features, author interviews and news of any author events.

Contents

Prologue   9

1 The Young Wythe   1

2 Williamsburg   15

3 Colonel Washington   27

4 The Young Jefferson   37

5 Revolution in the Air   47

6 Death and Taxes   63

7 Uncertain Times   79

8 Fasting, Humiliation and Prayer   93

9 Mr. Wythe Goes to Congress   111

10 Independence for Virginia   127

11 Reformers and Revisors   137

12 "Hither You Shall Go, But No Further!"   153

13 Yorktown   165

14 Constitution   181

15 Ratification   199

16 The House on Shockoe Hill   213

17 Slavery   229

18 His Last Great Case   241

19 Murder!   251

Contents

20 A Trial and an Appeal   265

Epilogue   279

Postscript   281

Notes on Sources   287

Select References   303

Index   311

Acknowledgments   285

He was my ancient master, my earliest and best friend; and to him I am indebted for first impressions which have had the most salutary influence on the course of my life.

Thomas Jefferson on George Wythe, 1806

Prologue

Early in June 1806, Major William DuVal wrote to the President of the United States, conveying the dreadful news that DuVal's neighbor, Chancellor George Wythe, had been poisoned by a member of his own household. DuVal went on to say that three of Richmond's most eminent doctors "pronounce his death to be certain in a day or two."

The president, Thomas Jefferson, deeply shocked, replied that "such an instance of depravity had been hitherto known to us only in the fables of the poets":

> I had reserved with fondness, for the day of my retirement, the hope of inducing him to pass much of his time with me. It would have been a great pleasure to recollect with him first opinions on the new state of things which arose so soon after my acquaintance with him; to pass in review the long period which has elapsed since that time, and to see how far those opinions had been affected by experience and reflection, or confirmed and acted on with self-approbation. But this may yet be the enjoyment of another state of being.

George Wythe had been Thomas Jefferson's teacher of law, his mentor and his friend. He had also been his colleague and close collaborator in the great events leading to American's independence and formation as a nation. An early though reluctant revolutionary, Wythe spent almost a year in debate at the Second Continental Congress in Philadelphia from 1775 to 1776. In 1787, he attended the convention in Philadelphia that hammered out the U.S. Constitution. The following year at the Virginia Ratifying Convention, Wythe, Edmund Pendleton and James Madison carried the day amid bitter debate, against anti-federalists Patrick Henry, James Monroe and George Mason.

Distinguished though this record was, Wythe made perhaps his most lasting contribution to the United States of America through his devotion to the education and mentoring of students of talent. He took into his home many private students, including William Cabell and Littleton Waller Tazewell, each of whom became governor of Virginia, and William Munford, distinguished lawyer and author. Jefferson had been his brightest star. From the age of nineteen, the future president spent five years reading law in Wythe's legal practice. Jefferson's father had died early, and in George Wythe he found someone to guide him to maturity. In his autobiography, Jefferson recalled that Wythe was "my faithful and beloved mentor in youth, and my most affectionate friend through life." More intimately, he once described Wythe as "my second father."

This is the story of the life and strange death of Wythe, a man determined, steadfast and courageous, yet described by another founding father, Benjamin Rush, as possessing "dove-like simplicity and gentleness of manner." As Jefferson put it: "His virtue was the purest tint; his integrity inflexible, and his justice exact."

1

The Young Wythe

Wythe's forebears—death of father—his mother and the mighty-willed George Keith—a homely picture of Wythe's tuition—a boy learns about slavery—legal studies—the young lawyer—the circuit in rural Virginia—the associate marries the master's daughter—an early death

When called upon to write a short biography of George Wythe in 1820, Thomas Jefferson noted that his friend was born in either 1727 or 1728, although conceding that he might be mistaken by a year or two. He was mistaken—it is more likely Wythe was born in 1726. This is because a will Wythe wrote in April 1803 indicates he was then aged seventy-six. The inhabitants of the house in which he was born, on the banks of Brick Kiln Creek on the northwest arm of the Back River, Virginia, were solid God-fearing folk who never made a fuss about birthdays, and nor did he. His forebears were of English–Scottish descent, planters of the middling sort, and, through three generations, justices of Elizabeth City County.

When the English arrived in Virginia in 1607 in the quest for gold or a river passage to a southern sea, they found instead the tobacco weed—and proved that it was possible to build an empire on smoke. George's great-grandfather Thomas Wythe took up land adjacent to the Back River some time before 1680. If he had gone farther inland to farm the rich black soil along the James River, his descendants might have been as rich as the Byrds, the Randolphs or the Carters.

Instead, the Wythes remained in Elizabeth City, where no one was wealthy enough to be called an aristocrat. Their plantation, Chesterville, lay inland from the salt marshes, barely above sea level, beside an anxious creek whipped by tides and floods, and when the wind blew from the north one could smell the salt turning the soil sour. The tobacco the Wythes grew was never of first-rate quality, but through hard work and perseverance Thomas made a go of it.

In 1680, the first Thomas Wythe became a member of the House of Burgesses, Virginia's first elected assembly, which sat in nearby Williamsburg. For his legislative duties he was paid two hundred pounds of tobacco, the commodity money of colonial Virginia. In the absence of a coherent system of coinage, tobacco leaf became negotiable as cash and coin. From the early 1700s, traders issued tobacco certificates with a value backed by warehouse inventories. Soon it became customary for taxes, bills of exchange, creditors and public officials to be paid either in certificates or in the leaf itself.

Despite the generosity of the burgess's stipend, it seems that Thomas Wythe was not taken with being a legislator, for he served one session and did not offer himself for reelection. Rich in respectability, if not wealth, when he died in 1693 or 1694, he left a house and an estate that included nine slaves, four hogsheads of tobacco, six silver spoons, sundry farm animals and two tracts of land.

Thomas Wythe II, who as eldest son inherited all, achieved much during his short life. At the age of nineteen he was appointed a local justice, and soon after married widow Ann Gutherick, the wealthy daughter of a prominent gentry family. The couple produced two children before Thomas died in 1694, aged twenty-four.

The next Thomas, the father of George Wythe of this book, inherited the frugally acquired Wythe fortune, and followed the family path of public service. He was the local magistrate, a vestryman of Saint John's Church in Hampton, briefly county sheriff, and a member of the House of Burgesses in 1718 and again from 1723 to 1726. Industrious as a tobacco farmer, and a shrewd investor, he bought a wharf on Hampton's busy port.

In 1719, he married Margaret Walker, the daughter of George Walker, a man who owned another Hampton wharf and commanded the battery on Old Point Comfort that overlooked the entrance to Hampton Roads. Margaret's grandfather was the celebrated preacher George Keith, a strong-willed Scot who during a turbulent life managed to antagonize Quakers and Anglicans on both sides of the Atlantic.

After being imprisoned many times in both Scotland and England for his Quaker beliefs, Keith had fled to America where, from the late 1680s, he tub-thumped his way through the middle colonies in the Quaker cause, denouncing slavery even before his own religion had officially condemned it. Always a querulous, contrary personality, he became embroiled in a doctrinal dispute with the elders in Pennsylvania. Disowned by the Quakers in 1692, he returned to England, where he eventually joined his old persecutors by being ordained in the established church.

To the astonishment and dismay of American Quakers, he re-emerged on their shores as an unbearable zealot and pamphleteer for the Society for the Propagation of the Gospel in Foreign Parts. Intent on denouncing the errors of Quaker mysticism, he traveled widely through the colonies. Keith's change of religion split his family. His daughter, Anne, had by then married George Walker, a Quaker, yet she adopted her father's Anglicanism. In 1703, Keith visited this family divided by religion and noted in his journal that his daughter "is fully come off from the Quakers, and is a zealous member of the Church of England, and brings up her children . . . in the Christian Religion, praised be God for it."

He left satisfied that he had set the family on the path to the true religion, but that was not to be. Soon after, George Walker forbade his wife to attend the Church of England. Dissent was in the Keith blood, for Anne did not accept his ruling. In an act which became the talk of Williamsburg, she presented two separate petitions to the Governor's Council complaining that her husband had "violently restrained" her and her children from attending the local Church of England.

Such a public challenge to her husband's authority was unprecedented, and it was with great reluctance that the council granted her a hearing. In judgment, husband and wife were each handed a small victory. George Walker was ordered not to interfere with his wife's free exercise of religion, but the council supported his right to bring up his children (who included George Wythe's mother, Margaret) in the religion of his choosing. By all accounts, the couple reconciled, and became a tolerably harmonious family of mixed faiths. Anne continued to attend the Church of England, and her husband hosted Quaker meetings in the family home.

*

George Wythe had no opportunity to know his father, for he died in 1729 when George was just three. Margaret Wythe was left a widow with three children to raise alone and a plantation to manage. Supervising a workforce of slaves cannot have been easy for a woman, yet she was a Keith. It seems she was also well read, for George Keith had been a firm believer in the education of women and insisted on instruction for his daughters and granddaughters. The English clergyman and writer, Andrew Burnaby, who visited Virginia in 1759–60, reported that Wythe's "perfect knowledge of the Greek language [was] taught him by his mother in the backwoods."

Thomas Jefferson confirmed the story: "He had not the benefit of a regular education in the schools, but acquired a good one of himself, and without assistance; insomuch, as to become the best Latin and Greek scholar in the State. It is said, that while reading the Greek Testament, his mother held an English one, to aid him in rendering the Greek text conformably with that."

Some historians, skeptical of this tale of unschooled genius, suggest that Wythe was educated at the grammar school at Williamsburg's William and Mary College, or the Eaton-Symmes Free School in Hampton, but no records exist to confirm his attendance at either. Thus it is permissible for us to imagine the homely picture of the widow Wythe sitting with her son at the kitchen table on an isolated, windswept farm in the New World, holding a Homerica before them as they joined heads to read tales of long-past adventures in a bounded sea far, far away.

Under the English law of primogeniture which applied in colonial Virginia, the first-born male child inherited his father's land as a matter of right. All of the Wythe family understood that the eldest male, Thomas the Fourth, would inherit Chesterville upon obtaining his majority, while the younger siblings, George and Anne, would inherit nothing—and their widowed mother's interest would be limited to dower rights of residence during her lifetime. George Wythe would need his education. As for sister Anne, her prospects, even more limited, were confined to marrying well.

*

George Wythe's childhood was intimately enmeshed with the institution of slavery. A tobacco plantation required slaves, just as it needed horses and carts. For a native American weed, tobacco required a lot of rearing, and the hands to do it—not skilled hands, but many. The planters of Virginia could not imagine how commercial quantities of tobacco could be grown without slaves.

Plantation life meant labor for every waking hour the heavens gave. Tobacco seed had to be planted in its own mound of soil, the weeds hoed out all summer, and caterpillars picked off the crop daily. When leafy green, it had to be pruned, plucked, tied into bunches, and slow cured in barns. Once dry, the leaf was cut and folded into hogsheads that were rolled to the wharf to await shipment to market. In his *Notes on the State of Virginia,* Jefferson told the world that growing tobacco was "a culture productive of infinite wretchedness":

> Those employed in it are in a continued state of exertion beyond the powers of nature to support. Little food of any kind is raised by them; so that the men and animals on these farms are badly fed, and the earth is rapidly impoverished.

Records indicate that in the 1690s two indentured servants and nine slaves worked Chesterville, so it is unlikely that Margaret Wythe could have done with fewer slaves, and possibly she possessed many more, as by 1767, Chesterville was home to thirty-two slaves. In such an environment young George Wythe would have learned, without being taught, that racial distinction was integral to slavery: that black men and women did not come into the house unless asked, that they deferred to white people, did not attend school, wore cast-offs and coarse woolens, ate different food, and lived in the slave quarters, one-room huts ganged in a line.

Although Wythe and his brother and sister, when small, probably played with the black children of Chesterville, they soon understood that their playmates were born to serve. None of this was questioned in Elizabeth City County, Virginia: African women worked in the laundry and the kitchen, their daughters and sons worked in the fields and their babies played under the sun.

*

To a landless youth adrift in colonial Virginia with little wealth and few connections, three paths to a more prosperous future were open: to take orders in the Church of England, to woo an aristocrat's daughter, or to become a lawyer. For George Wythe, his family's complex religious background made the first unlikely, as did his own questioning mind; while being small, young and painfully shy made him unqualified for courtship. So, around 1743, at the age of sixteen or seventeen, this boy of cloistered education began legal studies.

At that time there was not a single law school in America. The wealthy studied at the English Inns of Court, while the impecunious sought a clerkship with an established attorney, or studied alone. One suspects that none but a relation would take on such an unpromising law clerk as George Wythe: his offer of employment came from Stephen Dewey, an attorney who was married to his mother's sister and who had a thriving practice in Prince George County, upriver from Williamsburg.

He was a justice of the peace, a county representative in the House of Burgesses and king's attorney for nearby Charles City County. Wythe would later claim that he was treated badly by his uncle and learned very little from him: Dewey was rarely in the office and neglected his instruction. Wythe, as an underling's underling to Dewey's law clerks, spent most of his day on a high stool, copying in flowing hand wills, writs, deeds, pleas and affidavits. Whenever there was a quiet moment—which was not often—he was able to take a book from the shelves of his master's library, such as it was.

Dewey, like most colonial lawyers, probably owned few texts. Local legal scholarship barely existed, for English common law reigned supreme, and Sir William Blackstone had yet to write his famous *Commentaries on the Laws of England*. A rural lawyer in America probably had a well-thumbed copy of the *Institutes of the Laws of England*, by an earlier English judge, Sir Edward Coke; also, Bacon's *Abridgement*, Pigott's *New Precedents in Conveyancing*, and perhaps Francis's *Maxims of Equity*. Occasionally, Wythe was allowed to climb down from his stool to attend the local courts, where he could not fail to observe that the judgments dispensed by Virginia's rural magistrates bore little resemblance to the majesty of English law he had read about. On the other hand, perhaps he learned volumes about the cupidity of people, the complexity of human nature, and that law and justice were not the same thing.

After several years of clerking with neglectful Uncle Stephen, Wythe left Prince George County and returned to Chesterville. About this time his mother died. This was in 1745 or 1746. The cause and manner of her death is unknown, and it may be that he returned to his childhood home to be with her during her last days.

Upon the death of the widow Wythe, all dower rights were extinguished and George's brother became the absolute master of the family plantation. Chastened by this experience, it is no wonder George Wythe regarded primogeniture as a perverse system. When the American Revolution finally gave him the opportunity to rid Virginia of what he regarded as archaic English laws, he would work to have primogeniture abolished.

He was now a young man of almost twenty, with little to hold him at Chesterville. His sister Anne was no longer living at home, having made a tolerably advantageous match in marrying Charles Sweney from a Tidewater family at Sewall's Point. During his return to Chesterville, George must have spent some hours with his law books, because by early 1746 he was ready to qualify as a lawyer.

To do so he had to satisfy three prominent lawyers that he was competent in the law, and obtain from them a certificate of "probity, honesty, and good demeanor." One of those vouching for him was Stephen Dewey. Wythe submitted the signed documents to the General Court in Williamsburg, along with his fee of twenty shillings. He may also have been required to attend for an oral examination before a board appointed by the General Court.

On February 13, 1746, he was admitted to practice in the Caroline County Court. In a ceremony of oaths, he had to subscribe to the Test[1] designed to exclude Catholics from office, and swear that he had taken communion in the Church of England. He also had to swear his allegiance to George II, and—finally—that he would "truly and honestly demean myself, in the practice of an attorney, according to the best of my knowledge and ability." Thus both cleansed and burdened, George Wythe became an attorney, bristling with the confidence and naivety of youth.

Being a lawyer in the colonial period was not necessarily a prestigious or remunerative calling. Virginia was largely an agrarian society and many a planter held that a man should speak for himself, and that those who made a profession of speaking for others were slippery and officious characters who used artificial reasoning, half-truths and unintelligible statutes to defeat the cause of justice. In some ways this hostility was understandable, as there was no such thing as a code of ethic. Lawyers frequently put in feint defenses merely to delay, or brought actions that had no basis in law. Nor was it considered improper to prepare documents for one client, then at trial switch sides and argue for an opponent.

Little wonder that in 1645 Virginia's legislature banned professional attorneys from courts entirely. The preamble to this legislation raged in justification: "Many troublesome suits are multiplied by the unskillfulness and covetousness of attorneys, who have more intended their own profits and their inordinate lucre than the good and benefit of their clients." Eleven years later the ban was lifted to be replaced by a regime of licensing, oaths of office, and the regulation of fees. When George Wythe commenced practice the fee for a county court appearance was pegged by law at thirty shillings, alternatively three hundred pounds of tobacco.

---

1   The Test read: "I do declare that there is not any transubstantiation of ye Lord's Supper, or in ye elements of bread and wine, at or after ye consecration thereof by any person whatsoever."

Finding clients was the young attorney's main concern. Self-taught and inexperienced, Wythe faced a barren landscape. His solution was to discover a location poorly serviced by others of his profession. He applied for, and gained a position as associate in the legal practice of Zachary Lewis in Fredericksburg, Spotsylvania County, east of the Blue Ridge.

Lewis proved to be a hale man in his mid-forties, well satisfied with life—as indeed he deserved to be. A large, rambling house accommodated his large family: his wife, five sons and five daughters. Regarded as solid as a brass bull by his community, Lewis had built up an extremely profitable practice through plain dealing and cheerful bonhomie, augmented by an appointment as the King's Attorney for the county. He had so much work, that even with his son John in the practice, he needed another to share the load.

At first Wythe was a mere bag-carrier for Lewis, though as he became more at home with procedures and the rough and tumble of rural advocacy, he was entrusted with a few minor cases. It soon became clear why Lewis had taken him on—the younger man was to travel to the distant courts in surrounding counties, initially in the company of Zachary Lewis, later on his own. Within months Wythe had been admitted to courts in Elizabeth City County, Spotsylvania County, Orange County and finally into the nether reaches of civilization in the county of Augusta. At that time Augusta County extended, at least theoretically, all the way to the Pacific Ocean—most of it was territory unknown to white men. For practical purposes it ran to the Mississippi, and included much of what is now Indiana, Illinois, Kentucky, Michigan, Ohio, West Virginia and Wisconsin.

Wythe regularly rode with Lewis on the rural circuit, in company with other lawyers traveling from place to place, with their attendant clerks and slaves leading a string of horses carrying satchels of law books, writs, files and papers. In backwoods Virginia they rode along rutted roads where morning's ice turned to afternoon's mud puddles. They forded swollen rivers, crossed tree-clogged creeks and waded through marshes. They were rained upon, snowed upon, and suffered from seed ticks and chiggers.

They rode through hamlets where men and women surrounded by bare-footed children peered out in dark-eyed poverty from split-timber cabins. They entered immense woods broken only by the occasional patch of corn and tobacco. Often their party would not encounter another traveler all day. They ascended the foothills of the Shenandoahs where the Scots–Irish were engaged in a thirty-year war against the silent imperious forests, and a man wielding an ax from dawn to dusk might hope to clear half an acre in a month.

At each village, Lewis and his young associate met familiar opponents in familiar courthouses, drinking afterwards with them in taverns, and rising next morning to join the troop traveling to the next courthouse to make cause all over again. Typically, they argued in courthouses of clapboards or red brick fronted by an arcaded loggia of rounded arches and a pavement of flagstones. The justices usually sat on the same day that the local market was held, and the green out front resounded with the tumult of musicians and puppeteers, slave traders, itinerant preachers, women selling butter and eggs, and farmers in bearskin coats trading horses.

In the winter months, fires were set about the courthouse grounds. Court proceedings being the premier free entertainment, they always attracted a good crowd. Ten minutes before the magistrates took the bench, the courthouse vestibule would be filled with lawyers touting for business, witnesses rehearsing their evidence, and greybeards with time on their hands queuing to give silent witness to the proceedings. At the opening of the doors, the idle and the curious would elbow in to stand at the back of the court, while the gentry took the front benches. The audience, naturally interested in what was being said about their neighbors, friends and enemies, usually remained all day—except if some poor miscreant was sentenced to a public flogging. Then they hastened outside to the whipping post in the courthouse grounds and jostled each other as they counted down the magistrate's sentence, laid solidly on the offender's back. When the court rose, everyone retired to the nearest taproom to discuss, over a keg of cider, rum or brandy, the relative merits of the litigants, lawyers, witnesses and the justices' decisions.

His Majesty's justices were the gentlemen of the county, performing voluntary service, and presiding as required. Bewigged and dressed in embroidered coats, waistcoats, lace collars and cuffs, they sat on a raised bench under the king's arms. Most were not conversant with the finer points of the law, though knowledgeable about their neighbors, and aware of what the community thought passed for justice. If a jury was assembled to rule on a matter, it was likely that half its number could not read fluently and even fewer of them could write. This was a court of neighbors, who decided the issues according to clannish justice.

As with all young lawyers Wythe would rise, trembling but resolute, and dutifully explain to the court the impeccable legal logic which should lead it to a verdict for his client. As with most young lawyers, more often than not he lost. But he was a quick learner, and soon developed a modest persuasiveness to his presentation. Further, he began to appreciate that the justices would rarely tolerate the impertinence of words on paper challenging their sense of rectitude—flattery, folksy good humor and flaying one's opponent was the favored way. The public gallery and the jury (the latter so often influenced by the reaction of the former) loved a virtuoso attorney who waved his hands dramatically, and possessed an actor's range of voice and grimaces.

Lewis and Wythe worked the rural circuit for many months, and filled up their fee book with small fees for small matters. Sometimes they appeared against each other, and Wythe's pleasure was great when the victory was his. As they rode shoulder to shoulder to the next town, they pitted their wits over again as they discussed the flow of the case and picked flaws in each other's tactics.

Within months Wythe, much to Lewis's delight, established himself as an attorney of competence, well capable of riding the circuit unsupervised. To Lewis's further delight, a romance blossomed between his young associate and one of his daughters. The courtship moved at remarkable speed and, less than a year after his first arrival in Spotsylvania County, Ann Lewis and George Wythe became man and wife. Both were twenty-one.

Since food, drink and musicians were ordered for Christmastide, Zachary Lewis and his wife decided that the celebration of the Savior's birth would be followed by a wedding the very next day. There was the customary Virginian feast for such occasions: roast pork, minced pies, custards, wine trifles and candied fruit, washed down by a bowl of rum toddy, brandy or Madeira. One supposes that during the wedding breakfast the speechifiers indulged in the expected puns, describing the newlyweds as each other's Christmas gift, turtledoves and yuletide turkeys. Then, to the accompaniment of a French horn and violins, the guests danced a Virginian combination of elegant minuets and popular jigs and reels.

*

The court records which have survived from George Wythe's time in Zachary Lewis's employ show that, from July 1747 to September 1748, the young lawyer was very busy indeed. Although bread-and-butter matters of debt collection predominated, Wythe also argued cases in trespass, selling liquor without a license, assault and petty theft.

On his rural rounds he quickly learned that innkeepers, being the sole provider of food, drink and warmth within miles, needed to be treated civilly. Their usual fare was salted beef or ham, supplemented by duck pie or squirrel broth. Fresh vegetables were almost unknown. Cornpone toasted in hog's lard was ubiquitous. The common drink was whiskey, applejack, and rum: if one wanted to sleep soundly it was recommended to drink several jars before retiring. Guests usually shared a room, and occasionally a bed, with a stranger who always seemed to have a snore like a file on metal.

After bedding down in awful hostelries for days on end, it was a blessing for Wythe to be invited to stay overnight at the houses of the gentry. They were a mixed bunch. Some were so devoted to their sip of rum that they tottered through the day in a stupor. Others were sporting men whose lives revolved around horseracing, foxhunting, cockfighting and gander pulling (in the latter, mounted competitors galloped past a well-greased goose suspended by its legs, and attempted to tear its head off). Others, even more boorish fellows, chortled over the pleasures to be found in the slave quarters at night.

Yet some planters were sober and retiring, and regarded an intelligent guest carrying news of the outside world as a great prize. One such planter, expecting the lawyers on their rural circuit to pass by, had his slave stand on the roadway with a lantern held high in one hand and an invitation to dine with the master in the other. On such occasions George Wythe, with his knowledge of the classics, the philosophers and literature, more than paid his way.

The young lawyer did not sleep many nights with his new wife. He was frequently absent from home and eight months after their ceremony of marriage, he attended Ann's funeral. No information survives about the circumstances of her death, or Wythe's reaction to it. He was a widower at the age of twenty-two.

Just as he had moved on after his mother's passing, so now he looked again to the wider world. As soon as he was able to wind up his outstanding cases and settle his affairs with Zachary Lewis, Wythe left Fredericksburg and the family of his deceased wife. He did not return for close on twenty years. He must have parted on good terms with his parents-in-law, however, for the family relationship opened doors for him in the next chapter of his career.

2

Williamsburg

Wythe in the capital—about Williamsburg—a successful attorney—Governor Robert Dinwiddie—the gold pistole dispute—Attorney General Wythe—the House of Burgesses—the Governor's Council—Wythe becomes a Tidewater planter—Wythe remarries

George Wythe's cure for grief and an uncertain future was to carve out a career in the superior courts of Williamsburg, Virginia's capital and seat of government. When he arrived there in 1748, the "city"—for so it rather audaciously called itself—had its share of handsome structures. There was the three-story red-brick governor's palace, built in the style of an English manor and surrounded by English gardens. And there was Duke of Gloucester Street, long, wide, and level, which ran a majestic mile from the imposing edifice of the College of William and Mary to the Capitol. This thoroughfare was strewn with crushed oyster shells, which was as Virginians required, preferring as they did to ride their horses on unpaved surfaces.

In truth, the colonial capital was a drowsy village of little more than a thousand souls, one half in permanent servitude to the other. A mile-square checkerboard of half-acre blocks, in Williamsburg everything was within walking distance of everything else. A man could go to the woods at twilight, shoot a squirrel or duck, and return home in time to put his catch in the pot for supper. The place was under-endowed with passable roads, and over-endowed with taverns. Ale and rum were produced in abundance, and manufacture had no existence. The town's economy depended on slavery and even those whites who did not own slaves felt the trickle-down benefits.

Tobacco was the principal product of the colony, and the wealth of Williamsburg was locked in riverside tobacco warehouses. The Reverend Burnaby, during his travels to Virginia in 1759, noted the colony's beauty and natural abundance, but compared its development unfavorably with Pennsylvania's: "Viewed and considered as a settlement, Virginia is far from being arrived at that degree of perfection which it is capable of."

Colonial Virginia was structured on deference—women to men, black to white, and white to the wellborn. As a matter of course the great planters were the justices of the county, proctors of the church and commanders of the militia. It was said that if a man of rank had two chimneys atop his house, he made himself a major; if he boasted four, he was entitled to a colonelcy. Orbiting the great planters were county officials, town journeymen and dirt-poor farmers, all dependent on these father-kings for work, income and status. It was a traditional, stable society, where the yeomen and landless thought themselves fortunate to leave the running of the colony to their betters. The colony was their world entire.

As the site of the oldest enduring English settlement in America, Virginia had a long and continuing connection with the Crown. A good number of the so-called colony's "aristocracy" were Cavaliers hounded from England following the defeat of Charles I in the Civil War, while others were the younger sprigs of distinguished British families who came to the New World after watching their fathers' titles and wealth pass exclusively to their eldest brothers. Some were not aristocrats at all, but merchants of lowly origin who over several generations had made good. It was a common sneer of English visitors that the planter class, for all their airs and graces, would rank no higher than middle gentry in England's home counties.

An ideal aristocratic marriage was one where landed wealth married landed wealth, with the result that often Virginian's first families were a ravelment of cousins. Fiercely loyal to the Crown, these aristocrats aped themselves on the English squirearchy, wore imported clothes, sat on imported furniture, and read English magazines. They built pillared mansions, in which their coats of arms, authenticated by the College of Heraldry in London, sat over the fireplace in paneled rooms decorated with portraits of the lord of the manor astride his favorite thoroughbred. They toured to the home island every decade or so, and returned with their English manners and accents refreshed, outspoken that Virginia was the best place in the world and Europe was a cesspit of vice and corruption.

Thoroughly devoted to the established church, these untitled nobles believed that respect for property was the foundation of an ordered society, public morality and personal liberty. Yet, they understood that ownership of property brought obligations of service for the common good, by acting in public offices as justices, churchwardens and assuming political authority in the Williamsburg Assembly. Only a few modeled themselves on the perfumed courtiers of Europe with their reputed idleness and extravagance. Rather, Virginia's lords of the manor remained connected to the soil, and regularly rode their estates checking on the overseers and slaves, and the health of their animals and crops.

*

Twice a year, in April and October, the population of Williamsburg tripled, as the great men of the colony, their families, retainers and servants came to the capital for sittings of the courts and legislature. The inns and houses were crammed four or five to a room. Gentlemen attended to the business of the bench and chamber during the day, and balls, dalliances, dinners, gambling and the theatre occupied their evenings. Auctions of land, furniture, books and slaves were held at the Raleigh Tavern or opposite the courthouse in Market Square. English thoroughbreds and their Virginian-bred issue galloped over a mile course on the edge of town. Cockfights drew a devoted crowd. A northern visitor, Elkanah Watson described the scene at one such event:

Exceedingly beautiful cocks were produced, armed with long, sharp, steel-pointed gaffs, which were firmly attached to their natural spurs. The moment the birds were dropped, bets ran high. The little heroes appeared trained to the business, and not the least disconcerted by the crowd or shouting. They stepped about with great apparent pride and dignity; advancing nearer and nearer, they flew upon each other ... the cruel and fatal gaffs being driven into their bodies, and, at times, directly through their heads. Frequently one, or both, were struck dead at the first blow, but they often fought after being repeatedly pierced, as long as they were able to crawl, and in the agonies of death would often make abortive efforts to raise their heads and strike their antagonists.

This description caught both the opulence and crudeness of colonial Virginia. Burnaby, who clearly preferred the industry and initiative of the Pennsylvanians, also noted that the Virginian elite were "haughty and jealous of their liberties," but prone to "extravagance, ostentation and disregard of economy." In any case, it made Williamsburg promising, even exciting, legal territory for a talented and ambitious attorney.

*

Wythe had at least one significant contact within Williamsburg's legal fraternity. His father-in-law had married into the Waller family, making Wythe the nephew-in-law of Benjamin Waller. A member of Virginia's elite, Waller was an esteemed vestryman of the parish of Bruton and a member of the House of Burgesses for James City County. During his illustrious legal career, he had been city recorder, king's advocate, and then judge of the Vice Admiralty Court. He became Wythe's patron.

Before the year was out, Wythe was appointed clerk to two committees of the House of Burgesses—Propositions and Grievances, and Privileges and Elections. The first was concerned with complaints and petitions from electors; the second dealt with the privileges of the burgesses and the proper conduct of polls. The Privileges and Elections Committee was regarded as the more important as it dealt with matters such as ballot stuffing, drunkenness in the chamber, un-parliamentary language and charges of corruption. Wythe's role as clerk to both was to remain silent and record on octavo parchment the committees' deliberations. He performed these duties under the watchful eye of Waller, who sat on both committees.

As his new appointments were part-time, Wythe was still able to practice as a lawyer. His acquaintance with those on the burgesses' committees led to his engagement by some of the colony's most distinguished gentlemen. His self-effacing manner, devotion to their causes and prodigious memory appeared to satisfy their wants, and soon his list of clients expanded even more.

Thus, with an ample wind in his sails, he launched on a legal career largely dedicated to serving the needs of the gentry. Initially, he practiced in the neighboring counties of York and Warwick, and probably in some other counties, but those records are missing. He gave legal advice to John Blair Sr., member of the Governor's Council and auditor-general of the colony, and was an advocate for the Custis family, into which George Washington later married. The Warwick Court records show that on one occasion he unsuccessfully defended one Andrew Giles on a charge of "not frequenting his Parish Church." Giles was fined "five shillings or fifty pounds of tobacco."

Within four years of Wythe hanging up his shingle, his office hummed with clients and he was well on the way to becoming a comfortable, if not a wealthy, man. About this time he lent a substantial sum to his brother, Thomas the Fourth. The new lord of Chesterville was proving no more successful than his forebears in farming mosquito-ridden land better left to the fog, wild pine and brambles of honeysuckle.

Attorney Wythe's reputation grew: he became known as a man careful with words and wise beyond his years, a lawyer's lawyer and counsel to legislators. Where a case involved a dainty difficulty, other attorneys began to seek his advice. He devoted every spare moment to study of the law, and was never without a book in the folds of his cloak. With a memory stretching over classic Greek and Roman authorities, as well as English ones, he could find a point on almost any issue under the sun.

In 1750, Wythe was elected an alderman of the Common Hall which ran the city of Williamsburg. He also continued as clerk to the two committees of the House of Burgesses, from time to time vacating his stool in the Privileges and Elections Committee to act as advocate for one of those charged. Notably, in 1752 he appeared for his uncle Stephen Dewey, who faced an allegation that he had corruptly won the seat for Prince George County. A rival candidate, Francis Eppes, claimed that the night before the election Dewey had provided accommodation, food and drink for eighty voters. On polling day, Mrs. Dewey took a hogshead of alcoholic punch to the courthouse grounds, and her servants told the freeholders that if they voted for Dewey they could drink as much as they liked. Wythe, while conceding the truth of the allegations, convinced the committee that nothing improper had occurred: everyone knew that was how Virginia conducted its elections. Poor Eppes was ordered to pay the costs of the hearing.

Less than a decade after he had arrived in the capital, Wythe decided to concentrate his practice on the General Court, the supreme tribunal of colonial Virginia, presided over by the governor and five members of his council. Neither the governor nor the members were required to have legal qualifications, and most didn't. It was in that demanding arena that Wythe really made his name. The practice of law in the capital was quite different from the rough-and-ready justice of the county courts. Securing or resisting orders from the glassy-eyed governor and his fellow judges required an attorney with an excellent grasp of the law, a good head for figures, the right documents to hand, and a presentation that was lean and certain. Wythe excelled and soon attracted a loyal following of wealthy clients.

The gentry were great litigators, and in those days of inexact surveys, incompetent surveyors and badly kept records they were ever ready, like medieval knights, to hasten into battle in order to protect their estates. Wythe argued cases about land and reversions, remainders, indentures, ejectments and equitable titles—words not fully understood by the gentleman judges, let alone most of the lawyers and clients who relied so strenuously upon them. There were also lawsuits about lost wills, unsigned wills, ambiguous wills and forged wills. Writs flew claiming slander, bastard births, the seduction of wives, breach of promise and the defrocking of priests. There were disputes over inheritance involving baptismal records, entries in family bibles, midwives' depositions and nurses' confessions. Wythe also argued about runaway slaves, injury to slaves hired out and slaves who accidently set fire to neighbors' crops.

Above all in importance, there was debt recovery. Virginia's aristocrats were well practiced at overvaluing their income and undervaluing their outgoings, and when they came to grief, as they frequently did, they resorted to juggling IOUs, selling tobacco notes and rearranging bills of exchange with British merchants and their agents. If these measures failed, as they frequently did, they visited relatives and friends and obtained loans, sold land or slaves, mortgaged more of the estate, or pledged next year's harvest or the harvest after that. Wythe was sometimes engaged by debtors, at other times by creditors, so he was able to observe firsthand the frustration and outrage each side felt for the other. Not being connected by blood or marriage to any of the great families, he was seen as an impartial warrior. He was above the fray; he spoke softly and deliberately; if anything he understated his client's case.

Honor was everything to the aristocracy of Virginia, and Wythe learned matters of particular delicacy that required care in their presentation. Because it was good for business to foster a reputation for integrity and discretion, he adopted a sober garb of black breeches, gray silk stockings, a tie wig and few ruffles, and dressed this way for the rest of his life. He also learned to hold his tongue.

Even his stature gave the impression of prudence and good judgment. Physically he was a balding, spare man, who moved with a graceful step. George Munford, the son of one of his law students wrote: "His head was very round, with a high forehead; well-arched eyebrows; prominent blue eyes, showing softness and intelligence combined; a large aquiline nose; rather small, but well-defined mouth; and thin whiskers, not lower than his ears ... His face was kept smoothly shaven; his cheeks, considerably furrowed from loss of teeth."

*

The king's representative in Virginia during those years was Robert Dinwiddie, a deputy for a stay-at-home governor, the Earl of Albemarle. The governorship was a patronage post granted to old dependables of the empire, and its income was highly sought after by the well-connected—but only on the understanding that they did not have to forsake the comfort of home to live in a wilderness with colonials, slaves and Red Indians. So the appointee normally remained in Britain and sent a lesser man as lieutenant-governor. Albemarle's choice of Dinwiddie as his replacement turned out to be a most unhappy one.

Born near Glasgow, Scotland, in 1693, Dinwiddie had been the royal customs collector for the southern district of North America and Bermuda, a role which had convinced him there was money to be made in colonial administration. He had paid the Earl of Albemarle £3,300 for his appointment as lieutenant-governor and was determined to make good on his investment. Within months of taking the oaths of office in November 1751, he began demanding a fee of one gold pistole for writing his signature on land patents. Although the governor had obtained approval from the Virginia Council, the burgesses were outraged. No governor had dared impose a tax without the house's consent in almost half a century. It was not the amount of the fee (which in any case was substantial),[2] but the erosion of Virginian rights which upset the assembly. "Liberty and Property and No Pistole" became the catchcry of the elected representatives.

When the House of Burgesses stubbornly refused to ratify the imposition of the fee, Dinwiddie prorogued session after session during a year and a half of bitter and spiteful rhetoric from both sides. Dinwiddie's perceived shortcomings included that he was no aristocrat, much less a gentleman. How could the burgesses respect an ex-customs collector? Furthermore, he had lived in Virginia for some years before his appointment, during which period, according to Edmund Randolph (who regarded himself as a real aristocrat—well at least a Virginia one) he was but "the master of a little vessel trading in the river."

In protest at the governor's determination to impose the fee, the burgesses upped the stakes by dispatching the attorney general, Peyton Randolph, to London, to convince the English authorities that the fee was

---

2   A pistole was a Spanish gold coin worth about a pound sterling. As a guide to value, a pistole might buy a cow and its calf, or a handsome human-hair wig made in London.

unconstitutional. Dinwiddie was "wounded to the soul" by what he saw as disloyalty from his first law officer. He dismissed Randolph and began looking around for a replacement. His eye lighted on an up-and-coming lawyer, George Wythe. The young man was flattered of course, but the appointment was obviously a poisoned chalice. After some thought, Wythe accepted it provisionally, intending to yield to Randolph on his return. This proved to be a sensible move, because when Randolph came back from London, largely unsatisfied, he patched up his differences with Dinwiddie and resumed his old position. The ruling from the Privy Council was that the pistole fee could remain, though it would not be collected retrospectively, or collected at all for small land grants.

None of this hurt Wythe's reputation, and when house member Armistead Burwell passed away, Wythe was elected to the House of Burgesses as the representative for Williamsburg.

*

The balance of power in Britain, to which the sovereign and Parliament had adjusted to over a century of civil strife and revolution, was held in high reverence by Virginians, who replicated it in their royal colony. In the Williamsburg microcosm, the House of Burgesses represented the Commons, the Council was modeled on the Lords, and the governor was the colonial version of the king. In this way, so the theory went, all of society was represented.

The governor's potency lay in his power to prorogue or dissolve assemblies and to veto legislation. True to the British model, the governor and his council sat as an upper chamber of review, and the Council also advised the governor on matters of importance. Twelve in number and unelected, the councilors were appointed for life by the king, on the recommendation of the governor.

The House of Burgesses aped the seating arrangements, modes of address, etiquette and procedures of the House of Commons. The Speaker had his mace, gown and high chair, the sergeant-at-arms his staff, and the members had their chaplain, clerk, doorkeeper and long green benches. The house also took pride in being the longest-lived of all American assemblies, first meeting in 1619. Quaint and self-important it may have been, but this sense of tradition gave it the sureness to demand, as of inherent right, the same powers as the English parliament. Furthermore, according to a growing chorus, this authority meant that no taxes could be imposed on the citizens of Virginia unless the Burgesses first agreed.

If the Council was the lifelong home of the few, the House of Burgesses was a tobacco planters' club of ever-changing membership. There were no political parties in the Burgesses, just swirling, unstable allegiances and enmities based on geography, wealth, personality and family connection. Sessions were long and tedious and absenteeism was high. Never was the pressure of business such that speakers needed to hurry. Oratory was prized above all, particularly well modulated wit, and it often seemed to observers that the sense of what was being said mattered not so much as the manner of declaiming it.

This legislature, the British governor and his council administered a realm that extended westward over the Blue Ridge and the Allegheny Mountains, across the bluegrass plains to the Mississippi. It was an area double the size of France—though in a week's ride a traveler departing the capital would be quite of out touch with civilization.

*

In January 1755, Wythe's brother died. Although Thomas had married, he died childless, so George Wythe succeeded to his estate. Suddenly he was a Tidewater planter and the master of Chesterville with its house, slaves, storehouse and stables. Though it was the home of three generations of his forebears, Wythe had rarely visited since the death of his mother a decade earlier. Upon reading the will, he learned that Thomas had left most of the estate's slaves (undoubtedly worth more than the land) to his widow and to his sister, Anne. Wythe rode to Chesterville, inspected the property, found no allure in growing tobacco, appointed a manager, and turned his mount back toward Williamsburg. Nevertheless, tradition dictated that he fill his brother's former place on the bench of magistrates for Elizabeth City County. He became the fifth Wythe in succession so appointed, and the first who was legally qualified.

Now a member of the planter class (albeit barely profitably), and suitably connected in the city, Wythe was keen to complete the circle by marrying well. He was a very eligible twenty-nine when he first laid eyes on his future bride, Elizabeth Taliaferro. The Taliaferros were of the second rank of aristocratic families, but Elizabeth was pretty, intelligent and tutored in the treasures of the mind. She was all of sixteen, Wythe more than a decade older, but their age difference was within a range that would have been considered respectable.

Elizabeth's family name was Venetian, but the Taliaferros had been established in Britain for more than two centuries, and it was from there they emigrated to Virginia in the 1640s. Her father, Richard Taliaferro, in addition to being a substantial landowner, was an accomplished architect, and had designed several mansions for the great families with elegant simplicity and taste, as well as remodeling the governor's palace.

Wythe called on Elizabeth's father, and the match was agreed. The couple married a few months later.

As George Wythe left the Bruton Church with his bride on his arm, he surely reflected on the enormity of his good fortune. It was a mere twelve years since he had walked off Chesterville to become a law clerk in the office of a rural lawyer, and now he was being welcomed into one of Virginia's established families. His work day was an enjoyable round of meetings and debates in the courts, the House of Burgesses, and the Common Hall, followed by an evening meal at home, and reading beside a warm fire, before climbing the stairs to a satisfied sleep beside his young wife.

His father-in-law honored the union by gifting the couple a life interest in a charming house of Flemish bond brickwork, set in a large garden on the Palace Green, close to the governor's residence. Now known as George Wythe House, today it is visited by many thousands of tourists who flock to Colonial Williamsburg.

3

Colonel Washington

*The French in Ohio—Washington dispatched—the
French and Indian War—Braddock am-
bushed—Wythe and Washington seek political careers—rum punch and pork ribs—Wythe handles
Washington's legal affairs*

In the midst of his pistole dispute with the burgesses, Governor Dinwiddie's thoughts turned to the French. The British and the French had been at
each other's throats for more than half a century, their skirmishing broken
only by intermittent lulls of uneasy peace while the combatants renewed
their strength for further bloodshed. In the North American theatre, the
fundamental question was whether France or England should control the
continent. British colonists viewed with alarm French claims to an arc of
territory along the valley of the Saint Lawrence River, through the Great
Lakes and down the Mississippi to the river's mouth beyond New Orleans.

When fur traders reported that the French were forging alliances with
Indian people and building a series of forts between Lake Erie and the
Ohio, Dinwiddie was greatly concerned by the news. He was a sharehold-
er in the Ohio Company of Virginia, which had huge land claims of its
own. The governor sent an emissary three hundred miles through hostile
Indian territory and across a succession of mountains and rivers, to assess

the threat and inform the French that the Ohio Country was "notoriously known to be the property of the Crown of Great Britain." The man entrusted with this task was George Washington, a 21-year-old major schooled to arms on a middle-fortune plantation on the Rappahannock River.

When the fresh-faced Washington arrived at French Creek where it joined the Allegheny, the French intruders disdainfully brushed him aside, replying (as Washington recorded) that it was "their absolute design to take possession of the Ohio, and by God they would do it." Washington rode back over the mountains to a commendation from Dinwiddie (he's a "raw laddie") and promotion to lieutenant colonel.

The French, as good as their word, built more forts the following year. In retaliation, the British began fortifying a strategic fork on the Ohio River, and within months Washington was sent with the Virginia militia to protect its construction. As Washington's troops approached the Ohio, they stumbled on a French encampment. During the resulting skirmish the Virginians killed the officer-in-charge and stood by as their Indian allies knocked "the poor, unhappy wounded in the head, and bereaved them of their scalps." (Washington's words again.) Upon hearing of this outrage, the French commandant at Fort Duquesne charged at Washington's militia with a force of five hundred French and Indian warriors. After holding out for a day in intermittent drenching rain, and sustaining heavy losses, Washington was forced to sign a surrender document and limp home.

It was an ignominious reversal for the young officer.

Wars are costly, the war chest was empty and the House of Burgesses was locked in a struggle with Dinwiddie over his insistence he could impose taxes without legislative consent. In an attempt to loosen the purse strings, the governor recalled the assembly. The burgesses voted £20,000 for the war, but again they flexed their muscle. The funds were not to be spent by the governor as he saw fit, but under the supervision of a special committee of burgesses. George Wythe was one of those elected to membership.

With the defeat of Washington's forces in 1754, the French were poised to claim the Ohio and Mississippi river systems. Emotions ran high in the colonies. The message from pulpit and printing press was that unless the Gallic peril of popish tyranny and Indian savagery was resisted by force of arms, loyal British colonists would lose the heart of their continent and live in constant fear of invasion from over the mountains.

In the spring of 1755, a veteran British officer, Major General Edward Braddock, arrived in Virginia with two regiments of redcoats and a determination to regain control of the Ohio Country. Washington was already a colonel, but a colonel of the colonial militia, which did not count for much with the British. They had decreed that in *their* army, a colonial could not hold a rank higher than captain.

After that rebuff, and several other studied slights, Washington resigned his commission and rode away from military life, intending to return to farming his Mount Vernon estate. Yet, a few months later, when he had the opportunity to join General Braddock's staff as an unpaid aide-de-camp with the courtesy title of colonel, he agreed. Many were surprised that Washington consented to serve under Braddock, a brisk British bulldog with an explosive temper, little discretion to control it, and a distressing lack of manners.

Such was Braddock's determination to get at the enemy that he ordered a road be hacked two hundred miles through the wilderness of the Allegheny Mountains. After a sickly journey of several months dragging English artillery through a morass of dripping green, by July 9 the general's forces were closing in on the French stronghold of Fort Duquesne on the Ohio River. The British, augmented by Washington's Virginian Regiment, had the superior arms and numbers, and it now seemed to Braddock to be a straightforward matter of laying siege to the fort and cannonading the French into submission.

As his advance force of regular and colonial troops entered the dark arches of a forest a few miles from the fort, musket fire rang out. Several men fell. Another volley sounded and more fell. By the time Braddock's troops readied their own muskets, the enemy had faded away. In the deep undergrowth the French and their Indian allies, all clad in hunting dress, were practically invisible.

Suddenly, war whoops sounded on either side of the British, who wheeled around in confusion and fear. The officers, dressed in red coats and towering on horses, were easy targets. Shots rang out from both flanks and more died. Braddock rode up and down the column roaring frantic orders to hold steady as the French and Indians flitted through the trees picking off his men at will. In the next fusillade a musket ball grazed Braddock's right arm and entered his lung. He tumbled from his horse and thudded to the ground. Several more British officers fell, along with scores of their infantrymen. Washington and what was left of his troops bundled the comatose Braddock into a small covered cart, and hurried away through smoke and fearful disorder, leaving the dead and dying to their fate as the Indians rushed in to harvest a crop of scalps. In all, nine hundred British and colonial soldiers were killed or wounded in a few hours of slaughter.

As one of the few surviving officers, Washington took charge of the bloodied remnants of the demoralized army. All he could do was establish a defensive rearguard while he organized an orderly retreat over the mountains. Braddock, jostled along in the back of a covered cart, died after several days of dreadful pain. He was buried in the middle of the road he had constructed. Wagons were driven over the grave to disguise its location—thus denying the Indians a general's scalp. His last words were "We shall better know how to deal with them another time"—a poor prediction for, as the revolutionary war demonstrated, the redcoats never mastered the stealthy skills of forest warfare.

The French victory on the Ohio brought terror to Virginian hearts and an abrupt loss of confidence in England as protector. The French would continue to construct their inland fortifications. The Indians would be emboldened to pour down from the Alleghenies and attack outlying settlements. Virginia was now in greater peril than before Braddock's attempt to save the colony.

Washington was not caught up in the inevitable recriminations that followed the disaster: indeed, he won praise for his coolness and courage in shepherding his ragged army to safety. According to his report, the Virginia troops, unlike the panicky British, had "behav'd like men and died like soldiers." He regained the rank of colonel with the Virginia Regiment and was made responsible for the defense of the Virginian frontier, now wide open to attack from the French and Shawnee and Delaware warriors. It was a thankless, if not impossible task, protecting a line three hundred and fifty miles long with a lowly paid army, inadequate supplies and troops of uneven quality. He hanged deserters, yet still more deserted.

*

As the French and Indian War dragged on, George Washington and George Wythe, moving on parallel political paths, stood for election to the House of Burgesses. In 1755 Washington, then still an officer in the Virginia Regiment, offered himself to the voters of Frederick County, a frontier electorate fringing the lower half of the Shenandoah Valley. A few months later, Wythe contested the seat of Elizabeth City County.

Elections in colonial Virginia were occasions for people to travel to town, meet friends and celebrate. It was normal, indeed expected, for candidates to set up stands in the courthouse grounds before the poll, offering voters refreshments such as jugs of applejack, rum punch, ginger cakes and slices of barbecued hog. Wythe, as a matter of principle, refused to proffer such inducements. At the appointed hour he and seven opponents stood on the courthouse steps ready to make their campaign speeches. With considerable reluctance, the crowd quit hoeing into the food and drink, and drifted over to hear what they had to say. Wythe promised that, if elected, he would serve without payment. Another candidate said he would do the same, leading a heckler in the audience to call out that "he was glad of, as he found it very difficult to pay his taxes." The other candidates then puffed their way through speeches promising devoted service. Each had their circle of admirers who cheered their every word.

At last came the poll. As the clerk of the roll called out names, each freeman[3] came forward to announce his vote to the sheriff seated at a table under the courthouse portico. Some were so drunk they could hardly get the words out. As the clerk recorded the voter's choice, it was traditional for the candidate favored by the vote to bow and say something like "Your

---

3   Only white, Protestant, propertied males could vote. In more detail: an eligible voter had to be a man over twenty-one years and the owner of one hundred acres without a house or twenty-five acres with a house. A man whose wife had sufficient property to qualify as an elector could vote "in right of his wife." Electors wealthy enough to hold qualifying land in two or more counties could vote in both. As two members of the House of Burgesses were elected for each county, each voter recorded two choices.

vote is heartily appreciated" or "I shall prize that vote in my memory forever."

As some of Wythe's opponents' scores mounted to ten, then into double figures, he did not once hear his name called. The blood drained from his face as, one after another, the electors declared for others. Finally, a jeering, ribald cheer went up as someone voted for Wythe. No more support came his way. He had received only one vote! He was so discouraged that when called upon he did not even vote for himself. That gesture at least produced a smattering of applause.

Wythe was well known in the county: he had grown up there, and served as the local magistrate. What had gone wrong? Certainly his refusal to ply the voters with food and drink would have counted against him. Scholarly and puritanical by nature, Wythe had little in common with the voters drinking bumbo and supping on pork ribs in the tents of his opponents, all hearty fellows willing to share a jug with the refined and commoner alike. Moreover, in a ballot by open declaration, the smaller planters would have thought it in their interests to be recorded as voting for the local lord of the manor, rather than an absentee landowner who only visited the county to take the bench as a magistrate.

Or did Wythe's unpopularity with the freemen of Elizabeth City County stem from his activities as a local justice? Riding down to his old county seat to take on the role of a rural magistrate several times a year might have presented difficulties for Wythe—not with the law or the lawyers, but with those who sat with him. Up to eight of the leading citizens had the right to join him on the bench, and most were innocent of ever opening a law book. "As a judge," wrote B. B. Minor of Wythe, "he was not only fearlessly upright and independent, but able, punctual, attentive and industrious."

He could have added that Wythe did not suffer fools gladly. When Wythe became a judge he was intolerant of windy counsel, waffling witnesses and time-wasting court officials. A legalist in an era when more legalists were needed, he once declared that "compassion ought not to influence a judge, in whom, acting officially, apathy is less a vice than sympathy." At least some of the voters who took their vengeance on polling day would have appeared in his court; some perhaps he had sentenced to an hour or two of public humiliation in the stocks.

Washington, a man of only twenty-three, little known except for his part in Braddock's defeat, was also defeated in his poll, at Frederick County. Like Wythe, he had failed to provide drink and victuals for the voters. Unlike Wythe, he learned his lesson. When he stood in 1758 for the same seat, the electors were greeted on the courthouse green by the sweet persuasion of 28 gallons of rum, 50 gallons of rum punch, 34 gallons of wine, 46 gallons of beer and two gallons of cider royal—an average of more than a quart and a half for the 391 voters. Washington's supporters arranged this largess, as he was still a commissioned officer training his troops at Fort Cumberland. Afterwards, when it was clear Washington had won, they put on a ball. Then they sent Washington the bill, totaling thirty-nine pounds six shillings, which he duly paid.

But Wythe was not so compromising. When he recontested Elizabeth City County in 1758, just as before, he provided no hospitality. The result was that he received eight votes out of 242. Nevertheless, he won a place in the House of Burgesses. The founding charter of the College of William and Mary endowed the college with the right to nominate its own delegate to the Burgesses. The faculty, perceiving in Wythe a regular attendee of the Church of England and an experienced legislator, elected him. Thus on February 29, 1759, Wythe was there to witness Colonel Washington take his seat in the house.

The year before, Washington had joined a force of more than seven thousand men under the command of a British Brigadier-General, John Forbes, for a third stab at the Gallic enemy. After hacking a road from Pennsylvania through a rain-drenched fall wilderness, Forbes's army approached Fort Duquesne only to be informed by scouts that the French had burnt it to the ground. Nor would there be a forest battle—the enemy had floated away down the Ohio. The French, with their Canadian possessions under threat, their supply lines from Lake Erie overstretched, and their troops hemmed in by a British naval blockade, had decided it was impossible to defend the Ohio Valley.

General Forbes rebuilt the fort and named it Fort Pitt after the British foreign minister, William Pitt. (In time, it became Pittsburgh, Pennsylvania.) After that, the war went elsewhere. General James Wolfe captured Quebec in 1759 and the commander in chief of the British forces,

Jeffery Amherst, took Montreal the following year. It was the end of the French and Indian War. The hostile Gallic force over the mountains, which for long memory had been Virginia's fear, was vanquished forever. After humbling the French at the Treaty of Paris in 1763, Great Britain became the most powerful nation on Earth—leaving the French cherishing an insatiable desire for revenge.

After Washington returned from service with Forbes, he resigned from the army. Disillusioned with the failure of the Virginia Assembly to supply his army adequately, and irritated that although he was a full colonel in the Virginia regiment he remained just above captain in the British army, he resumed farming his sadly neglected estate. It would be seventeen years before he returned to soldiering, and that would be in very different circumstances indeed.

When Washington entered the House of Burgesses for the first time, he had just returned from his glorious, if anti-climactic journey to Fort Duquesne. The house passed a resolution thanking him "for his faithful services to His Majesty, and this colony." When Washington rose to acknowledge the honor he "blushed, stammered, and trembled," until the Speaker called "Sit down, Mr Washington, your modesty is equal to your valor; and that surpasses the power of any language that I possess."

Washington remained a member of the Virginia House of Burgesses until the eve of the revolution. At first, he displayed no recognizable stamp of future greatness. In a chamber barely ten paces across, this six-foot-two warrior sat uncomfortably as an upright man on a bench too small for his bulk. His contributions to debates were few and marked by commonsense rather than wisdom. Amiable rather than charming, he was popular with the other members despite a degree of aloofness.

Roger Atkinson, one of his contemporaries, wrote: "He is a modest man, but sensible, and speaks little—in action cool, like a bishop at his prayers." Thomas Jefferson recalled:

> I served with General Washington in the legislature of Virginia before the Revolution, and during it with Dr. Franklin in Congress. I never heard either of them speak ten minutes at a time, nor to any but the main point which was to decide the question. They laid their

shoulders to the great points, knowing that the little ones would follow of themselves.

Others saw Washington as a well-intentioned country gentleman
stiffened by a firm sense of duty and a singular ability to concentrate,
but overly concerned with perceptions of his dignity and courtesy. Like
Wythe—indeed, like most of the burgesses—he was not a natural revolutionary. Carefully measuring his response to each perceived British
infringement of Virginian freedoms, he moved by increments through
protest, rebellion and independence, finally to war.

*

Wythe came to know Washington on a personal level when the colonel
engaged him to defend his interests in a multi-party action that caused
Washington much grief and Wythe much poorly remunerated work. The
most striking aspect of the whole sorry affair was how William Clifton
managed to resist the claims of creditors for so long. He owned two thousand acres, just across Little Hunting Creek from Washington's estate
at Mount Vernon. When Clifton defied his creditors' demands for possession of the land, an exasperated judge, weary of hearing the claims
of four mortgage holders, Clifton's wife and Clifton himself, ordered a
compulsory sale at the Alexandra Court House in February 1760. Washington attended. He was the successful bidder for 1806 acres of Clifton's
best pastures. He paid £1210, and perhaps he thought he had obtained a
bargain. In fact, it was only the beginning of his problems. Two of the
mortgagees declined to deliver title, another threatened to appeal to England's Privy Council, and Clifton himself refused to vacate. The whole
mess went repeatedly back to court. Each time the litigation moved at a
snail's pace toward some illusory finality, Washington journeyed down
from Mount Vernon (a four-day ride he seemed to enjoy) to dine with George and Elizabeth Wythe.

Certain that Wythe was handling matters satisfactorily, he would conclude discussion as quickly as possible and repair to the Raleigh Tavern
for a round or two of cards. This litigation extended over three decades!

Astonishingly, it was still on foot as Washington besieged Boston in 1776. The commander in chief took time out from battle to write to a letter to his advisors contemplating the next move. He did not get clear title until 1791, well after Clifton's death.

4

The Young Jefferson

Governor Francis Fauquier—Wythe sups with the new governor—the radical William Small—Thomas Jefferson at the governor's palace—the molding of the young Jefferson—Jefferson studies law—Jefferson in love—the "partie quarree"

By the time Washington and Wythe took their places in the Burgesses, the erratic and arrogant Governor Dinwiddie had suffered a disfiguring stroke and departed the colony with nary a fond farewell from his colonial subjects. His replacement, Francis Fauquier, was another substitute governor and as erratic as his predecessor, but cultured and charming. The gossip that accompanied him to Williamsburg said that he had been forced to depart England's shores because in the space of a few years he had tumbled from wealth to straitened gentility through gambling.

Further, so the talk went, he had attempted to restore the family fortune by taking on Lord Anson at cards. Anson was famous throughout the empire for setting off on a circumnavigation of the globe with six warships and returning with only one—but stuffed full of five hundred thousand pounds worth of Spanish treasure. Perhaps Fauquier should have known better than to chance all against such a wily character, because by the time he rose from the baize he was destitute. The story goes that Anson, in an act of charity, then arranged for his former opponent to be given the lieutenant-governorship of Virginia.

Not that Fauquier was devoid of gentlemanly qualifications for the post. He was a fellow of the Royal Society, had an interest in all manner of things scientific and philosophical, and before leaving England had written a well-regarded monograph entitled *The Ways and Means of Raising Money for the Support of War Without Increasing the Public Debt*. His paper argued that a tax on necessities would ultimately be passed onto the consumer, and everyone, especially the poor, would suffer. Fauquier suggested a graduated tax on higher incomes. He was ignored, of course.

Fauquier held other views one might not expect in a British viceroy. Pleading for better treatment of American Indians, he once wrote "White, Red or Black; polished or unpolished, Men are Men." His compassion extended to the mentally ill, and over several years he repeatedly reminded the House of Burgesses of its failure to establish a hospital for the insane. This complex man was also a gourmet and a bacchant. An invitation to his table was a treat, with the very best of French wines and English cooking—which meant something like baked lamb pasty, and vegetables in cheese and herbs, followed by pudding, custard, cream and brandy.

Not surprisingly, the governor looked every moment of his fifty-six years. To the general population he was tactful, amiable, charming, and they esteemed him as the complete gentleman, such as one might find inhabiting the novels of Goldsmith or Richardson. He arrived in Williamsburg accompanied by his decorative wife, Catherine, a refined Cumberland heiress. After probing Virginian society, she decided against being cocooned in a minor outpost of empire, and returned home with one of their sons.

Some assert that Fauquier was responsible for spreading the curse of gambling among the Virginian aristocracy. According to Burk's *History of Virginia* (1805), Governor Fauquier "visited the most distinguished landholders in the colony, and the rage of playing deep, reckless of time, health or money spread like a contagion amongst a class proverbial for their hospitality, their politeness and fondness for expense."

After the graciousness of Georgian England, Fauquier pined for repartee and intellectual debate, rather than gossip and a keen discussion of bloodlines in horses and humans. He decided to assemble a discussion group, and out of the many, handpicked George Wythe and a member of the William and Mary faculty, William Small, to join him for coffee at the palace. Wythe had met the governor several times in service as a minor member of the legislative assembly, and for an ambitious attorney intent on carving out a legal and political career, the invitation was an opportunity to be seized.

As he soon learned, coffee was rarely to be seen at Fauquier's suppers; instead conversation was lubricated by copious quantities of wine and spirits. In the midst of one of their discussions, the governor announced his desire to encourage viniculture in the colony by donating an annual award for the best in wines. By evening's close he had charmed Wythe into drafting the rules of the contest.

Their companion, Small, was a Scot with a Master of Arts from Aberdeen. While he was still in his early twenties, the Bishop of London, who was chancellor of William and Mary, had nominated him to teach mathematics at the college. It did not take long, after Small's arrival at Williamsburg in 1758, for the college elders to develop reservations about the wisdom of the bishop's choice. At the time, William and Mary was primarily a training ground for the Church of England. Founded in 1693, and named for King William and Queen Mary, the college breathed to the rites of the established church, with prayers at dawn and dusk. Its academic year followed the church calendar and its professors were required to subscribe to the Thirty-Nine Articles of Religion.

Small was the only lay academic on a faculty otherwise comprised of clergy. He arrived brimful of the impieties of the Scottish Enlightenment, with its emphasis on scientific reasoning and Hutcheson's radical thought that virtue lay in the greatest good to the greatest number. With all the attributes of an over-confident young man of breeding, Small soon became a buzzing bee within the confined bottle of William and Mary, questioning beliefs, debating the power of kings and quoting Voltaire. He never feared upsetting others. Sparks flew at a faculty meeting in 1762 when he insisted that it be recorded that he did not agree with the order that "every Master has the Right to inflict such punishment on a Scholar behaving in an indecent and irregular Manner as he shall think proper."

His teaching methods were as radical as his politics. To the consternation of the professorial board he departed from William and Mary's tried and true method of instruction in Latin by virtue of memory and recitation. Instead, Small stood at a rostrum, lectured in English, and invited his students to respond in the Socratic method of reciprocal inquiry. Then he would lead them into the garden to inspect nature by day and the stars at night. Historian Martin Clagett writes of "a long-time legend" that Small, Jefferson and fellow student John Page once ascended the cupola on the roof of Rosewell, the Page family estate, to examine the stars with the aid of a telescope. On other occasions, Dr. Small had his students light fires under open paper balloons and watch them fly over the James River—then ask if, one day, men might hitch a ride.

The college hierarchy may well have come down hard on Small, save that shortly before his arrival, five of the six professors had been dismissed in a power struggle with the Board of Visitors and he was one of the few left standing. This meant that he was obliged to teach ethics, belle-lettres and rhetoric as well as mathematics. Indeed for much of Jefferson's undergraduate education, Small was his only teacher.

*

Meetings between Fauquier, Small and Wythe proved so enjoyable to the governor that they developed into regular soirées of political and philosophical debate. Enlightenment's skepticism was washing from Europe onto Virginian shores, and it seems that Fauquier enjoyed enticing Small into bursts of radicalism, be they anti-clerical, anti-monarchy or contempt of the Virginia aristocracy, so that he could smile indulgently and tut-tut.

Small, a ruddy man of fiery disposition, played his role well. The governor's part was Socrates: with a polished and cutting wit softened only slightly by courtly manners, by adroit questioning he led his companions to reveal more of themselves and the political mood of Virginia than they intended. He took the contra view just for jest, setting the younger men as kittens chasing a ball of string, and often after several hours' debate Wythe would return to his house still unsure of the governor's real opinions. Nevertheless, Fauquier became his great friend.

One evening, Small told Wythe and the governor about a lanky youth from Albemarle County who had been boarding at William and Mary for the past two years. The boy's name was Thomas Jefferson—Tall Tom, as he was known to other students. Despite his stumbling hesitancy in conversation, he had a remarkable native intelligence and a quickness of mind that Small thought was sure to delight his companions. He described how master and student had taken to walking on the college lawns, then farther afield down country lanes, discussing anything that came into their heads—astronomy, mathematics, philosophy, religion.

From his first encounter with the governor, Jefferson charmed Fauquier, who expressed the wish that the youth attend all their future soirées. The four met irregularly over the next two years. It was an unusual group: a cultivated Englishman approaching sixty, a self-taught colonial in his mid-thirties, an opinionated Scot a decade younger, and a loose-jointed, countrified youth of nineteen.

Jefferson was the only one of the four to write about this friendship circle around Fauquier: "at his table, Dr. Small & Mr. Wythe, his *amici omnium horarum* [friend of all hours], & myself, formed a *partie quarree*, & to the habitual conversations on these occasions I owed much instruction." On another occasion, he wrote: "At these dinners I have heard more good sense, more rational and philosophical conversations, than in all my life besides. They were truly Attic societies."

It is tempting to let the mind's eye picture the foursome gathering in the palace library on a hot summer evening to debate Locke on the social contract, or the unsolvable problem of why evil prospered in a world of God's design, or whether Bolingbroke was correct in doubting that God would have restricted his knowledge to the Jews. As the butler, a black dressed in the wig and livery of a courtier at the court of Louis XV served drinks, Jefferson and Wythe, the untraveled provincials, might sit in awe listening as the other two spoke of the sights and pleasures of London—the theatres, the magnificent buildings, the intellectual ferment of the clubs and societies. Then discussions moved on to political economy, history, philosophy, religion and medicine.

One can imagine Fauquier making his points over draughts of Madeira, yet keeping his wits in perfect assembly, Wythe, holding his hand over his glass at every round, Small, drinking less than the governor but still losing his way as the decanter emptied, and Jefferson drinking little, but listening intently and absorbing much. Perhaps the youth, after long reflection, contributed his ideas in his hesitant, stumbling way, though in such an economy of words that the older men felt compelled to take note.

Small and Fauquier had their favorite hobbyhorses ready to prance around Jefferson, and religion was certainly one of them. Influenced by the Scottish Enlightenment, Small questioned claims that the established church was the sole repository of religious truth. Fauquier was a hair's breadth from being a Deist. Wythe, according to one of his students, was "without religion", instead following "that great command, Do unto all men as thou wouldst they should do unto thee." Others said he was a Deist.

The group surely traversed Hobbes, Hutcheson and Montesquieu, with their presentation posies of the ideal form of government. The irony of discussing the rights of man in a colony where 40 percent of the population were slaves could not have escaped these four intellectuals. Small owned no slaves. Wythe eventually freed his. Jefferson would acquire many, but free only three, all from the Hemings family. Fauquier, who had seventeen slaves attending to his needs, wrote that he found slavery "in its nature disagreeable to me." Why not free them, Small might well have asked. The governor's answer appeared in his will, written in 1767: he considered that his "situation" had made it necessary for him to own slaves, even though it constantly gave him "uneasiness." By which he meant that everything he did was a symbol of the monarch's will, and Virginians expected a royal governor to set an example of being attended by black servants.

*

In the fall of 1762, Jefferson became a student-at-law in the office of George Wythe. The pupilage was arranged by William Small as a "measure of his goodness to me." Wythe was then thirty-five, and his student nineteen—in classical terms the ideal ages for tutor and tutored. Jefferson took lodgings at the Market Square Tavern, a five-minute walk from Wythe's house.

The course of reading Wythe prescribed for his student is not fully recorded. That Wythe made *Coke on Littleton* his student's staple is known because of Jefferson's vociferous complaint to a friend: "I do wish the devil had old Coke, for I am sure I never was so tired of an old dull scoundrel in my life." Jefferson also purchased a number of law books including the *Attorney's Practice in the Court of the Kings Bench*, the *Practice of the Court of Chancery Practice*, and the *Attorney's Pocket Compass* and *Grounds and Rudiments of Law*. But the course of instruction Wythe set was far wider than the minutiae of law, for the record of Jefferson's purchases at Williamsburg's bookshop also included volumes of Milton's works, Hume's *History of England*, Stith's *History of Virginia*, Yorick's *Sermons*, Sale's *Koran*, Bacon's *Philosophy* and the Thoughts of Cicero. Furthermore, Jefferson had access to Wythe's own extensive library of moderns and classics.

Years after completing his own studies, Jefferson wrote a list of recommended reading for a young law student. If one assumes this grand list reflected his own experience with Wythe, it might be said that Wythe designed a plan of study that progressed through all ages in all disciplines. Thus Jefferson would have read belles lettres, rhetoric, logic, ethics, physics, metaphysics and mathematics. Of the ancients, Wythe would have offered Epictetus, Tacitus, Homer, Xenophon, Horace, Seneca, Cicero, Livy and Plutarch. Of the moderns, Pope, Hutcheson, Lord Kames, John Gay and the three Ss: Smollett, Sterne and Swift. Of drama, Shakespeare, Steele, Congreve and Addison. He would have rounded out the year's study for Jefferson by recommending texts on agriculture and botany. But above all, Wythe imparted to the young man a love of learning for its own sake, and the fundamental view that in both law and life reason should prevail.

Of his studies Jefferson later wrote: "I was bold in the pursuit of knowledge, never fearing to follow truth and reason to whatever results they led, and bearding every authority which stood in their way." When the courts were in session, Jefferson was commanded by his master-at-law to "attend constantly." Wythe also took him to debates of the House of Burgesses so he could learn the intricacies of parliamentary procedures and observe how laws were made.

In the evenings, after master and pupil had dined with Elizabeth, they would retire to Wythe's study of glass-fronted bookcases on the upper floor. Both men were fluent in Greek and Latin, and as candles burnt low, they would discuss the wisdom of the day's readings. Then Wythe would close his eyes and bathe in the sound of a youthful voice reading from the greats. At a late hour, Jefferson would pack up his books and walk across Palace Green to his tavern lodgings—only to reappear at Wythe's door at dawn to report on some revelation he had discovered in Plato or Kames.

The years Jefferson spent under Wythe's tutorage were not so much a pupilage in law, but a training for life. Or as history now appreciates, a preparation for greatness.

Yet sometimes it seemed that Jefferson was unlikely to see his studies through. In December 1762, he fell in love with pretty Miss Rebecca Burwell. Wythe watched in dismay as his student moped around Williamsburg, practiced excessively on his violin, and daydreamed of his beloved's bright blue eyes and flaxen hair. Miss Burwell was a couple of years younger than Jefferson, but far from being overwhelmed by his stuttering overtures she showed little interest in them. Deeply hurt, he retired to his home at Shadwell for the Christmas recess, a miniature portrait of Rebecca clutched to his breast, and a huge reading list from Wythe for company.

Perhaps prophetically, the portrait was destroyed in a cloudburst. Jefferson wrote to a friend about this tragedy,

> And now, although the picture be defaced, there is so lively an image of her imprinted in my mind, that I shall think of her too often, I fear, for my peace of mind; and too often, I am sure, to get through old Coke this winter; for God knows I have not seen him since I packed him up in my trunk in Williamsburg.

After a break from his studies lasting nine months, Jefferson returned to Williamsburg and moved into lodgings near Wythe, ostensibly to resume his studies. Presented with the opportunity to again make a fool of himself, he approached Miss Burwell with a proposal of marriage. She refused, and giving certainty to her decision, promptly became engaged to another. Only then did Jefferson throw himself back into his studies, with all the grim determination of a man spurned.

At that time in Virginia, it was possible for an apprentice lawyer to be admitted to practice after six months' study. By 1764, after more than two years reading under the colony's leading attorney, Jefferson's knowledge of the law far exceeded most new lawyers, yet he hesitated. It seems he felt he had much more to learn from his master. Nor was he under any pressure to earn an income. Upon turning twenty-one, he inherited as his share of his father's estate some three thousand acres in Albemarle County and the slaves to work them. Each time Jefferson left on a periodic inspection of his properties, Wythe perhaps expected a letter saying he was abandoning his studies to become a gentleman planter but no, at the end of each summer, like a migrating bird, he left his country estate and returned to Williamsburg for the winter months. He followed this practice over the next three years.

Jefferson studied under Wythe's guidance for five years, off and on. His father had died in 1757, so it seems possible that during this period he looked upon Wythe as a substitute parent or, as he characterized it in his mature years, "a second father." Certainly he felt the need of a guiding hand, as he later reflected: "When I recollect at 14 years of age the whole care and direction of myself was thrown on myself entirely, without a relative or friend qualified to advise or guide me, and recollect the various sorts of bad company with which I associated from time to time, I am astounded I did not turn off with some of them, and become as worthless to society as they were."

One winter, Jefferson received a singular compliment when Governor Fauquier invited him to play second violin in the palace quartet. The dramatic music of Handel was then the rage. Dressed in embroidered coats, lace-ruffled cuffs and periwigs, the musicians assembled each week in the ballroom: Jefferson, the governor (harpsichord), and two notables of the Virginia aristocracy, John Randolph (first violin) and Robert Carter (German flute).

These few years, a decade before Virginians threw themselves at the throats of their British masters, were the happiest of Wythe's life. He found huge delight in his personal and professional life: in his marriage to Elizabeth, in tutoring a student of Jefferson's ability, in his success as an attorney, and above all in the scattered hours of friendship and debate he shared with Fauquier, Small and Jefferson in the parlors of the palace. How precious these times were none of them could foresee, for within a few short years the *partie quarrée* would be shattered by conflict and death.

5

Revolution in the Air

*The Two Penny Act—Wythe and the Parson's
Cause—introducing Patrick Henry—Henry and the
Parson's Cause—Henry as a lawyer—protest
against stamp duty—the newest member of the
House of Burgesses—an assault on priv-
ilege—Henry's fifth amendment*

Considered in isolation the Parson's Cause was no more than a duck-pond
squall over how much tobacco the clergy of the Church of England should
be paid for their religious duties. Yet it is possible to see it as the conjuring
up of a rebellious spirit that would eventually diffuse through the thirteen
colonies and inspire a revolution.

Tobacco was not just legal tender in Virginia, it was the colony's
only significant export. Unfortunately, it was a distressingly unstable
commodity on which to found a community's wealth. Prices fluctuated
alarmingly, and periodically crops failed. When tobacco went well, the
colony prospered; when prices fell, spirits faltered. Everyone's spirit
faltered during the seasons of 1757–58, when unusually cold springs followed by two dry summers led to poor harvests. The House of Burgesses
responded by passing remedial legislation, called the Two Penny Act. It
provided that debts, contracts and salaries payable in tobacco could be
paid in cash at a rate of exchange of twopence per pound of leaf. This

was supposed to be a temporary emergency measure. Governor Fauquier assented to it without seeking London's approval, which proved to be a grave mistake for his career.

Although the new rate of conversion applied to a wide range of transactions, it fell with particular harshness on the clergy of the Church of England, who complained that this was not reform but robbery. For years, priests had been paid an annual stipend of 16,000 pounds of tobacco from the county coffers. Now they were paid twopence a pound. The clergy argued that with the price of tobacco at sixpence a pound, their remuneration had been devalued by two-thirds.

The priests rallied. They met in conclave, protested to the authorities in London, commenced lawsuits and released a snowstorm of pamphlets. Reverend Jacob Rowe, a professor at William and Mary, went so far to declare he would not administer the sacrament to those members of the Burgesses who had voted for legislation. (He recanted after the house ordered the sergeant-at-arms to take him into custody for contempt.)

George Wythe, as the nominee of the clergy-dominated William and Mary College in the Burgesses, made a speech to the assembly urging that the clergy be given their tobacco. Neither his address, nor the clergy's protests, produced a flutter of sympathy from the house. Soon after, the Professor of Divinity at William and Mary, the Reverend John Camm, hurried to London to protest about this unwarranted attack on the Anglican Church. After alarming the Bishop of London and the Archbishop of Canterbury with tales of persecution, he appeared before the Board of Trade and the Privy Council. He must have performed well because, soon after, a report went up to the King in Council, causing it to disallow the Two Penny Act. The Council also rebuked Governor Fauquier for approving the laws in the first place—adding that if he incurred the royal displeasure again he may be recalled.

Fauquier felt obliged to write to his London masters in explanation. Not only had the measure been a temporary one to ease a burden on the people, he said, he was merely following a precedent set by the last governor:

> And I conceive it would be a very wrong step for me to take, who
> was an entire stranger to the distresses of the country, to set my face

against the whole colony by refusing a bill which I had a precedent for passing. Whatever may be the case now, I am persuaded that if I had refused it, I must have despaired of ever gaining any influence either in the Council or House of Burgesses.

He received no reply.

Fauquier was so outraged by Camm's tale-telling that when the reverend gentleman came strutting up to the palace clutching the king's writ outlawing the Two Penny Act, the governor's temper got the better of him. The Reverend William Robinson, who had accompanied Camm, described what happened:

He came out and called with great violence—Call my negroes, says he, call all my negroes, in high wrath. When the negroes were come, look at him, mark him, says he, that you may know him again, & running his finger close up to my face: & if this gentlemen ever hereafter approach my gates, take care that you do not suffer him to enter them.

But if the news that the house's legislation had been put at naught by London was greeted with pleasure by the men of cloth, most Virginians were dismayed. Pamphlets and broadsides appeared, flaying the clergy as worldly and rapacious (they "wanted an opportunity of feasting as largely as they could on all, both rich and poor," said one). In turn, the churchmen hinted darkly at the growing influence of the Baptists and Presbyterians over the sinews of government.

A few years later, Wythe, as the presiding justice at the Elizabeth City Court in Hampton, was called upon to decide a bitterly fought action that was a consequence of the Parson's Cause. A local cleric, the Reverend Thomas Warrington, a gentleman of high religious principles and a stubborn sense of what was his due, was not content with the restoration of his annual stipend of 16,000 pounds of tobacco. He determined on suing the county collector of parish levies for the short payment of his stipend during the several years it took for London to overrule the Virginian legislation.

The case was heard in 1763, with Wythe and five other gentlemen on the bench, and a jury of twelve empanelled. The jury wisely returned a special verdict on a matter of law—leaving Wythe to rule whether the Two Penny Act was effective before it was disallowed by George II and his council. Warrington and his supporters, remembering Wythe's speech of 1759 in the Burgesses urging that clergy be exempted from the act, perhaps expected a favorable decision. Instead the court dismissed Warrington's claim. It seemed clear-cut to Wythe. The King in Council had merely disallowed the Two Penny Act; it had not said the act never existed. Thus, during the period covered by Warrington's claim, the act was effective and he was not entitled to back pay.

That was not the end of the matter, for another parson brought a similar case nine months later, one that catapulted an attorney called Patrick Henry to public notice.

*

Thomas Jefferson enjoyed telling the story of his first meeting with Patrick Henry. Jefferson was only sixteen, and on his way to Williamsburg to study at William and Mary College, when he was invited to stay at a Colonel Dandridge's house in Hanover County for the Christmas season. Every evening a man in his mid-twenties walked up from a neighboring property to join in the music and dancing. This was Henry. Jefferson recalled:

> His manners had something of the coarseness of the society he had frequented; his passion was fiddling, dancing and pleasantry. He excelled in the last, and it attached everyone to him.

A few months later, the fiddler appeared at William and Mary to call on Jefferson, and announced, with a great show of familiarity, that he was in Williamsburg to obtain a license to practice as a lawyer. Jefferson was astonished. Henry boasted that he had spent a single month in the study of law before obtaining his license. This was perhaps hyperbole: others said his legal training was six weeks to nine months of reading just one text, Coke's *Commentary on Littleton*. In any case, Henry gained his license. He was well connected in Hanover County. His father was a magistrate and his uncle an influential clergyman, and somehow he managed to satisfy several respected attorneys of his ability in argument, although perhaps not in his knowledge of the law. By the time he knocked on Wythe's door he had been examined and passed by Robert Nicholas and the brothers, Peyton and John Randolph. Wythe, after some hesitation, signed as well.[4]

Wythe did not see Henry for some time after that. While he was busy in Williamsburg's superior courts, Henry waited for clients in a tavern he ran for his father-in-law, opposite the Hanover courthouse. There, he offered free legal advice to the rough-hewn imbibers at the bar, entertained travelers on his fiddle, and occasionally ventured forth to argue a case across the road. Yet he managed to lose money, surely one of the few men in Virginia selling liquor and practicing law to do so.

After three years of hanging around court, appearing at reduced fees for poor clients (who rarely paid anyway), Henry made himself famous in the course of a single morning. The Reverend James Maury, like the Reverend Warrington, had demanded compensation from county officials for the years he was underpaid while the Two Penny Act was in force.

Henry took no part in the first day's hearing, because the collector of parish levies had hired another attorney, John Lewis, to argue the defense. The day concluded with the justices (one of whom was Patrick Henry's own father) finding the law was in Maury's favor because the act was void from the beginning. Lewis, believing all was lost, withdrew from the case. When the court resumed three weeks later the jury would have the simple task of calculating how much Maury was owed. Looking around for a replacement, the collector of parish levies found Patrick Henry serving bumbo in the tavern across the street. Henry leapt at the chance.

By the time Maury's case resumed it had become a cause célèbre. The growing number of Presbyterian, Calvinistic and New Light dissenters who inhabited Hanover County seethed at being taxed so that tobacco

---

4   Jefferson claimed that "Mr. Wythe absolutely refused" to sign. However court documents show otherwise—Wythe did sign Henry's application to practice.

could be given to prelates of a church spreading what they regarded as doctrinal errors. This was only one of a number of privileges afforded the Church of England that rankled them. Anyone holding public office had to subscribe to the articles of the Anglican faith, and the only legal marriages were those conducted before Church of England ministers. Magistrates could fine and jail those who did not attend Sunday service at the established church. Dissenting preachers were hounded by authorities and their meetinghouses licensed.

All this was anathema to Dissenters who believed a new land meant new freedoms. Thus when Henry elbowed his way through the courthouse doors every available space was filled by the opposing sides. On one side of the public gallery stood rows of grim Dissenters in buckskin breeches and coonskin caps, squaring off against twenty or so smooth-faced ministers in clerical-gray coats and white bibs.

No one recorded the incendiary things Henry said in court about the greed of priests, their holding of multiple appointments to parishes, or devotion to farming their glebes rather than saving souls. These were common topics for barroom ranters, and hardly exceptional. But what he dared say about King George was savored in repetition for years to come.

Defiantly, Henry stood and praised the Two Penny Act. It was a good law; it served the community's need in times of distress. But the king, said Henry, raising his voice in great severity, "by disallowing acts of this salutary nature, from being the father of this people has degenerated into a tyrant, and forfeits all rights to his subjects' obedience!"

A shocked silence followed these words. It was astounding to the citizens of Hanover County that King George could forfeit his right to anything, let alone obedience. Some in the body of the court hissed treason, but they in turn were silenced by murmurs of support from the Dissenters.

Raising his voice above the uproar, Henry condemned the clergy for defying Virginia's own legislature. The community had no further need of ministers such as these, he said, as he waved dismissively at the priests opposite him. Roars of approval rose from one side and hisses of outrage from the other. Henry turned and pointed to the jurymen, and said:

that excepting they were disposed to rivet the chains of bondage on their own necks, he hoped they would not let slip the opportunity which now offered, of making such an example of him [Maury] as might, hereafter, be a warning to himself and his brethren, not to have the temerity, for the future, to dispute the validity of such laws.

It was all over by lunchtime. The jury awarded Maury a paltry one penny and, proud of a job well done, they marched manfully onto the green to be greeted by thunderous applause from the crowd outside. Calls for Henry grew to a roaring demand. So bidden, Henry appeared at the courthouse doors. He was lifted on high by willing shoulders and paraded around the forecourt to the adulation of the multitude. None saw the ministers leaving by a side door.

Thereafter, Wythe occasionally met Henry around the county courts, perhaps accompanied by an admiring yeoman whose case he was pursuing with much declamation but little application of legal knowledge. Jefferson once haughtily observed that Henry was "totally unqualified for any but mere jury causes." Even Henry's worshipful biographer, William Wirt, conceded that Henry was "woefully deficient as a lawyer." As someone who had served his country as attorney general (1817–29), Wirt was surely well placed to judge. He claimed that Henry "was not only unable to draw a declaration or a plea, but incapable it is said, of the most common and simple business of his profession, even of the mode of ordering a suit, giving a notice, or making a motion in court."

Often, Henry would refer to a case supposedly in support of his client's interests, only to have the judge explain that it supported a contrary principle. Such niceties never fazed the audacious Henry, who believed a bold assertion of the law generally turned out for the best. He had no Greek, and precious little Latin. Rather than being abashed by his deficiency, he appeared to rejoice in it. Backwoods American was his vernacular and he was a champion at it. Natural became "naiteral", learning became "larnin'", angling became "anglin'" and earth became "yearth". This "orator of nature", as he came to be styled, relied on his closing address to the jury. He possessed an uncanny ability to have each juryman feel as if he was speaking solely to him, as a plain man, as if both were sitting around a potbelly stove on a snowy night.

Wrote Wirt:

> he understood the human character so perfectly; knew so well all its strength and all its weaknesses, together with every path and by-way which winds around to the citadel of the best fortified heart and mind, that he never failed to take them, either by stratagem or storm. Hence he was, beyond doubt, the ablest defender of criminals in Virginia, and will probably never be equaled again.

Cross-examining prosecution witnesses, Henry would ridicule them until they were reduced to a state of stutters and jerks—then triumphantly inform the court that their demeanor indicated they were telling lies. On other occasions he would turn to the members of the public crowding the court, and enlist them to his cause by referring to some irrelevancy such as a horse race, a local trollop, or an esteemed tavern owner. Soon he would have the onlookers chuckling or sneering as the occasion demanded, thus overwhelming whatever good sense the jury retained.

One Patrick Henry story in particular has become legendary: the case of the stunned turkey and the well-fed wagoner. It was a typical market-court shenanigans. A team of wagon horses had trampled a turkey underfoot, and the wagoner and his passenger were accused of throwing it into the cart and driving off. The wagoner agreed to take a whipping rather than be sent to jail, but the passenger insisted that he was wholly innocent. Henry, to the contrary, contended that the man was "a party, present, aiding and assisting." The passenger's denials were going well until Henry rose to address the jury, saying "He tells you he had nothing to do with the turkey—and I daresay that is true (dramatic pause of which Henry was a master)—at least not until it was *roasted*." With much eye-rolling, and whirl of his tongue, Henry dragged *roasted* into such a comic extension that the whole court collapsed into a fit of laughter, and with that the jury jollied the passenger to inglorious defeat.

Many years later after he obtained revolutionary fame, Henry again triumphed, appearing for a man accused of seizing two steers from a

Mr. Hook and delivering them to Washington's army. The case was all but lost until Henry stood before the jury. He painted a distressing picture of the general's troops, shivering with cold and hunger as they marched in threadbare uniforms under a leaden sky, marking their course in the snow with the blood of their unshod feet.

Henry asked the jurymen: "Who would not have fed this starving band as it trudged through the snow? Who amongst you would not have opened the doors of your house, the very portals of your breast to receive that little band of famished patriots?" He cupped his hand to his ear. "But hark, what notes of discord are there which disturb such a wintry scene. Hark, what can I hear? Why, there is a human cry echoing through the mist. It is from Mr Hook. He is calling for his missing animals: *Beef! beef! beef!*" Henry's mournful mocking produced a paroxysm of laughter, then a rumble taken up by the courtroom audience: *Beef! beef! beef!* It was followed by a cry for tar and feathers, as Mr. Hook fled the courthouse.

After his triumph in the Parson's Cause, Henry carried his packet of law books farther west to the "hill-'n-holler" county of Louisa. It is said that on court days he would go deer hunting with his cronies, and then rush into the courthouse still wearing buckskin breeches and leggings. With a pair of saddlebags draped over his arm, he would take the first case to be called. While bearded men with guns milled outside, he would rant and bamboozle the justice and jury, winning more often than not. His clients, whatever the outcome, regarded it as worth Henry's fee just to watch him humiliate the opposition. The orator of nature accepted whatever his rural clients could afford—be it peach brandy in demijohns, leathers, cows, or the hire of a slave for a quarter of a year.

*

In the spring of 1764, ships furrowing up the James River brought letters from London announcing that Parliament intended to impose a new tax in the form of stamps on all documents issued in the colonies. It seemed a reasonable proposition to the British. The expense of wresting North America from the French had drained the Treasury, and now it faced the cost of permanently stationing troops in the colonies to defend its possessions. Much gallant British blood had been spilt for Americans; it was time they paid the costs of empire.

The Virginia House of Burgesses did not see the tax in quite the same way. In a spurt of activity, this house regarded by Britain to be of subordinate rank, resolved to send a memorandum of concern to King George, an address of disapproval to the House of Lords, a remonstrance to the House of Commons, and a friendly communication to Massachusetts, in support of its objections to the same tax.

Wythe was now the elected member for Elizabeth City County, having at last won the seat in May of 1761. He was made a member of the Committee of Correspondence charged with drafting some of the protest. Putting pen to paper in his "remonstrance" to the House of Commons, he found himself expressing a hostility to Britain he hardly knew he possessed. No matter how adroitly he skirted the issue, what was being said would offend London. According to Jefferson, Wythe wrote "with so much freedom, that, as he told me himself, his colleagues of the committee shrank from it as bearing the aspect of treason, and smoothed its features."

Wythe tempered himself in a redraft, though his colleagues were still not satisfied, and further passages were excised. Even so the finished communication contained enough spirited language in the opening sentences to make Virginia's opposition to the taxes unmistakable. It defiantly insisted that "it is essential to British liberty, that laws, imposing taxes on the people, ought not be made without the consent of representatives chosen by themselves."

Fauquier, of course, was aware of Wythe's role, and may even have seen his first draft and suggested it should be toned down. The governor was dismayed that a dispute not of his making had placed him on opposing sides to many in Virginia, especially Wythe and Jefferson. He suspected that Virginia's hostility to the mother country was set to become more strident.

*

In 1765, Patrick Henry entered the House of Burgesses as an elected representative for Louisa County. In the Burgesses, the natural opposition to

Henry's leveling rhetoric came from the Tidewater gentry, whose estates sat on peninsulas of fertile land between rivers beating to the rhythm of the sea. In uplands Louisa County, tobacco ships could not go, but poor German, Scots and Irish immigrants could. It was there that Henry established his political base by defending backwoodsmen in court, playing the fiddle at country dances and attacking the privileges of the wealthy.

Within days of taking his seat, Henry, not yet a man of thirty years, was shouting and haranguing the elders of the House of Burgesses in a most alarming manner. It was not difficult to sniff out scandal in the patronage-ridden Burgesses, but Henry's target quite took the breath away. The Speaker of the assembly was John Robinson, a scion of the aristocracy and a man of culture and impeccable manners—in short the very image of a Virginian gentleman. He owned three hundred slaves and forty thousand acres of the best Tidewater land. For twenty-eight years, splendid in his full wig, cassock and gold-laced surplice, he had kept firm order with grace and avuncular wit from the Burgesses' gabled Speaker's chair. He was also treasurer of the colony and acquainted with everyone of importance in the colony.

A few days after Henry took his seat, the venerable Robinson, in a voice of sympathetic concern, reminded the house that many planters had fallen deeply in debt and faced ruin. Not that it was their fault: they had been betrayed by British merchants who, after enticing them to borrow beyond their means, were now cutting back on credit. He suggested that the government raise £240,000 from England at 5 percent interest, and use the bulk of it to establish a loan office to tide distressed planters over their difficulties. Members of the house, particularly those of great wealth and great debt, thought it a sound proposal.

Robinson's plan was set to pass into law until Patrick Henry asked for leave to be heard. Dressed in a flaming scarlet cloak, his head covered by a wig so moth-eaten that it showed patches of bald card beneath, the newest member of the house, without the courtesy of polite preliminaries, proceeded to birch Robinson's proposal. There were murmurs of protest, but Henry continued right on gnawing at the aristocracy, to the delight of the upcountry members who for years had been too reticent to criticize their social betters.

Student-at-law Thomas Jefferson was observing proceedings in the chamber when Henry launched his attack: "I can never forget a particular exclamation of his in the debate, which electrified his hearers ... 'What, sir!' exclaimed Mr. Henry, 'is it proposed then to reclaim the spendthrift from his dissipation and extravagance by filling his pockets with money!' "

Yet Henry's oratory availed nothing against implacable self-interest. When the vote was taken, the mountain counties were with him but the Tidewater majority carried Robinson's plan. When it was placed before the Governor's Council, however, such was its odor that it was defeated there.

"From this moment he [Henry] had no friends on the aristocratic side of the house," wrote Wirt. Rather than ridiculing the representative for Louisa Country for "his vicious and depraved pronunciation and homespun coarseness of his language," the aristocracy now "looked upon him with envy and with terror."

The following week, Henry threw another firebrand into the temple of talk. By then, the house had been sitting for a month and its session was drawing to a close. The temper of the assembly was fretful. As Fauquier told his London superiors, "The colony is greatly indebted to Great Britain ... which renders them uneasy, peevish and ready to murmur at every occurrence." Earlier in the session news had reached the House of Burgesses of Britain's response to its letters of protest. Parliament had passed the Stamp Act! As an additional insult, Virginia's London agent wrote that the law had been enacted after a most cursory debate before a half-empty chamber. It seemed that the carefully labored remonstrations of the Committee of Correspondence to the king, Lords and Commons had been read by no one, or completely disregarded, if they had.

Summer had come early, and Williamsburg was dripping with humidity and buzzing with mosquitoes. The burgesses were anxious to return home, which for many lay a ride of several days away. A few members made desultory speeches expressing anger and dismay at the news from London, then in a mood of bitter acceptance most began to pack up for an early departure. Not so a handful who remained behind, plotting a more vigorous response. They gathered in a conspiratorial huddle around Patrick Henry.

The next day, as the first order of business, Henry stood up and read a series of resolutions objecting to the Stamp Act. The first declared that the settlers of Virginia brought with them and transmitted to their posterity all the rights of the inhabitants of Great Britain; the second, that royal charters granted by James I had admitted the same; the third, that taxation by the people or their representatives was a characteristic of British freedom; the fourth and final resolution that this most ancient colony had enjoyed these rights without interruption.

Attendance by this stage had thinned to about a third of the delegates, thirty-nine of 116. After a bitter debate, the house adjourned to the following morning. The next day Wythe gathered up Jefferson and took him with him to the Capitol to observe the excitement. Jefferson stood in the doorway, listening in awe as Henry proceeded with his four resolutions, plus an additional one he had drafted overnight for good measure. He "appeared to speak to me as Homer wrote," said the awestruck Jefferson. "The debate was most bloody."

Henry, raising his voice clear above the din, roared the words that have gone down in history: "Caesar had his Brutus, Charles the First had his Cromwell, and George the Third ... [amidst calls of treason, Henry straightened himself to his full height, and gathered his breath] ... and George the Third may profit from their example."

There was a buzz of outrage from Speaker Robinson. "Traitor! Traitor!" called some in the house. Brothers John and Peyton Randolph, Virginian aristocrats to their bootstraps, rose from their seats demanding Henry withdraw his comments. "I well remember the cry of treason," wrote Jefferson, "the pause of Mr. Henry at the name of George the III, and the presence of mind with which he closed his sentence."

Henry looked around the chamber with the fire of conviction coursing through his veins. There were more calls of *traitor*. The protests were only sauce to Henry. He turned directly to his accusers, and in the exultation of the moment spat out: "If this be treason, make the most of it." His resolutions were put to the vote. The first four resolutions followed the earlier remonstrations to the British government, though shorn of their ornate language. They passed easily. The fifth, much stronger, passed by one vote. It read:

That the General Assembly of this Colony have the only and sole exclusive right and power to lay taxes and impositions upon the inhabitants of this Colony, and that every attempt to vest such power in any person or persons whatsoever other than the General Assembly aforesaid has a manifest tendency to destroy British as well as American freedom.

The portly attorney general, Peyton Randolph, his face a purple sheen of indignation, huffed out of the chamber, muttering words that Jefferson, standing in the lobby, overheard: "By god I would have given 500 guineas for a single vote." Patrick Henry, well satisfied with his day's work, left Williamsburg for home.

*

The foregoing account of Henry's assault on the Stamp Act is a conventional one, the stuff of legend, and somewhat short on historical evidence. None of the thirty-nine burgesses present that day wrote an account of what happened, and no record of the debate appears in the journal of the house.

However, there was another observer standing beside Jefferson in the doorway of the Burgesses that day. He was an agent of the French government, a spy perhaps, and it was not until 1921 that his account was discovered in the Paris archives of the Service Hydrographique de la Marine. The version of this unknown Frenchman substantiates the tradition of Henry's initial boldness, then rather punctures the legend of Henry's defiance when accused of treason. His journal entry for May 30, 1765, read:

Set out early ... and broke fast at York, arrived at Williamsburg at 12, where I saw three Negroes hanging at the gallows for having robbed Mr Walthoe of 300ps.[5] I went immediately to the assembly which was sitting, where I was entertained with very strong debates

---

5   Spanish pesos. The Frenchman's journal is in poor English. The present author has made slight corrections.

concerning duties that the parliament wants to lay on the American Colonies, which they call or style Stamp Duties. Shortly after I came in one of the members stood up and said he had read that in former times Tarquin and Julius had their Brutus, Charles had his Cromwell, and he did not doubt but some good American would stand up in favour of his country, but (says he) in a more moderate manner, and was going to continue, when the speaker of the house rose and said, he, the last that stood up had spoken treason, and was sorry to see that not one of the members of the House was loyal enough to stop him, before he had gone so far, upon which the same member stood up again (his name is Henery) and said that if he had affronted the speaker or the house, he was ready to ask pardon, and he would show his loyalty to His Majesty the King G. the third, at the expense of the last drop of his blood, but what he had said must be attributed to the interest of his country's dying liberty which he had at heart, and that the heat of passion might have led him to have said something more than he intended, but, again, if he said anything wrong, he begged the speaker and the House's pardon.

Jefferson, apparently fascinated by these scenes of dissension among his elders, attended the Capitol the next day. There he saw Peter Randolph at the clerk's table leafing through the journals of the house. Randolph turned to the young witness and explained that he was in search of a precedent to allow him to expunge the record of the previous day's unseemly vote. Evidently he found one, for that afternoon he and a number of like-minded members voted to expunge the fifth resolution from the record, then marched to the printer's office to ensure it was removed from the press. Thus Randolph prevented the inflammatory fifth resolution from appearing in the journals of the House of Burgesses. However, Henry's supporters won handsomely in the wider record of public opinion, for several newspapers printed six resolutions purportedly adopted by the assembly. The mythical sixth read:

That His Majesty's liege people, the inhabitants of this Colony, are not bound to yield obedience to any law or ordinance whatever, designed to impose any taxation whatsoever upon them, other than the laws or ordinances of the General Assembly aforesaid.

The *Maryland Gazette* even published a seventh:

That any Person who shall, by speaking or writing, assert or maintain, that any person or persons, other than the General Assembly of this colony, have any right or power to lay or impose any tax whatever on the inhabitants thereof, shall be deemed an enemy to this, His Majesty's colony.

As the news of Henry's outburst traveled north, it appeared to readers that the newest member of Virginia's House of Burgesses, far from exposing the Virginian assembly to a squall, had set loose a threatening storm.

6

Death and Taxes

The governor dissolves the assembly—the Stamp Act—scandal in the Burgesses—Wythe promoted—the Townshend Act—illness and death of Governor Fauquier—Fauquier's will—his views on slavery

In dismay, Governor Fauquier sent a copy of the first four resolutions (but not the censored fifth) to the lords of the Board of Trade in London. After outlining what had happened in the house, he commented: "The most strenuous opposers of this rash heat were the late speaker [John Robinson], the King's Attorney [Peyton Randolph] and Mr Wythe; but they were over powered by the young, hot and giddy members. I have heard that very indecent language was used by Mr Henry a young lawyer who had not been a month a member of the House; who carried all the young members with him."

These were perplexing times. There was Peyton Randolph calling Henry a traitor, yet a decade later he ended up as president of the Continental Convention charged with drawing up a declaration of independence. And Wythe's opposition to Henry's resolutions also seems surprising, given his own role in remonstrating with the House of Commons over its Stamp Act. Perhaps he had taken the view that once Parliament had enacted the Stamp Duty Acts, his duty as a lawyer was to accept the new order. Perhaps he was repelled by Henry's methods rather than his actual demands—that Henry had usurped the procedures of the house by putting forward his resolutions when the house was two-thirds empty. Or was he irritated that a newcomer, an upstart, in a coltish presumption of power had shown scant respect for his more experienced seniors and exposed them as timid?

If a majority of the members of the House of Burgesses had been in attendance it is more than likely Henry's resolutions would have been defeated. Right up until the eve of the revolution most of them continued to regard themselves as British, and would have bowed before King George if ever he felt inclined to visit Williamsburg. Their protests against the stamp duty extended no further than claiming the rights of Englishmen as if they had never left home; and, in particular, the right to set their own level of taxation. They wanted freedom within the empire, not freedom from it. Certainly no heart was bold enough in 1765 to conceive of a separate nation, much less to think of pitching into battle against the greatest power in the world—one that had so recently whipped France and Spain into submission.

The day following the drama of the Stamp Act Resolves, Governor Fauquier, standing tall in his silk robes of office, dissolved the House of Burgesses without "the civility of a parting speech," and ordered fresh elections. He was gambling on the voters of Virginia delivering a rebuke to Henry and his ilk, by returning a more moderate crop of burgesses. In truth, the governor played straight into the radicals' hands by demonstrating the kind of high-handedness of which they complained.

The ballot held several months later produced only four new members. Henry and the other radicals were all returned. Fauquier had failed to appreciate that while Virginians might grumble that the House of Burgesses was a palace of planter largesse, this did not mean they would tolerate its arbitrary dissolution, or allow others to attack it. Over a century, Mother England, distracted by tumultuous civil disturbance, the removal of kings and internecine wars with European kingdoms, had by imperial neglect convinced Virginians that the House of Burgesses administered the colony. Men who were tyrants on their own plantations were not likely to accept tyranny from a distant island.

Wythe was reelected by the voters of Elizabeth City County. It did not seem to matter that he rarely visited the place, and refused to fund a grogfest, or make pork barrel promises. The colony bubbled with anger against authority, and because he had ruled against the clergy in the Parson's Cause, and was known to have drafted the remonstrations against Parliament's Stamp Duty, he was respected as a man to speak out for Virginia's rights.

Fauquier, alarmed at the temperature of the burgesses, decided it prudent to advise London of his plans to give them time "to cool." Despite the fresh elections he did not call the House of Burgesses together for over a year. In the meantime, greatly wounded by the turmoil in his realm, the governor retreated to his palace. Jefferson continued to play violin in the governor's quartet, and although he and Wythe were still welcome in the governor's parlor, the feeling had changed. Whereas in the past they gave full flight to theories of freedom and equality, now they hesitated lest they cause the governor discomfort. It was not the time or place, not while the slogan "no taxation without representation" was on everyone's lips.

Moreover, the old partie quarrée had been broken up by the departure of its fourth and most lively member, William Small. In the fall of 1764, after a stay in Virginia of almost six years, Dr. Small had returned to England to purchase scientific apparatus for the college. After several months in Britain, he decided not to follow the purchases he had dispatched. He was tired of the squabbling ecclesiastics at William and Mary, and the provincial life of Virginia. But his departure left a gap that could not be filled.

The governor had grown to love Virginia and its people, and it saddened him to move among such discontent. Fauquier's position was difficult. He was enjoined by London to uphold the prerogatives of the Crown while somehow recognizing that Americans had the rights of Englishmen. The Treasury in London wanted regular remittance of revenue, while the colonists demanded control over revenue-raising and how it should be spent. The British saw Virginia as an outlying community dependent on and subject to the mother country. The colonists saw themselves as local rulers within the king's domain. Britain demanded obedience. Virginia reserved the right to resist.

Fauquier found it especially galling that, despite the royal power he represented, the only forces under his direct command were the footmen and gardeners of the palace. The Virginia militia, although nominally under his control, was in reality a part-time army of farmers, whose allegiance was to the local squires who led them out on a monthly muster on the village green, followed by cider, beer and games. Even if the governor wanted to arrest one of the radicals, he had no means of doing so. His position conveyed power and authority but, in truth, he was quite defenseless and dependent entirely on moral suasion.

If he wrote a dispatch seeking instructions, a reply could take months—if it came at all. The Board of Trade, the Privy Council, the secretary of state and the lords of the Treasury all purported to reflect the king's pleasure or parliament's will. Depending on which official was in ascendance, Fauquier could be praised or overruled for any particular action he took. Adding to his difficulties was the perception in Whitehall that he was too close to the colonials to be reliable.

*

A few powerful voices in the British Parliament took the side of the colonies and urged repeal of the Stamp Act. They included William Pitt, the Elder, a man greatly admired on both sides of the Atlantic for directing Britain's victorious war against the French. He told the House of Lords he could only see dissention and unrest if Britain ignored colonial rights. Edmund Burke, parliament's great orator, agreed, and forecast that taxing Americans against their will would be as hard as shearing a wolf. He was right. Boston led the way. A mob smashed the stamp office with axes, then holding firebrands to the night sky, surrounded the stamp distributor's home. They hung a straw-man on an elm tree and torched it. The stamp distributor, horrified at the sight of his own representation in flames, resigned the next day. Twelve days later, hooligans sacked the home of Massachusetts's lieutenant-governor.

If one colony exploded in rampage, another soon matched it. In New York, stamp agents were tarred and feathered, and traders who purchased stamps were attacked. There were violent protests in Pennsylvania, South

Carolina and Georgia. It seemed that every night, in half a dozen cities along the seaboard, citizens resisting the Stamp Act prowled the streets forcing shopkeepers not to sell products imported from Britain. Secretive patriotic groups, styling themselves the Sons of Liberty, sprang up, initially in Boston, later in New York and then month by month, as the protests spread, in almost every colony. Their members and supporters manhandled British loyalists and destroyed their property. In most regions the mere threat of violence was enough to cause stamp distributors to resign.

*

One day in October 1765, Governor Fauquier was taking his ease in the Exchange Coffeehouse, near the Capitol in Williamsburg, when his attention was seized by the sound of a mob crying "One and all" as they followed a man striding hurriedly down Duke of Gloucester Street. Fauquier stood up. To his astonishment he saw that the man was his royal stamp tax collector, Colonel George Mercer. The crowd caught up with Mercer on the Capitol steps, and in an angry chorus demanded he resign. Mercer broke free, seeking sanctuary in the coffeehouse. The mob followed, baying for Mercer to answer its question. Fauquier boldly pushed his way forward—risky perhaps, but he had judged the crowd's mood for, at a cry of "See the governor, take care of him," the multitude parted. The governor stood shoulder to shoulder with Mercer, as the crowd demanded that the tax collector satisfy them: Would he resign his post? Stubbornly, Mercer said he would give his answer at the Capitol at five the next day. In the words of Fauquier:

> The crowd did not yet disperse, it was growing dark and I did not
> think it safe to leave Mr. Mercer behind me, so I again advanced to
> the edge of the steps and said aloud I believed no man there would
> do me any hurt, and turned to Mr. Mercer and told him if he would
> walk with me through the people I believed I could conduct him safe
> to my house, and we accordingly walked side by side through the
> thickest of the people who did not molest us; tho' there were some

little murmurs. ... When we got home we had much discourse on the subject. He asked what he should do; in return I asked him whether he was afraid for his life, if he was, it was too tender a point for me to advise him; if not, his honor and interest both demanded he should hold the office.

The following afternoon Mercer stood on the Capitol's steps, and before a large and threatening crowd, read a long statement which concluded with the declaration that he would not distribute stamps. A cheer of triumph went up and Mercer was let depart in peace.

As Fauquier wrote to the Lords of Trade in London, what disturbed him most was that those baying for Mercer's blood were "chiefly if not altogether composed of gentlemen of property in the colony—some of them at the head of their respective counties, and the merchants of the country."

His report of this incident ended on a somber, if somewhat piteous note:

Thus my Lords I have in a candid and undisguised manner set the naked truth before you: and submit my conduct through this whole affair to your Lordships judgment. I must confess that I have never in the course of my life been in a situation which required so much circumspection. I have often been at a loss to form a judgment for myself how to proceed; and have often been dissatisfied with my determinations; and should have been glad of your Lordships superior abilities to assist me in my conduct.

Fauquier's correspondence concluded, tellingly, with the tactful complaint that London had failed to keep him informed: "I even have not the common notice of there being such an Act, as it has never been sent to me, but my zeal to promote his Majesty's service never let me take this into consideration."

*

By the time the Stamp Act came into effect in November 1765, every stamp distributor in Virginia had been chased from office. Newspapers sold free of stamps, custom officers released cargo without stamped papers, citizens entered into mortgages and leases without bothering about stamps, and agitators took pride in handing out their unstamped pamphlets.

When Fauquier took the bench as chief judge of the General Court he had to suffer the embarrassment of being told that none of the writs had been stamped, so by virtue of Britain's own law, they were a nullity. He adjourned proceedings and rode back to his palace, a greatly troubled man. Throughout the colony, the lesser courts followed suit, the justices saying they were not reopening their doors until spring, much to the relief of debtors and the dismay of creditors. Virginia owed something like two million pounds to British bankers and merchants, and not a few of the gentry faced bankruptcy or sale of the family estate—giving rise to the oft-heard jibe that the larger the debt, the greater the patriot.

As the population adjusted readily to disobedience to the Crown, while fearing that any day a man-of-war would appear out of the fog to bloody their rebel noses, Britain backed down. To the utter surprise of all, the Stamp Act was repealed.

Everyone took credit. In Boston the Sons of Liberty claimed the repeal was due its campaign to "persuade" agents not to sell stamps. Others said thanks should go to James Otis and the Stamp Act Congress[6] which convinced traders not to import British goods. Those who lobbied Whitehall said it was because British merchants fearing a downturn in trade had demanded it; others praised Benjamin Franklin, the American statesman who had been sent to London by Pennsylvania to tell the committeemen of the House of Commons that Americans would only submit by force of arms.

Loyalists said it showed the goodness of the king and the common sense of parliament, while gentlemen of property, watching drunken crowds dancing around celebratory bonfires in Boston and New York, saw it as a horrible

---

6 On the motion of James Otis, the Massachusetts House of Representatives sent a letter to the other colonies suggesting a meeting of the various houses to protest against the Stamp Act. In October of 1765, delegates from nine colonies met in New York. Virginia, New Hampshire, North Carolina and Georgia did not attend. After two weeks of turbulent debate the congress drafted a Declaration of Rights and Grievances, centered on the demand that "no taxes be imposed on them but with their own consent."

victory for mob violence. The House of Burgesses in Williamsburg, in a paroxysm of relief, voted funds for the erection of a statue of King George. The effervescence soon subsided and the proposal was shuffled off to a statue committee, where, not surprisingly, the idea languished.

Meantime, Patrick Henry's reputation rose to new heights. The "orator of nature" was now known throughout the colonies as a man ready to oppose an empire that reached across oceans and was determined to make the American colonies slaves to its bidding.

In a churlish afterword to the repeal, Britain passed the Declaratory Act of 1766 which insisted that Parliament "had, hath, and of right ought to have, full power and authority to make laws and statutes of sufficient force and validity to bind the colonies and people of America, subjects to the crown of Great Britain, in all cases whatsoever."

These imperialistic dictates were eerily similar to those of the Irish Declaration Act of 1719–20 that had turned Ireland into a crown colony. It was sobering for Americans to realize that despite their protests, the mother country still regarded colonial legislatures as little more than provincial debating societies.

*

Soon after the colonies' triumph, Virginia's most revered legislator, John Robinson, passed away from the "torment of the stone." It was Robinson who, while Speaker of the House of Burgesses, had promoted a scheme to create a loan office for debt-ridden planters, only to have it scuttled by Patrick Henry. Barely had this eminence been laid to rest with full and sentimental ceremony when whispers began to emerge from Treasury that the man thought as honest as a presbyter had filched immense sums from the colony's coffers and distributed them to his friends. The amounts were enormous, rumored to be over one hundred thousand pounds.

Details were hard to come by because a goodly number of the aristocratic clique in the House of Burgesses had been beneficiaries, and they refused access to the accounts. Patrick Henry and Richard Henry Lee smelt blood, and began hounding the Treasury for names and amounts. Over time, in dribs and drabs, details emerged.

There was nothing sophisticated about Robinson's methods. When paper currency issued to fund the French and Indian War was called in, rather than burning it Robinson lent it to the colony's notable families to meet their debts—through an excess of kindness of the heart it seemed, because he personally gained nothing. His accounts for the loans were in disarray, and most of the borrowers, claiming innocence, said they thought the loans were from Robinson and not from public funds.

Then, in another scandal involving the Robinson clan, Colonel Chiswell ran his sword though an unarmed merchant in a tavern argument, killing him. Chiswell was John Robinson's father-in-law, and a former burgess himself. There was public outrage when he was granted bail by a court of his friends despite facing a charge of murder.

The controversy took a dramatic twist. On the eve of his trial Colonel Chiswell suddenly died. His doctor declared he succumbed to "nervous fits, owing to a constant uneasiness of the mind." An angry mob, suspecting that Chiswell's death was a ruse so he could flee to England, stormed the family plantation of Scotchtown in Hanover County, and blocked the funeral procession. They told the bereaved family that they would not move until the coffin was opened. The lid was prized off, but the corpse was so blackened it was impossible to identify the body. Only after close acquaintances of the deceased came forward to say that indeed it was the colonel, was the burial allowed to proceed.

These tawdry scandals had two consequences. First, they enhanced Henry and Lee's reputation as champions of the people. Second, and more surprisingly, they emboldened other critics of the establishment. Until the Robinson and Chiswell affairs, Virginia's docile press had rarely printed items that reflected poorly on the legislature, the aristocracy or the governor. Instead it filled its columns with news lifted from London, New York and Philadelphia, official notices, obituaries and shipping news.

Once citizens put pen to paper and tasted the pleasure of traducing the well-fed, they looked around for other victims to savage. Readily at hand was a royal governor feigning power and authority, but in truth quite defenseless. Fauquier, disillusioned, wrote home to his superiors: "Everything is become a matter of heat and party faction; everything is contested; a spirit of discontent and cavil runs through the colony."

*

Wythe was not one of those favored by Robinson, nor did he have any role in exposing the sorry affair. His life was already busy enough without taking on the role of a public addresser of wrongs. He was counselor, conveyancer, mediator, drawer of wills and drafter of documents. All this besides his service as occasional magistrate in Hampton, legislator in Williamsburg and attorney of the General Court. In 1786, he was elected mayor of the Common Hall of Williamsburg, becoming responsible for oversight of the repair of roads, the regulation of fairs, the fire service, and the night watch from ten o'clock to dawn.

It was during these years of public service that Wythe gained the reputation of being one of those rarest of creatures, a lawyer little interested in money. He declined to appear in bad cases and was neglectful in sending accounts to his clients. Once he wrote:

Sir: The suit wherein you were pleased to do me the honor to engage my services, was last week brought to trial, and has fully satisfied me that you were entirely in the wrong. Knowing you to be a perfectly honest man, I concluded that you have somehow or other been misled. At any rate I find that I have been altogether misled in the affair, and therefore insist on washing my hands of it immediately ... I hasten therefore to enclose you the fifty dollar note you gave me as a fee, and with it my advice, that you compromise the matter on the best terms you can ...

I have just to add, that as conscience will not allow me to say anything for you, honor forbids that I should say anything against you. But, by all means compromise, and save the costs. Adieu—wishing you that inward sunshine, which nothing outward can darken.

Geo. Wythe

No wonder that the Reverend Lee Massey of Fairfax County once called George Wythe "the only honest lawyer he ever knew."

After the scandal of the Robinson fraud, it was deemed essential to separate the offices of Speaker and treasurer. Robert Carter Nicholas was appointed to the latter role, and Peyton Randolph moved to the Speaker's chair, leaving the position of attorney general vacant. Governor Fauquier favored Wythe for the appointment. Unfortunately, the appointment was not within his gift, so he penned a gushing letter of support to his Whitehall superiors:

> He is a gentleman of a most unexceptional character for his knowledge of the law, his candor, integrity and inflexibility. May I presume to ask Your Lordship's interest to procure His Majesty's confirmation of my nomination. I should not dare to ask this particular favor did I not think it for his Majesty's service to promote men who have constantly and uniformly supported government and all His Majesty's requisitions on the house of Burgess where he [Wythe] has as much weight as any member.[7]

Wythe was not the only one interested in the position. The post of attorney general was a grace-and-favor appointment that the British gifted to old reliables. The influential Randolph family lobbied connections in Whitehall for one of their own, John Randolph.

It was a measure of Fauquier's waning influence in London that Wythe thought it wise to seek support from Benjamin Franklin. Wythe had met Franklin when the scientist and statesman attended William and Mary College in March 1756 to receive an honorary degree for his experiments on the electrical nature of lightning. Wythe wrote to him, suggesting Governor Fauquier's recommendation would be more effectual if it was known that "such a promotion would be in any degree pleasing to Doctor Franklin. If you incline to honor me with your patronage in this competition, you will perhaps be partly instrumental in producing that rare phenomena a contented mind." If Franklin backed Wythe's appointment he was ignored, as was Fauquier. London appointed John Randolph.

---

7   *unexceptional*: presumably Fauquier meant to write exceptional. *inflexibility*: meaning incorruptibility, or as London might understand, not one to be persuaded by colonial allegiances to ignore instructions.

Fauquier may not have had the authority to make Wythe the colony's attorney general but he could offer him the post of clerk of the House of Burgesses. Wythe readily accepted. Despite its lowly-sounding title, it was an influential position which gave him administrative control of the business of the assembly, and made him privy to proceedings in the committees. To accept the appointment, he had to resign from the House of Burgesses. Others might have the frontline glory, Wythe was now strategically placed to guide the legislative program of the house and have a hand in drafting every bill presented. All this while he continued in the private practice of law.

Wythe took his role as clerk to the house as a great honor. From a London merchant he ordered a "robe, such as worn by the clerk of the house of commons, but better than the one I had before from mr. Child, which indeed was scandalous." (Nothing is known of the history of that inadequate garment.) He also ordered an inkstand, one hundred skins of writing parchment and "balls and other apparatus, such as are used by the house of commons in balloting." This letter reveals the absence of upper-case letters for titles in Wythe's correspondence. The practice reflected Wythe's Quaker heritage. The Society of Friends believed that displays of honor only encouraged pride.

*

In 1767, "Champagne Charlie" Townshend, Britain's wayward chancellor of the exchequer, imposed another impost on the American colonies—this one on everyday items entering American ports, such as lead, painters' colors, paper, glass, flint and tea. All justified, Townshend thought, because the money would be used to pay British troops and royal officials such as judges and governors. Remembering the widespread American resistance to the Stamp Act a few years earlier, this eccentric lawmaker authorized customs officers to break into warehouses and homes to ensure compliance.

At first there was little resistance to the duty, and a pleasing sum tinkled into the king's coffers. Then gradually, during the fall of 1768, opposition began to spread from colony to colony like seeds from a thistle.

The winds of opposition blew strongest from Massachusetts. Samuel Adams, a member of the legislature there and a key mover in the protests of 1765, declared that he would not eat, drink or wear anything British, and drafted an open letter for Massachusetts to send to the other colonies calling on them to join in a struggle against "infringements of their natural & constitutional rights." Protests spread. In New York and Boston marchers demanded shopkeepers cease selling British goods, while the Sons of Liberty patrolled the ports, intent on hindering the landing of British merchandise. Citizens everywhere signed non-importation agreements and distributed pamphlets bewailing the British plot to reduce American freedoms. Mobs attacked customs agents.

Wythe did not immediately join the boycott of British goods. As late as August 1768, he wrote to John Norton and Sons of London, purveyors of fine goods to the colonies seeking:

an elegant set of table and tea china, with bowls of the same of different sizes, decanters and drinking glasses, an handsome service of glass for a dessert, four middle sized and six lesser dishes, and three dozen plates of hard metal, 100 skins of writing parchment proper for enrolling our acts of assembly on several bundles of best quills, two pieces of blanketing and as many rolls for servants[8], 10 or 12 pairs of shoes and two slippers for myself ... The goods have not come to hand, neither have I yet had an account of sales of the tobacco. If they have not sent, nor design to send the goods, I desire you will be so kind as to let me have them, with a bonnet for mrs. Wythe. ... A few days since I desired you would procure for me a handsome well built charroit.

*

In his role of clerk to the House of Burgesses, Wythe was delegated to act as messenger to the governor explaining resolutions passed in the as-

---

8   Norton would have understood that the order of "rolls for servants" meant Wythe required a standard of cloth suitable for slaves.

sembly. As the resolutions became increasingly hostile toward the policies Fauquier was obliged to implement, these discussions must have grieved both men. Wythe could not fail to observe that his friend's health was failing. Fauquier's wife and children had returned to England, and he seemed lost and lonely in the palace. He had no answer to the growing unrest in his dominion, and despite writing long letters to his superiors in London he received little guidance or support.

At the approach of winter, the governor retreated to Yorktown, to the house of William Nelson, to recuperate. He remained absent from Williamsburg for many months. Of his infirmity nothing is known, apart from a reference in the *Virginia Gazette* of William Rind[9] to "a lingering illness and the severest attacks of the most excruciating pain submitted to ... with a fortitude and resignation known to but few." Wythe was not a man to keep a diary so there is no record of him visiting the governor in Yorktown, although surely he did. It is likely they recalled happier times of their discussions with Jefferson and Small, and wondered if the bitterness between America and Britain would, or could, be peacefully resolved.

Fauquier died on March 3, 1768, in the governor's palace at Williamsburg. He was sixty-five, and had presided over the colony for nearly ten years. There was heartfelt grief in Virginia at his passing, for despite the harsh political differences between him and the people, he was known as an honorable and humane man. Rind's *Virginia Gazette* said that "he was vigilant in government, moderate in power, exemplary in religion, and merciful where the rigor of Justice could by any means dispensed with." The *Virginia Gazette* of Purdie and Dixon paid tribute in a black-framed announcement: "He was a Gentleman of most amiable disposition—generous, just and mild; and possessed, in an eminent degree, of all the social virtues."

Jefferson, looking back more than fifty years later, described Governor Fauquier as "the ablest man who ever filled [the] office."

Fauquier's last will and testament was a composition of the Enlightenment. After describing his body as "an uninformed mass of clay" he directed physicians to open his body so that:

---

9   At this time there were two Virginia Gazettes. This occurred because when the original *Virginia Gazette* ceased publication, two rival newspapers adopted its name.

the immediate cause of my disorder may be known, and that by these means I may become more useful to my fellow creatures by my death than I have been in my life. I insist this and make it part of this my last will ... After this examination of my body, if necessary, I will that it be deposited in the earth or sea as I shall happen to fall, without any vain funeral pomp and as little expense as decency can possibly permit; funeral obsequies, as it had long appeared to me being contrary to the spirit of the religion of our Blessed Saviour, who on a proper occasion said, Let the Dead bury their Dead, follow thou me.

He then turned to the morality of slave owning. Because the laws of Virginia forbade him freeing the seventeen slaves he owned, he had made the best provision he could:[10]

It is now expedient that I should dispose of my slaves, a part of my estate in its nature disagreeable to me, but which my situation made necessary for me; the disposal of which has constantly given me uneasiness whenever the thought has occurred to me. I hope I shall be found to have been a merciful master and that none of them will rise up in judgment against me in that great day when all my actions will be exposed to public view . . . But it is not sufficient that I have been their master in my life. I must provide for them at my death by using my utmost endeavors that they experience as little misery during their lives as their unhappy and pitiable condition will allow. Therefore I will that they shall have liberty to choose their own masters, and women and children shall not be parted; that they shall have six months allowed them to make such choice, during which time they shall be maintained out of my estate; that my executors shall take for them of such masters as they shall choose 25 percent under the then market price.

---

10   An act of 1723 declared that no slave could be set free except with the permission of the Governor's Council *and* as a reward for meritorious service, for example, saving a white person's life, or revealing a slave rebellion.

An audit of Fauquier's estate valued his slaves at £758. One child, valued at £7.10s, died before sale. The remainder, sold to nine purchasers at a 25 percent discount as his will ordered, realized £587.10s.

Despite the governor's last instructions, no doctor would slice into his body, and the city insisted on a funeral suitable for its royal representative. His coffin was carried in procession, accompanied by the dignitaries of the legislature, church and militia, to the Bruton Parish Church, where he was laid to rest under a flagstone in the northern aisle.

Wythe was named in the will as one of four executors though, as a lawyer, prime responsibility fell to him. It took over four years to settle Fauquier's estate. The governor's financial affairs were chaotic and poorly documented. He had left many creditors and scanty assets scattered across the colony and the British Isles. An inventory of his Virginian possessions reflected his interests: 76 gallons of rum, 210 pint bottles of Malmsey wine, 36 dozen bottles of old cider, two microscopes, a camera obscura, a telescope, 300 books, numerous musical instruments, 30 packs of cards, and a huge collection of imported garden seed.

7

Uncertain Times

A new governor—Jefferson joins the House of Bur-
gesses—Jefferson tries slave reform—protests
against British imposts—the Boston Massac-
re—death of Botetourt—Governor Dunmore rules
Virginia—the difficult Edmund Pend-
leton—Washington raffles slaves—Somerset frees
Britain's slaves—Jefferson takes a bride

Six months after Fauquier's passing, a British man-of-war hove up the James River as night was falling. On board was His Excellency Norborne Berkeley, Baron de Botetourt. This was a fully-fledged governor, Virginia's first in sixty years, not a lieutenant substitute for another who preferred the comforts of home. Moreover, he was a peer of the realm, an honor his family could trace back to the fourteenth century.

The new governor had a treat in store for his subjects and, anxious to attract a good turnout, after landing at Yorktown he sent messengers on horseback along the peninsula to spread the news that he was on his way. His Excellency arrived in Williamsburg riding in a dazzling cream carriage trimmed with gold beads and scrolls, and led by eight milk-white horses with harnesses of polished silver. The carriage was a gift of the Duke of Cumberland, and only recently had Botetourt arranged for the heraldry of Virginia to be painted over the Cumberland crest. After such a spectacular entrance, it was something of a disappointment for the crowd assembled at the palace gates to see that the man who alighted from the carriage did not look much like nobility. He was elderly, stocky, overweight, thick-necked, ruddy and possessed of a knobbly nose. That night, fireworks erupted overhead, cannons boomed and the folk of Williamsburg raised their glasses to the king and his noble representative sent to live among them.

Polite enquiries were made in London, where it was learned Botetourt had been a member of the House of Commons for more than twenty years before his elevation to the peerage, and was renowned there for never missing a day's sitting or making an interesting contribution to debates. Still a bachelor, it seems he had been something of a rake in his younger days and had been foolish with women, drink and gambling. It was rumored that he had come to Virginia to escape his creditors.

Among his many titles was Groom of His Majesty's Bedchamber, which the common folk of Virginia thought hilarious, and which led them to assume he was a fop and a fool. They were only partly wrong. Nonetheless, he was approachable, affable, gentlemanly in conduct and did his best to be charming and personable. A man of religious conviction, he aligned himself with the clergy at William and Mary College and favored them with endowments from the public purse. There at least he was honored. Not so in the Burgesses.

The governor presided over the opening of the assembly in May 1769, and made a rather earthbound address, at his most pointed saying, "I have nothing to ask, but that you consider well, and follow exactly, without passion or prejudice, the real interests of those you have the honor to represent; they are most certainly consistent with the prosperity of Great Britain, and so they will forever be found, when pursued with temper and moderation." The members listened politely, thanked the governor for his "very affectionate speech," and departed.

At the start of the session, Wythe, as clerk of the house, had had the extraordinary pleasure of swearing in the recently elected representative for the County of Albemarle, one Thomas Jefferson. It was just two years since Wythe had led his erstwhile pupil into practice at the bar of the General Court. At first Jefferson had traveled widely for work, riding from courthouse to courthouse and practicing in most counties of Virginia. Soon, thanks in part to his aristocratic connections, he had attracted the very best of clients: the Carters, Randolphs, Byrds, Pages and Lees.

Wythe and Jefferson sometimes appeared in matters together. Occasionally, they opposed each other. In one such case, Jefferson appeared for Samuel Howell, who sought his freedom. His great grandmother, a white woman, had lain with a black man and for that offence her baby girl was bound out as a servant to the churchwardens until the age of thirty-one. Under the law of Virginia, this girl's daughter inherited her mother's sentence of being a servant for thirty-one years. She gave birth to Howell, who was similarly burdened. Howell, being twenty-eight at the time his case was heard, had three more years to serve.

Jefferson conceded that the law's purpose "was to punish and deter women from that confusion of species, which the legislature seems to have considered an evil"—but then pressed the point that according to the law of nature all men were born free, and everyone came into the world with a right to his own person which included the liberty of moving and using it at his own will. This argument was obviously based in the liberal philosophy of John Locke, who had written that "every Man has a Property in his own Person." It would be wicked, Jefferson continued, to extend the original sentence of bondage to "grand-children and other issue more remote."

The law was entirely against Jefferson—so much so that the judges did not bother to hear Wythe in defense. It had ever been the law of Virginia, backed by statute, that the status of the child was determined by the status of the mother—in other words, if a child was born while the mother was a slave then the child was a slave, and so on in perpetuity. Further, this rule applied to conditions attached to a mother's bondage.

Soon after taking his seat in the Burgesses, Jefferson backed a measure of the most adventurous kind: he sought to alter the law so that masters had the right to free their slaves. Realizing he had neither the orator's skill nor, as the newest member of the house, the standing to shepherd his bill through, he prevailed on Colonel Richard Bland, a respected elder of the house, to propose it. Jefferson would second the bill. The debate did not get far. An uproar of opposition arose even before the poor colonel had finished his speech. He was attacked from all sides, one member going as far as denouncing him as "an enemy of his country." He "was treated with the grossest indecorum," said Jefferson.

Jefferson must have learned much from the manhandling his proposal received that day. Never again in his long political career did he again sponsor legislation to free slaves. It was, of course, naive for him to expect support for black freedom from a house of planters (though his bill gave no freedom to slaves, only to the conscience of masters). There is no record of the debate, but it seems probable that Bland made the argument that because slaves were property, their owners should be able to treat that property as they pleased—even to releasing it, just as the owner of a caged bird might lift the latch.

The burgesses did not see it that way. Freed Africans were seen as the natural allies of their enslaved brethren. In the Tidewater, where half the population was in bondage, the prospect of blacks, free and enslaved, combining in a servile insurrection, chilled white people. What was more, so the arguments of self-interest ran, slaves were generally better fed and clothed, more content, and in point of sobriety, virtue and moral character better off, than the free colored population.

*

Within days of Jefferson's failed bill the House of Burgesses was pitched into a livid battle with Governor Botetourt, and any resentment against the tyro legislator was soon forgotten, for this time he was counted among the majority.

The catalyst was a letter circulated by the Massachusetts representatives asking sister colonies to join them in resisting the Townshend duties. The House of Burgesses sat late on May 16, 1769, laboring over resolutions asserting its sole right to tax and condemning British plans to send those accused of treason to London for trial. As clerk of the house, Wythe remained until the session finished, then retired to his office to transcribe the resolutions into the official journal. He wrote with a sense of urgency, for he feared that when Botetourt learned of the house's resolutions (and there were some in the Burgesses who would run to him) he would dissolve the house before the protests could be recorded.

He still had his pen in hand when the governor's secretary knocked on his door and demanded entry. Wythe locked the door and managed to hold him off until he recorded the resolutions in the journal record. At noon the following day, the governor summoned the burgesses to the chambers of the Council. While the members of the house stood in mutinous silence, the governor, dressed in scarlet for the occasion, declared in offended tones: "Mr. Speaker and Gentlemen of the House of Burgesses, I have heard of your resolves, and augur ill of their effect: you have made it my duty to dissolve you; and you are dissolved accordingly."

Jefferson's first legislative career had lasted a mere ten days!

The spurned legislators trooped down Duke of Gloucester Street to the Apollo Room of the Raleigh Tavern, hitherto known to the populace of Williamsburg as a dancing parlor. Glowing hot with indignation, speaker after speaker declared it intolerable that Britain had assumed the right to tax the colonies as oft and in what measure it pleased. After the assembly elected Peyton Randolph as moderator (the man who had been so outraged by Henry's Stamp Act speech a mere four years earlier), Colonel Washington took the lead. He introduced a resolution drafted with his Northern Neck neighbor, George Mason, urging a campaign to refuse to import British goods (listed in exhaustive detail, be it spirits, wine, cider, perry[11], beer, linen, plate, watches, clocks, slaves, silver, linens, woolens, etc., etc.). This was readily passed by the Raleigh Tavern assembly. Peyton Randolph was the first to sign, Richard Henry Lee the fifth, George Washington the seventh, Patrick Henry the eleventh and Thomas Jefferson the sixteenth. Wythe, not being a member of the house, did not sign. Afterwards, the tavern assembly, as loyal Britishers, drank a toast to the good health of the king, the queen, the royal family and Governor Botetourt.

*

Poor Baron de Botetourt assumed he had been appointed the monarch of Virginia, only to learn that his subjects were proud, quarrelsome and dis-

---

11   An alcoholic drink made from pear juice.

obedient, and that he was powerless to do much about it. He fumed, but eventually accepted that the seat of government was now in a hostelry a short distance from his palace. Then he did the only thing he could and that was hold a ball.

Even that turned into a political protest.

All the women wore discarded clothes or homespun Virginian cloth, thus showing they had no need of British silks, satins and brocades! Governor Botetourt watched with resigned tolerance as the women pranced their defiance. The governor departed early to the palace. Suddenly the Virginian planter class, accustomed to drowning in opulence and debt, had found a new fashion in thrift.

*

In Virginia, bans on imported British goods were enforced in relative peace, but such was not the case in Boston. Since October 1768, British regiments had been garrisoned in the city to patrol the streets, muskets at the ready, playing cat-and-mouse with patriots who lay in wait with cudgels for customs agents nervously going about their business. Merchants placing orders for British goods were taken roughly in hand by the Sons of Liberty. The provocation of a standing army in their city so incensed Bostonians that it was remarkable that seventeen months elapsed before real violence broke out.

On a chilly day in March 1770, apprentice boys out on a lark began throwing snowballs at the British soldiers guarding the customs house. Jack tars and Irish dockers emerged from nearby public houses to join in. Amid the whoo-hoop of Indian calls, the crowd threw stones, oyster shells and chunks of ice at the hapless troops standing guard. One of the soldiers fell, causing his gun to discharge. The mob, roaring in fury, pressed forward. Amid the panic the redcoats fired, felling three on the spot. Two more were ferried away to die in the arms of friends. In all, eleven people in the crowd were shot. Samuel Adams now had the "Boston Massacre" to write about. Paul Revere's engraving of the blood of innocents trickling onto the icy ground was printed by the thousand to appear on parlor walls throughout the colonies, reminding all of the bestiality of the occupier.

In London, on the very same day as the massacre, events were moving toward a resolution of the crisis. In parliament, Lord North, the leader of a new ministry of the king's friends, proposed the repeal of the Townsend duties. The truculent Townshend had died in office and after a suitable time of mourning, his policies died with him.

The British backed down, not through shame at American protests that the duty infringed sacred rights, nor through fear of mob violence, but because the bans on imported goods had proved so ruinous to English manufacture and trade. With utmost ill grace, Lord North loudly proclaimed that Parliament still reserved the power to legislate directly for the colonies—if it so wished. To prove his point, a token tax was retained on tea, no more than a few pence a pound, but an irritant, nonetheless.

Virginia gratefully returned to pastoral peace. Hostility to the British had hummed and buzzed ferociously for almost three years, only to die as a bee at the end of summer. Twice now, the colonies had faced down the mother country; surely Britain would not presume to interfere with American rights again.

The fervor of protest had taken its toll on Botetourt, just as it had on his predecessor. Pale, puffy and bewildered that good manners and trotting up and down the streets of Williamsburg in his magnificent royal chariot had not calmed the people, he died in office in October 1770.

After an elaborate funeral, his remains were interred in the crypt beneath the Wren Chapel at William and Mary College, and the assembly allocated funds to have a marble statue of him placed in a prominent position in the Capitol. Most in Williamsburg bore him no ill will, for it was appreciated that the policies he had to enforce were not his own.

His replacement was another real governor: John Murray, fourth Earl of Dunmore, a Scottish nobleman of ancient blood, descended from the royal house of Stuart. Dunmore had previously been governor of New York, where he had been irritated at being told what to do by a worship of merchants. Now, he was about to be instructed by a clutch of self-anointed aristocrats; an experience he would find even less agreeable.

Everyone in Williamsburg agreed that the best thing about Lord Dunmore was his wife. The countess was beautiful, wellborn and gracious. At a palace ball to welcome her in 1774, she delighted all with how gracefully she managed the hoops of her gown as she danced the minuet. Her husband on the other hand was a popinjay of excitable disposition, whose supreme achievement was to rush Virginia to revolution.

Dunmore initially created a favorable impression. He brought to the palace a library of 1300 books, one of the largest collections in the American colonies, three organs, a harpsichord and a piano. He also frequently wined and dined influential members of the Burgesses, including George Washington. He even invited Thomas Jefferson, by then a self-taught architect as well as a lawyer, to submit plans for an extension at the College of William and Mary.

*

How times had changed for Wythe since Fauquier's day. Lord Dunmore, by right of office, presided as chief justice of the General Court. Wythe despaired of appearing before him. The governor had no legal training, and understood the law in confused measure and justice hardly at all. He would rush to judgment on a whim and likely as not was incisively wrong. He made it clear he regarded Wythe as a tedious time-waster with his numerous precedents and arguments based on the classics. Whenever Wythe rose to address him, His Excellency's face smoothed to patient condescension, he cocked his head, hooded his eyes and listened to not a word.

Wythe loathed the governor, and he also loathed Edmund Pendleton, the attorney who was his frequent opponent in court. Their rivalry as lawyers, and later as judges, was destined to extend over five decades. For two men who disliked each other so well, their upbringings were surprisingly similar. Both were descended from English stock of modest wealth. Pendleton's father died four months before his birth so, like Wythe, he was brought up by his mother. He barely attended school, yet achieved social advancement and prosperity through the practice of the law, just like Wythe. He became a burgess and later a judge, as did Wythe. Both lost their wives early, married again, yet remained childless. And like Wythe, Pendleton was slow to embrace the revolutionary cause.

There the similarities falter. Whereas Wythe was small, spare of frame, content in his own company and wary of familiarities, Pendleton was a large boat of a man, tall, assured, gracious and out-going. He had never learned languages and unlike Wythe scattered no classical decorations through his addresses in court. Pendleton was four years' Wythe's senior and had learned to lord it over him on the rural circuit early in Wythe's career. Later, at the small Williamsburg bar, he was the opponent Wythe feared most.

Attorney General William Wirt knew both men well, and wrote a piece comparing them as advocates:

> He [Wythe] carried his love of antiquity rather too far; for he frequently subjected himself to the charge of pedantry; and his admiration of the gigantic writers of Queen Elizabeth's reign, had unfortunately betrayed him into an imitation of their quaintness. Yet, with all this singularity of taste, he was a man of great capacity; powerful in argument; frequently pathetic; and elegantly keen and sarcastic in repartee. He was long the rival of Mr. Pendleton at the bar; whom he equalled as a common lawyer, and greatly surpassed as a civilian: but he was too open and direct in his conduct, and possessed too little management either with regard to his own temper or those of other men, to cope with so cool and skilful an adversary. Though a full match for Mr. Pendleton in the powers of fair and solid reasoning, Mr. Pendleton could whenever he pleased, and would whenever it was necessary, tease him with quibbles, and vex him with sophistries, until he destroyed the composure of his mind and robbed him of his strength.

The case would start, and Wythe would erect an impregnable factual and legal barricade, while Pendleton in the manner of a grand lord would tell the jury this was a very simple case. He would assure them that, unlike Mr. Wythe, he would not attempt to hide justice under legalese as complex as a ship's rigging. Instead he would tell them about the people involved. And then, despite Wythe's unheeded protests, he would say that his client's wife, or son or whoever, had recently died after coming back from the Indian wars, and he was an honest man, and a verdict against him would bring ruin. Wythe would object that this had nothing to do with the case, when in fact it was the only thing the jury found interesting.

Jefferson also testified to Pendleton's adroitness as an advocate, calling him "the ablest man in debate I have ever met with":

> He had not indeed the poetical fancy of Mr. Henry, his sublime imagination, his lofty and overwhelming diction; but he was cool, smooth and persuasive; his language flowing, chaste and embellished, his conceptions quick, acute and full of resource; never vanquished; for if he lost the main battle, he returned upon you, and regained so much of it as to make it a drawn one, by dexterous manoeuvres, skirmishes in detail, and the recovery of small advantages which, little singly, were important altogether. You never knew when you were clear of him, but were harassed by his perseverance until the patience was worn down of all who had less of it than himself.

Governor Dunmore was an easy mark for flatterers like Pendleton. Once, Wythe and a junior lawyer arrived at Dunmore's court, and observed with dismay that Edmund Pendleton was their opponent. Pendleton had come without his associate. He bowed to the bench and asked for a continuance, or postponement. Dunmore refused, saying: "Go on Sir, for you'll be a match for both of them."

This, said in front of a room full of lawyers and citizens, was more than Wythe could take. He bowed deeply to the governor and retorted in a tone heavy with sarcasm: "With your Lordship's assistance." Dunmore felt the stroke and glared at Wythe in barely disguised fury. Pendleton who never lost an advantage, nor ever gave one, set his face in a feigned expression of horror for all to see, and said not a word.

Another time, after losing again to Pendleton despite his opponent's argument being as watertight as a leaky umbrella, Wythe stamped back to his office muttering to a sympathetic friend that he would be better off quitting the bar and preaching from a pulpit. "You had better not do that," came the reply, "for, if you do, Mr. Pendleton will go home, take orders, and enter the pulpit too, and beat you there."

Although Pendleton was never accepted as a member of Virginia's aristocracy, very early in his career he gained the confidence of the men he served, thanks to his staunch conviction that government should be in the hands of those with property, and that slavery, being beneficial to society, was here to stay.

In 1769, Pendleton joined with George Washington and seventeen other gentlemen in a scheme to raffle slaves. It came about because a bankrupt planter, Bernard Moore, owed more money than his assets could possibly bring. Relying on Virginia's passion for gambling, the creditors decided to hold a lottery with Moore's possessions as prizes: that is six parcels of land, one hundred head of cattle, a team of horses and fifty-five slaves bundled into thirty-nine lots. To increase the number of prizes, some married couples were split up, and their children balloted separately. At ten pounds each, the 1840 tickets sold well. The lottery, drawn by dice, ran over three nights at Shield's Tavern, and caused high excitement. Washington's diary showed he attended every night.

During these years, Washington engaged Wythe as his lawyer in several matters. Once, when Washington purchased a plantation between the York and Rappahannock Rivers as guardian for John Parke Custis, he consulted Wythe. He wanted to know if the vendor, William Black, had the right to sell. In an opinion of Delphic complexity and reservation, Wythe concluded that Black did. Washington purchased, only to be blocked by Mrs. Black who, probably at the urging of her husband, claimed dower rights and refused to execute a transfer. Washington described Black as a "worthless scoundrel, who seems to be adept in every species of artifice and rascality." This assessment proved accurate, as it took several months, and Wythe's assistance, before the transfer of land to Washington was achieved.

*

Wythe rarely visited Chesterville. It was some thirty miles from Williamsburg, a day's ride away, and going there involved an overnight stay. Unlike Jefferson, Washington and Henry, who retreated from the buffeting of public life to their country estates to savor the tranquility of being attended by familiar Africans, Wythe seemed to feel guilty about accepting service from enslaved humans.

To escape from the unwanted responsibility of Chesterville, he employed a series of managers. He probably considered selling the plantation, although given its ownership by four generations of Wythes he may have thought this would be tantamount to betraying the family. Eventually, sometime around 1771, Wythe approached a planter on Hog Island, across the river from Jamestown, to manage it for a half-share of the profits. The man was a Scot with the grand name of Hamilton Usher St. George. Newly arrived in the colony, he came with an admirable reputation as a scientific farmer familiar with the latest European techniques. He must have known how to drive a hard bargain, because he agreed to manage Chesterville only if Wythe would board his teenage son in his house in Williamsburg, and instruct him in Latin and the rudiments of the law.

Nor was that the end of it. In 1771, Wythe wrote to London, explaining that he was "about building a small house," and placing an order for four hundred panes of crown glass, forty-eight joints for shutters and a number of locks and hinges. He instructed the hardware to be shipped to Hampton, which suggests he was providing the demanding St. George with a second dwelling.

*

In the winter of 1772, English newspapers carried the astonishing news to Virginia that a law lord had freed the slaves of Britain. It became the talk of every tavern, plantation and drawing room in Virginia, occasioning much anxious debate about the judgment's effect on colonial slaveholdings.

A slave named James Somerset, taken to London as a servant by his Virginian master, had quit service and "absolutely refused" to return. Not for long though, for the runaway was seized by his master and confined in irons in the *Anne and Mary*, a ship lying in the Thames and bound for Jamaica. Anti-slavery campaigners got wind of the slave's abduction and obtained a writ of habeas corpus, forcing the master to produce Somerset before Lord Mansfield of the King's Bench.

In a trial that ran for months and gripped the attention of the British,

Mansfield eventually ruled that slavery was so odious to English ideals of freedom, it could only be maintained if there was a positive law supporting it. He searched the statutes and the common law and, not finding any authority authorizing bondage of human beings, declared, "The black must be discharged."

So there it was. No doubt Wythe's opinion was sought by uneasy citizens. Had the judge taken leave of his senses? What arrogance had led England to declare their air too pure for slaves to breathe! Could the judgment apply in the colonies? How could someone's property be stripped away without compensation? Wythe would have reassured them. True it was if Virginians took their enslaved domestics to England they might never be recovered, but *Somerset* had no application in the colonies. Parliament would not dare interfere with colonial rights of ownership. The British would not forgo the riches of the African trade which had garnered the merchants of Liverpool imperial wealth. Nor would *Somerset's* case apply to the gathering of slaves in Africa, nor on the high seas, nor when they reached American shores.[12]

Still, it was a jolt to Americans' understanding of the world. The English, great beneficiaries of the slave trade, were suddenly describing it as odious. Americans saw the Old World as profane and corrupt, yet an English judge had at one stroke unshackled a whole people. It was said at the time of the *Somerset* decision there were as many as fifteen thousand slaves in Britain.

*

In the early months of 1770, Shadwell, the family home of Jefferson in Albemarle County, burnt to the ground. Jefferson took it very badly, not so much the loss of the building that his pioneering father had built, but the destruction of his substantial library and papers on matters legal, com-

---

12 Some argued that *Somerset* decided no more than a person could not be taken out of Britain to be enslaved. However, in practical terms the decision meant the end of slavery in Britain. In 1826 *Somerset* was narrowed somewhat by Lord Stowell of the British High Court of Admiralty, when he ruled in *The Slave, Grace* that because Grace had voluntarily returned to a slave colony (Antigua) she reentered bondage.

mercial, private and philosophical. Neighbors rallied, sending him hinges, locks and pulleys. Wythe sent cuttings of nectarines, apricots and vines, a Latin verse urging fortitude and a promise from Mrs. Wythe that "she will send you some garden peas." Fortunately Jefferson had the money to restore his library. Within two years, in a flurry of acquisitions from booksellers mainly in London, he had collected twelve hundred replacement volumes which he set on shelves in a manor house that he had begun to erect on a wooded summit a few miles from Shadwell. Its construction was a mammoth task, as the top of the mountain had to be first leveled and water carted from the creek below.

A few years later he married the daughter of a wealthy aristocrat, Martha Wayles Skelton. Her father, John Wayles, was a planter, slave trader and lawyer who outlived three wives, before taking to bed one of his slaves, Betty Hemings, who bore him six children. Martha, widowed at age nineteen, was twenty-three when she married Jefferson. She was charming, greatly accomplished in music and conversation, and admired for her graceful beauty.

When Martha's father died in 1773, the Jeffersons came into an estate that consisted of some 11,000 acres and 135 slaves—though unhappily their inheritance was burdened with heavy debts to English merchants. The struggle to clear this debt became Jefferson's lifelong task, strained though it was by his extravagant tastes, and interrupted by his perpetual busyness, and by revolutionary and presidential duties. Jefferson continued to build his house, which he called Monticello. He designed it in classical Palladian style and, to mock its wild surroundings, he faced it toward the untamed west.

8

Fasting, Humiliation and Prayer

*A Boston tea party—a day for fasting and pray-
er—Jefferson's Summary View—Lord Dunmore's
War—Chief Logan's speech—Congress con-
venes—Henry declares himself an American—Henry's Liberty or Death—Dunmore takes the
powder—war in Massachusetts—Dunmore aban-
dons the palace*

A silly prank—a dress-up party meant as a bit of a jaunt—ignited the
next crisis with Britain. Samuel Adams's patriots, dressed as Indians, and
shouting "The Mohawks are come," jumped from Griffin's Wharf onto
three ships in Boston Harbor. They smashed open tea chests with hatchets
and tipped the contents overboard, to the cheers of hundreds watching
them onshore.

The citizens of Williamsburg read about it in the papers, smiled indulgently and continued on with their normal business. It is unlikely that
any of them foresaw how a few empty tea chests bobbing around in the
harbor portended war, much less the painful separation of America from
the empire.

In fact it was not the Boston Tea Party which set the colonies alight,
but the British reaction to it. George III made it clear that Massachusetts
must be punished. Parliament responded with legislation that the colonists

dubbed the Intolerable Acts. The port of Boston would be closed to trade until the dumped tea was paid for, its popular town meetings were forbidden, and British troops were quartered in public buildings and in citizens' homes. Because no colonial jury could be trusted to convict, Britain ordered that those charged with capital offences were to be taken to England for trial. Emotions ran high; rebellion was in the air. The British sent troops from Nova Scotia to restore order. Within Boston itself, British soldiers patrolled at night. Outside the city boundaries, royal authority collapsed.

In Williamsburg, politics returned as the topic of choice. A duty on tea hardly mattered to Virginians, who preferred coffee or whiskey and regarded tea as little better than swamp water. But tea was no longer the point. Britain had demonstrated yet again that it would not hesitate to impose its supremacy by the most draconian of laws. The lockdown of Boston was seen as brutal. Punishment of Massachusetts was deemed punishment of all thirteen colonies. Were Americans prepared to submit supinely while the empire passed any laws it wanted to enforce its authority?

In 1773, Jefferson returned to Williamsburg to be in the thick of the ferment. From then on, his role was patriot and statesman: he never practiced law again. As the radicals' newest recruit, he met with Patrick Henry, Richard Henry Lee and Francis L. Lee. Together, they decided to revive the Burgesses' Committee of Correspondence, established under Governor Fauquier in 1759, but since fallen into disuse. Its revitalized aim was to monitor British attacks on American rights and correspond with sister colonies in rallying opposition and promoting united action. By early 1774, ten colonies had set up similar committees.

The Williamsburg committee also drafted a resolution for the House of Burgesses condemning "the hostile invasion of the city of Boston, in our Sister Colony of Massachusetts Bay," and calling for a "Day of Fasting, Humiliation, and Prayer, devoutly to implore divine Interposition for averting the heavy Calamity, which threatens Destruction to our civil Rights and the Evils of civil War."

Most in the house voted for it, including George Washington. Wythe, taking a modest step toward rebellion, placed his signature at the bottom, adding after his name C.H.B. (Clerk of the House of Burgesses). The next day Lord Dunmore demonstrated his extraordinary ability to overreact. Convinced the Virginia Assembly was a pest-house of dissent, Dunmore summoned the burgesses to the council room, where he waved a printed copy of their resolution in the air and declared, "I have in my hand a paper published by order of your House, conceived in such term as reflects highly upon His Majesty and the Parliament of Great Britain, which makes it necessary for me to dissolve you; and you are dissolved accordingly."

The members trooped down Duke of Gloucester Street to the Raleigh Tavern, just as they had when Botetourt was governor, and continued their debates there. After accusing Great Britain of "reducing the inhabitants of British America to slavery," they announced their refusal to buy goods imported by the East India Company (importers of the tea dumped in Boston harbor), and made their momentous call for their sister colonies to meet in a Continental Congress "to deliberate on those general measures which the united interests of America may from time to time require."

The day of fasting and prayer was duly held on June 1, the day the British closed the port of Boston. Jefferson declared it a great success: "The people met generally, with anxiety and alarm in their countenances, and the effect of the day thro' the whole colony was like a shock of electricity, arousing every man and placing him erect & solidly on his centre."

*

Buoyed by this propaganda triumph, Jefferson picked up his pen to write a fusillade of anti-British resolutions that were adopted by the freeholders of Albemarle County at a boisterous meeting in July 1774. He then retreated to his mountaintop at Monticello to elaborate further on these resolutions in a weighty essay, later published as *A Summary View of the Rights of British America.*

When he had finished this paper, Jefferson set out for Williamsburg. Taken ill with severe headache on the road to the capital, he returned home and sent a servant with a copy of his paper to his cousin Peyton Randolph, the dismissed Speaker of the House of Burgesses. Wythe was among a select audience invited to Randolph's house to hear it read. Jefferson hoped his *Summary View* would be endorsed by the men in Randolph's house as a guide to the Virginian delegates sent to the Continental Congress in Philadelphia. Instead, they drew back as if touched by a hot poker.

Jefferson had written in a rage. The tone of disrespect was apparent from the opening paragraph, in which he designated King George as "no more than the chief officer of the people." He followed this with cheeky advice and a dire warning: "Kings are the servants, not the proprietors of the people. Open your breast Sire, to liberal and expanded thought. Let not the name of George the third be a blot on the pages of history ... The whole art of government consists in the art of being honest. Only aim to do your duty, and mankind will give you credit where you fail."

The *Summary View* went on to chronicle British iniquities: they had not answered American complaints, they denied Americans justice, they punished the innocent along with the guilty, they inflicted heavy taxes on the colonies. Throughout he wove the metaphysical argument that Anglo-Saxon liberties had merely been suppressed, but not eliminated, by William the Conquer at the Battle of Hastings. These very liberties had been carried by settlers to the new world where they had blossomed anew—leading to the bold assertion that Americans had the natural right to govern themselves.[13]

Yet, after these bold words, Jefferson faltered. Logic led him to revolution, but prudence forbade it. Instead, he beseeched the king not to push the colonies into disconnection from Britain: "It is neither our wish nor our interest to separate from her. We are willing on our part to sacrifice every thing which reason could ask to the restoration of that tranquility for which all must wish."

Jefferson's polemic may have been too much for the gathering in Randolph's home, but braver souls published it in Williamsburg and Philadelphia—absent the author's name, or his permission. In Britain,

---

13   In his autobiography of 1821, Jefferson noted wryly that he "had never been able to get anyone to agree with me but Mr. Wythe. He concurred in it from the first dawn of the question ... Whether Mr. Henry disapproved the ground taken, or was too lazy to read it (for he was the laziest man in reading I ever knew) I never learned: but he communicated it to nobody."

Edmund Burke republished it, and several years later in the midst of the Revolutionary War, Virginia relished the story (probably apocryphal) that King George had read it in a black fury.

*

Governor Dunmore, seemingly unconcerned at the rumblings of revolt from the planters and lawyers in his realm, decided it was a good time to fight Indians. Like Fauquier and Botetourt, Dunmore was short of money, but whereas his predecessors attempted to live within their means, Dunmore's hungry plan to restore his family's fortune was to grasp as much Virginian land as he could. As well as owning four large estates in the settled districts, he aligned himself with land speculators and began granting them large chunks of frontier land over the ranges, south of the Ohio River.

When, as expected, the Shawnee began killing intruders, open warfare broke out on the Ohio frontier. Colonel Michael Cresap joined settlers in the massacre of a peaceful encampment of Mingo people who had until then declared themselves friends of the white man. Many of the women and children murdered were relatives of Chief Logan, the son of a pro-British Indian leader, who in revenge aligned the Mingos with the Shawnee cause. Now with two Indian nations to fight, Dunmore, perceiving a "danger of annoyance from the Indians" (as he expressed it), assembled a militia of seasoned soldiers, adventurers and frontiersmen to restore peace. Thus commenced what became to be known as Lord Dunmore's War. Assuming personal command, Dunmore split his troops in two and rode at the head of one column while the famed Indian fighter Colonel Andrew Lewis led the other. Lewis fell upon Chief Cornstalk and his Shawnee braves at Pleasant Creek on the Kanawha River, and in a day of hand-to-hand fighting broke Shawnee resistance and forced them to cede their claims over Kentucky.

Chief Logan, now a prisoner of the militia, wrote a speech which he sent by messenger to Lord Dunmore. Its quiet dignity so impressed Jefferson that he copied it from a newspaper and many years later included it in his *Notes on the State of Virginia*:

I appeal to any white man to say, if ever he entered Logan's cabin hungry, and he gave him not meat; if ever he came cold and naked, and he clothed him not. During the course of the last long and bloody war, Logan remained idle in his cabin, an advocate for peace. Such was my love for the whites, that my countrymen pointed as they passed, and said, "Logan is the friend of white men." I had even thought to have lived with you, but for the injuries of one man. Col. Cresap, the last spring, in cold blood, and unprovoked, murdered all the relations of Logan, not sparing even my women and children. There runs not a drop of my blood in the veins of any living creature. This called on me for revenge. I have sought it: I have killed many: I have fully glutted my vengeance. For my country, I rejoice at the beams of peace. But do not harbour a thought that mine is the joy of fear. Logan never felt fear. He will not turn on his heel to save his life. Who is there to mourn for Logan?—Not one.

Dunmore returned triumphant to Williamsburg without personally firing a shot. Greeted as a conquering hero, he named his newborn daughter Virginia, and to the delight of the colony held a ball to celebrate her birth. With his popularity restored, he promptly recommenced his war with the dismissed burgesses—now calling themselves the Virginian Convention.

*

In August 1774, while Dunmore was absent fighting Indians, the Convention met in Williamsburg's Raleigh Tavern. With passions running high, the group passed resolutions drafted by Jefferson for the non-importation of slaves and tea and the non-export of tobacco. Rather letting his indignation run away with him, Jefferson averred that patriotic Virginians would abstain from that brew identified with British repression:

Considering the article of tea as the detestable instrument which laid the foundation of the present suffering of our distressed friends in the town of Boston, we view it with horror, and therefore resolve that we will not, from this day, either import tea of any kind whatever, nor will we use or suffer, even such of it as is now at hand, to be used in any our families.

The Convention elected delegates to the congress of colonies to be held in Philadelphia in September. Acting on the belief that if one wanted to control the torrent, one must be there at the source, both radicals and the conservatives jockeyed for inclusion. Jefferson put his name forward but was not elected. The meeting settled on Peyton Randolph, Benjamin Harrison, Edmund Pendleton, George Washington, Richard Bland, Richard Henry Lee and Patrick Henry. The first three were counted as conservatives, while Washington and Bland were there to make sure neither they nor the radicals, Henry and Lee, gained the upper hand.

There was so much contention about the Virginian position, that the delegates were sent off with instructions to say that while the blockade of Boston continued, Virginia would not trade with Britain. And if that did not work, unspecified resistance and reprisal would follow—a vague brief which left the delegates scope to vote for a little or a lot.

Twelve of the thirteen American colonies were represented at the meeting in Philadelphia. Canada and Georgia both declined to attend. At this stage there was no war to run, so the members were free to contemplate the future in abstract and to hope that at the very brink Britain would concede what the delegates wanted (although what that was brought forth many opinions).

For Wythe, waiting in Williamsburg, it was a period of unwelcome inactivity. The courts had closed and the House of Burgesses remained dismissed. A Committee of Safety was formed to enforce the non-importation rules. Wythe, taking another step toward being a revolutionary, offered himself as a member. It soon became the real executive within the colony, replacing the powerless governor ensconced in the palace. In November a bag of feathers, suspended over a barrel of tar, appeared in the main street of Williamsburg as a warning to shopkeepers not to trade in banned goods. In frustration Dunmore wrote to London "There's not a Justice of Peace in Virginia that acts, except as a committee-man."

Anyone wondering what was being decided in Philadelphia had to rely on rumor, scanty newspaper reports, or letters from the fifty or so delegates, which were passed hand to hand among the favored few. It seemed that as fall passed and winter neared, the most exciting event had been Patrick Henry's electrifying speech made in response to squabbling about how many votes each colony should be allowed.

Dressed in a suit of parson's gray and peering through rimmed glasses, Henry, in his unrefined drawl, made his famous declaration:

Fleets and armies and the present state of things show that government is dissolved. Where are your landmarks, your boundaries of colonies? We are in a state of nature, Sir … The distinctions between Virginians, Pennsylvanians, New Yorkers and New Englanders are no more. I am not a Virginian, but an American!

This was novel imagining indeed; that the thirteen colonies, and perhaps Canada as well, could throw off the British yoke and create an American nation in its stead—a United States of America! It was both a fearful and thrilling possibility. But how to do it? Henry had no plan in tow. Henry never had a plan in tow.

After seven weeks of inconclusive debate, Congress adjourned, united only in its resolve for an economic boycott of British goods, a declaration of colonial rights and an appeal to the British Parliament for a remedy of grievances. It agreed to convene again in Philadelphia the following year—little realizing that by then Massachusetts would be a battlefield.

*

In the new year, the second Virginia Convention met in March at Richmond, some fifty miles upstream from Williamsburg on the James River, and at that time a hamlet of about six hundred souls. Its largest building was Saint John's Church, a white-framed edifice atop a wooded hill. About one hundred and twenty delegates from all the counties of Virginia squeezed uncomfortably into its high-backed pews. George Wythe was there, somewhere toward the rear of the assembly. The more notable attendees, Thomas Jefferson, George Washington, Benjamin Harrison, Richard Henry Lee, George Mason, Edmund Pendleton and Patrick Henry sat to the fore. Outside, Richmond's curious jockeyed to stand on tiptoe and peer in through the open windows.

By unanimous vote Peyton Randolph, Speaker of the House of Burgesses, was elected president of the Convention. The first few days of debate were taken up with hesitant protest at Britain's behavior, solemn pledges of Virginia's loyalty to the Crown and the composition of addresses to Nova Scotia, Georgia, Florida and Quebec asking for their support. On the fourth day of discussion, Patrick Henry could control his impatience no longer. He rose to present a series of resolutions calling for the establishment of "a well regulated militia ... for the protection and defense of the country."

The response was shocked silence, then a succession of influential delegates, including Richard Bland, Benjamin Harrison and Edmund Pendleton, rose to speak against the motion. It was not the time to take up arms, they said. Patriots should exercise a dignified patience. If they provoked Britain to hostilities, where were the colonies' sinews of war? Their ordnance? Their soldiers? Their generals? Who was to pay? The colonies were naked and defenseless. Opinion in Britain was turning in favor of their protests. The sovereign was looking on American suffering with an eye of pity. Compromise was still possible.

Henry demanded to be heard. A hush fell over the church as he rose. He looked around. Then, half-hidden by the high pew from which he spoke, he began the speech that was to fire the revolution. "Mr. President, it is natural for man to indulge in the illusion of hope," he said:

We are apt to shut our eyes against a painful truth—and listen to the song of that siren hope, till she transforms us into beasts ... Suffer not yourselves to be betrayed with a kiss ... We have petitioned—we have remonstrated—we have supplicated—we have prostrated ourselves before the throne. ... Our petitions have been slighted; our remonstrances have produced additional violence and insult; our supplications have been disregarded; and we have been spurned, with contempt, from the foot of the throne. In vain, after these things, may we indulge the fond hope of peace and reconciliation. There is no longer any room for hope!

There was quiet. He picked up an ivory letter opener, and held it in one hand as he continued in a voice soft, yet cracking with emotion: "There is no retreat, but in submission and slavery! Our chains are forged. Their clanking may be heard on the plains of Boston! The war is inevitable—and let it come!! I repeat it, sir; let it come!"

There was a stirring in the church. A few voices cried out in support; others in dissent. Henry continued:

It is in vain, sir, to extenuate the matter. Gentlemen may cry Peace! Peace!—but there is no peace. The war is actually begun! The next gale that sweeps from the north will bring to our ears the clash of resounding arms! Our brethren are already in the field! Why stand we here idle? What do you wish for gentlemen? What would you have? Is life so dear, or peace so sweet, as to be purchased at the price of chains and slavery? Forbid it, Almighty God!

Henry's shoulders slumped, as if in submission; he dropped his head and crossed his wrists as if bound in chains. There was a long silence. Then he looked around the church with his brows knit, his mouth clenched in determination. He held the letter opener aloft.

"I know not what course others may take," he said, his voice rising to a crescendo: "But as for me, Give me liberty, or give me death!"[14]

The letter opener flashed toward his heart.

All eyes, wide with horror, were on him. He bowed dramatically and took his seat. No applause was heard. Instead, the congregation in the church, as one, let loose a breath.

After the trance of a moment, several members started from their seats. "To arms! To arms!" they shouted. The cry was taken up by others, then by yet more, then a discordant chorus: "To arms! To arms!" The clamor

---

14   Henry's speech first appeared in 1817 in Henry's biography, written by William Wirt. But how accurate is it? Undoubtedly it is a romanticized reconstruction obtained from memory years later, especially from that of Judge St. George Tucker who attended the convention when a young man. However the judge is likely to be a reliable source, and many others recollect that Henry made a rousing speech that day, which turned the convention in favor of his resolutions.

for action echoed around the church, to be taken up by those in the garden outside.

Richard Henry Lee seconded Henry's resolutions, and Jefferson spoke "closely, profoundly and warmly" in support. The vote was taken and the resolution was passed by five votes.

In that little church on a hill in rural Virginia, men buzzed around a committee of Washington, Jefferson, Lee, Pendleton and Henry as they created a paper army preparing for war against the world's most powerful nation: "That each company of infantry consist of sixty-eight rank and file, commanded by a captain, two lieutenants, one ensign, four sergeants, and four corporals. And that they have a drummer, and be furnished with a drum and colors; that every man be provided with a good rifle, if to be had, or otherwise with a common firelock. Bayonet, and cartouche-box, and also with a tomahawk, one pound of gunpowder, and four pounds of ball at least, fitted to the bore of his gun; that he be clothed in a hunting shirt, by way of uniform."

So the detail of provisioning went on: each horse troop was to consist of thirty, exclusive of officers; every horseman was to be provided with a good horse, bridle, saddle, with pistols and holsters, a carbine, or other short firelock, a bucket, a cutting sword or a tomahawk.

Even as they prepared for war, old habits died hard. The last order of business at the convention was to pass a unanimous resolution thanking "our worthy governor, Lord Dunmore, for his truly noble, wise and spirited conduct, on the late expedition against our Indian enemy."

Virginians during these troubled years might be thought of as a coffle of men tethered by tangled strands of opinion, loyalties and faiths as they moved down a road to a fearful future. Every now and then someone like Henry would step forward and shout out what many had been thinking, but in full voice it sounded too frightening, too dangerous, so the nervous closed ranks. Then, as the timid assured each other that their demands were reasonable, they would edge forward. Meanwhile the outspoken had already moved on, and were roaring more unspeakable things, so the faint-hearted drew back, gasping, "It is not time! It is not time!"

*

Late on the night of April 21, Wythe was back in his bed in Williamsburg, when he heard shouts, then drums sounding an alarm. Thinking it could only mean fire, he quickly dressed and went out to stand on the Palace Green, looking in vain for sparks spiraling skyward. Then he noticed several men running down Duke of Gloucester Street. He followed men holding lanterns aloft as they entered the public magazine. The story was told afresh for each new arrival. The king's marines had forced the locks of the magazine, loaded barrels of powder onto a dray and fled into the night. The city's gunpowder had been stolen!

A duty on tea might excite the citizens and merchants of Boston, but not Virginians. However Dunmore's "rape of the powder" (as a contemporary dubbed it) was a different thing entirely. Mayor Dixon immediately wrote to Dunmore demanding an explanation and the immediate return of the people's property. An angry mob threatened to march on the palace. To a deputation led by Peyton Randolph, Dunmore gave the disingenuous reply that he had heard of the possibility of a slave insurrection, so he had ordered the powder be kept safe on the British man-of-war *Magdalen* at anchor on the James River. His lordship suavely assured them that should the slaves revolt, the gunpowder would be returned within the half-hour.

In truth Dunmore was acting on instructions from London, but then he went far beyond anything London might have approved. Working himself up in a fearful rage during a chance meeting with a city alderman, he warned that if any British official were harmed by mob violence he "would declare freedom to the slaves, and reduce the city of Williamsburg to ashes." Adding for good measure, "I have once fought for the Virginians, and by God I will let them see I can fight against them."

Randolph was prepared to leave it at that. Not so Patrick Henry. From his base at the Hanover courthouse he dispatched emissaries to scour the countryside for men willing to march on Williamsburg to recover the powder. As hundreds of armed men rushed to join him, his plans were overruled by his own Hanover County officials, who feared what Henry might do if given charge of the county militia.

Then sensational news arrived from Massachusetts of a fierce battle between the British and a farmers' militia. Hundreds had been killed. Massachusetts was at war.

*

Just before twelve o'clock on a frosty April night, seven hundred British troops marched out of Boston with orders to seize the rebel armory in Concord and Lexington. Their leaders planned a surprise attack, but as the sun rose, the British were still nine miles from Lexington, striding down county lanes. Then they heard the tolling of church bells. Alarm guns sounded, and in the far distance trumpets called to tell the minutemen to rise from their beds and take up arms. The famous ride of Paul Revere had spread the word that the redcoats were coming.

The British marched onto the village green at Lexington and, as they halted in drill order, they were unnerved to hear the beat of a drum as a citizen army, dressed in an assortment of rustic uniforms, formed up before them in ragged battle lines. For several tense minutes the adversaries faced each other, then a single shot rang out. This was the "shot heard round the world." From whence it came no one knew for certain. Some said later that the British fired first, while others saw a flash of powder from the upper window of the tavern, and yet others heard it come from behind a wall. Both sides, already on a nerve edge, opened fire. The steadier redcoats had much the better of the exchange. After the first salvo the farmer-soldiers fled across the green and vaulted the fence beyond, leaving eight of their companions lying on the grass as their lives oozed away.

After the mayhem on Lexington Green, the British tramped on to the Concord armory. They arrived to find the colonists had emptied it. The redcoats then began the return march to Boston on a day of humid heat. It proved to be a journey of eighteen miles of death, down winding country roads. More than a thousand shooters had descended on Concord to join the hunt for the British enemy. At every turn the local militia, hiding behind rocks, fences, trees and bridges, picked off their target.

After the snipers fired at the enemy from one vantage point, they ran through woods to wait for them at the next. The road to Boston, as it climbed a heavily forested hill, became another place of slaughter. The British broke ranks and made a panicky dash across fields, only to be pushed back into formation at bayonet point by their officers. They formed a moving defensive square and continued their retreat. By the time they limped back to Boston, more than 273 of their number had been killed or wounded. The American casualties were 89 killed or wounded.

Buoyed by their victory, hundreds of militiamen picked up their rifles and left their farms to surround Boston, locking the British in. The siege of Boston had begun. It would last eleven months.

The news sent a chill of fear through the colonies: the British would not remain leashed after such carnage. There would be retribution, there must be retribution. Emboldened by the news from Boston, the Hanover elders gave Henry permission for his march on Williamsburg. By early May, to the cheers of the citizens of the county, he led one hundred men armed with muskets, pikes and tomahawks out of town and on the road to the capital. They sang patriotic songs as they passed through towns and villages and by the time they approached Williamsburg, Henry had 150 or more to command.

Once Dunmore heard news of the thrum of marching feet he called the Council's president, Thomas Nelson, and the colonial treasurer, Robert Carter Nicholas, to his side. These two realized that the danger was just as much Virginia's as Dunmore's. If Henry's force stormed the palace and captured or killed the governor, the insult to the Crown would be unbearable, and the response was bound to be furious and bloody. The fiery governor was adamant he would not return the gunpowder. Dunmore sent his wife and children to *HMS Fowey*, at its mooring in the river, and brought forty marines into the palace. He again warned that if there were an attack on the palace he would issue a declaration freeing Virginia's slaves.

For three days, there was a tense standoff. Eventually Dunmore was persuaded to a compromise. A messenger was sent to Henry with a promissory note for £330, the value of the gunpowder. After tense negotiations the word came that Henry had accepted. The crisis was over. Lady Dunmore and the children returned to dry land.

Without firing a shot, Henry had taken his demands to the brink, had pushed the governor to an abject cave-in, and had shamed the moderates. The glory was all his.

Even as calm returned to Williamsburg, Dunmore dug himself deeper into ignominy with another miscalculation. He issued a proclamation declaring Henry and his supporters in rebellion, and asking Virginians "to oppose them and their designs by every means." All that did was present Henry with another badge of honor. A few days after being damned by Dunmore, Henry set off to the Second Continental Congress in Philadelphia, escorted by the Hanover Volunteers in a raucous procession of fife and drum as far as Hooe's ferry on the Potomac. There he was farewelled with repeated huzzas and wishes of Godspeed.

Soon after these dramas, Dunmore recalled the Burgesses. The British prime minister, Lord North, had drafted a peace offer for the colonies to consider and Dunmore wanted it read to the House. Upon hearing the news Peyton Randolph relinquished his role as president of the Continental Congress, and hastened home from Philadelphia to resume his role as Speaker.

Wythe, as clerk to the Burgesses, filed in with the others to listen to Dunmore reveal Britain's path to peace. In essence, Lord North proposed that the colonies might collect their own taxes if they were sufficient to meet the administrative and defense costs specified by London. Several months beforehand, that might have satisfied the Americans, but not now. There was no mention of the lifting of the punitive measures against Massachusetts.

Whatever slim chance there was of Virginia responding sympathetically to Lord North's proposal was shattered several days later. On the orders of the governor, a spring gun had been set in the Williamsburg magazine, and it wounded several youthful intruders. Mr. Purdie of the *Virginia Gazette* wrote that those responsible warranted "the opprobrious title of MURDERERS." Such was the popular outrage that, within days, two hundred armed men appeared to assume the self-appointed task of protecting Williamsburg, and mob-raided the governor's palace in search of weapons.

A week later, on June 8, Williamsburg awoke to the astonishing news that the royal occupants had abandoned the palace. Dunmore's servants told the tale of the governor, his six children and Lady Dunmore, holding a baby of six months, creeping out the back entrance of the palace in the dead of night and boarding a carriage. His Lordship and his family were now residing on a British warship anchored in the York River.

During these inconstant times Virginia still recognized Dunmore as the king's representative and in the weeks that followed delegates called on the waterborne governor to have him sign official documents. They assured him the people meant him no harm, much less his wife whom everyone in Virginia admired: he should return to the palace. Dunmore remained suspicious, so he bobbed around off Yorktown, sighing about the cramped conditions, mosquitoes, and the company of sailors.

The members of the House of Burgesses soon tired of traipsing down to the river to wait on the governor. They told him if he wished to rule he must return to the palace. Lord Dunmore declined, fearful of being held hostage. This gave the burgesses an additional grievance—that of willfully withholding the powers of government from the people. And because by the laws of nature it was ordained that citizens should combine for the common good, it was right and proper for the people to assume control of the colony.

*

As the winter of 1775 approached, the governor was still afloat, Virginians ruled through their representatives, and there was peace in the land. Men who had been loyal to the Crown through generations became disloyal overnight, and bragged about what they would do if ever a redcoat should cross their path. But if this was a revolution, it was one of the most amiable in history. The courts were closed and customs officials laid low. Shopkeepers, apprentices and farmers drilled on the Market Square in musket presentation, priming and ramrodding, but rarely firing, as gunpowder could not be spared.

It was a defining moment for George Wythe when, clad in an old black jacket (his version of a hunting shirt), he picked up a musket which hitherto had only shot at squirrels, and joined a line of villagers and shopkeepers at militia training on Williamsburg's green. Marching he could do, although after a few hours along unmade roads every muscle in his legs ached and his complexion turned from chalk-white to pink. Eventually he was referred to the officer-in-charge, who tactfully applauded his enthusiasm but suggested that he could contribute more by advising the Virginian convention on matters of law.

The only other time Wythe took up arms was five years later, during Benedict Arnold's invasion of Virginia. The clash must have been a matter of public amusement because William Tatham wrote about it in jocular fashion to Jefferson. Wythe and several friends were out on a partridge shoot when they saw some British soldiers attempting a landing in a creek. The British were repulsed "much to the soldierly credit of old Chancellor Wythe, and one or two other Gentlemen who took a pop at them."

Although there were still nests of royalists in the colony in 1775, by and large they went unmolested. A few of the more outspoken were tarred and feathered, several had patriots' bricks thrown through their windows, and some were raided for guns and ammunition. This had the effect of quieting the others. It was a case of adapt, flee or be crushed. Most adapted, taking the canny option of lying low until the issue was decided one way or the other on the field of battle. Several loyalist clergy at William and Mary College set sail for home, while Professor Gwatkin, who also served as the governor's personal chaplain, felt it his duty to escort Lady Dunmore and the children to safety in Britain.

John Randolph, Virginia's attorney general and a member of the illustrious Randolph family, was not one of those prepared to hide his attachment to the Crown. After publishing a pamphlet urging his fellow Virginians to accept their natural dependency on the mother country, he left for Britain, taking his wife and two daughters with him. His only son, Edmund, remained behind, as did John's brother Peyton. Years earlier John Randolph had played in Governor Fauquier's quartet with his cousin Thomas Jefferson. Before departing he sold his violin to Jefferson for thirteen pounds. Within days of John Randolph's departure, a mob ransacked his house.[15]

Those who fled to England took their chances. A Mrs. Rathell's decision to leave Virginia was rung out of her by economic necessity. Her

---

15   Once settled in London, Randolph became a leading member of the Association of American Loyalists, a sad little group that whiled away its time in coffeehouses on the Strand drawing up memorandums on how to solve the "colonial question", and seeking recompense for property left behind. He died in England in 1784, an exile in needy circumstances. Randolph's last wish was to be buried in Virginia. His daughter carried his remains home to Williamsburg and interred them in the chapel of William and Mary, near others of his family.

shop in the Duke of Gloucester Street, which sold every sort of British import from brocades to brushes, was shunned and her livelihood destroyed. She had no interest in gentlemen's talk of liberty; all she knew was that after nine years in Virginia she was forced to return to England as poor as she had left it. Tragically, she died when her ship sank within sight of Liverpool.

9

Mr. Wythe Goes to Congress

Wythe at Congress—Washington becomes Com-
mander in Chief—Battle of Bunker Hill—Wythe and
John Adams take a walk—Franklin at Con-
gress —Wythe writes an (Un)animated Ad-
dress—Tom Paine's Common Sense

The Second Continental Congress assembled in Philadelphia in May 1775
to consider preparing for war against Britain—in fact the colonies were
already at war. The debate was whether they should be. Revolutionary
forces had Boston under siege, and all the colonies were arming while the
British amassed an armada bristling with guns and troops to bring America to heel. Yet the delegates' discussions in the Philadelphia State House
dragged on.

As the months passed, several Virginians resigned due to illness or
military appointments, and George Wythe was one of those elected to
take their place. Because he was likely to be away for many weeks, he
asked his wife to accompany him. On the day of their departure the local
militia formed a guard of honor outside their front door and insisted on
a discharge of muskets as the couple walked to their coach. Wythe was
forty-nine and Elizabeth thirty-six when they embarked on this journey,
and it was the first time either of them had ventured outside the boundaries of Virginia.

It took the Wythes six days to reach Philadelphia via Gooch Ferry, Fredericksburg, Baltimore and Wilmington. Rarely did their coach exceed five miles an hour. Wythe must have asked himself, as he was bounced up and down on his sitting bones, how it would ever be possible to unite communities across such vast distances; it was a five-week ride from one end of the thirteen colonies to the other. The task of creating a positive unity of purpose from a common sense of fear and apprehension awaited the men called to Philadelphia.

No sooner than George and Elizabeth Wythe had reached their destination, they were afflicted with smallpox, probably picked up from one of the inns en route. They spent a vexing week with thundering headaches and festering sores, confined to their lodgings on Chestnut Street a few blocks away from the State House. By the time Wythe was well enough to take his seat in Congress during the second week of September, a decision of enormous significance to the looming war had been made.

Shouldering a sense of his own destiny, George Washington had arrived at the Congress in May wearing the buff and blue uniform of a colonel in the Virginia militia. He was the tallest man in the room by a good half-head, and the only one in uniform. Now that the delegates could observe him closely, he was undoubtedly the most soldierly-looking.

On June 15, Washington stayed away from the assembly, alone in his lodgings, so it is said, awaiting the call. His appointment by the Congress was unanimous. The only obvious alternative was General Artemas Ward, in charge of the siege of Boston. However, as a Virginian, Washington's appointment served the purpose of bringing the South to the fore in the campaigns in Massachusetts and New York.

The next day he again presented at the Congress in uniform. President Peyton Randolph asked him if he would accept "supreme command." Rising in his seat, but not approaching the rostrum, Washington made a short acceptance speech of remarkable modesty:

Mr. President, though I am truly sensible of the high honor done me in this appointment, yet I feel great distress from a consciousness that my abilities and military experience may not be equal to the extensive and important trust. However, as the Congress desire it, I will

enter upon the momentous duty, and exert every power I possess in
their service, and for support of the glorious cause.

He concluded by ruling out the possibility that he should be paid:

> [I]t may be remembered, by every gentleman in this room, that I,
> this day, declare with the utmost sincerity, I do not think myself
> equal to the command I am honored with. As to pay, sir, I beg leave
> to assure the Congress that, as no pecuniary considerations could
> have tempted me to accept this arduous employment at the expense
> of my domestic ease and happiness, I do not wish to make any profit
> from it. I will keep an exact account of my expenses.

This refusal of remuneration signified to Congress his adherence to the
true values of a Tidewater aristocrat of Virginia, with his emphasis on service, duty and self-sacrifice. Such men did not accept wages.

   Then without ceremony, emotion or doubt, Washington bade the assembly farewell. The task ahead of him was overwhelming. If he was
burdened by the realization he did not show it. True, he was commander
in chief of the Continental Army, but when he walked out of that Congress, it was as a force of one, namely himself. He had no arms or stores
and Congress had yet to provide him with a war chest. There was not even
a nation to fight for, as the Declaration of Independence was still a year
away. He had not served in any military capacity for seventeen years, and
that had been under British command.

*

A few days later the corridors of the Philadelphia State House were abuzz
with news coming out of Massachusetts of the Battle of Bunker Hill. The
British, confined in Boston by rebel forces, had decided to seize two strategic hills, Bunker and Breed, overlooking the city across Boston Harbor.
Supported by a naval cannonade, their troops had alighted from longboats,
assembled in splendid red lines, fixed their bayonets, and scrambled up
an incline in a charge intended to break the rebellion then and there. The

Americans, protected by earthworks, were ordered to hold their fire until they saw the whites of the enemies' eyes.

Under withering fire the British were repulsed, regrouped and repulsed again. The defenders, peering over their fortifications, viewed an area quilted with the red coats of the dead and dying. Although the Americans were running short of ammunition, they reasoned that the British would not try again. Yet they did, and with their third assault, overran the fortifications, firing on the American enemy as they fled. Both sides suffered dreadful casualties, yet little had been achieved: the siege continued with the siege line further back.

Congress initially saw the battle as a loss, then as a victory, by which was meant that although the hills had not been held, the colonial militiamen had showed extraordinary bravery and had killed many more than had been killed. That is how men reason in times of war.

*

The Congress Wythe joined in September 1775 was no assembly of the common man protesting against wrenching inequalities inflicted by a rapacious overlord. It was a forum of lawyers, wealthy merchants and large landowners, objecting to the imposition of taxes without their say so, and to the British occupation of Boston. Not a few delegates were surprised at their own audacity in attending what was in essence a protest meeting against the British; even more were shocked to discover that several of their fellow delegates were planning a complete overthrow of the royal order. Right into the early months of 1776 perhaps a third of the delegates were still looking for a compromise with Britain, a third were wobbling toward independence, and another third, uncomfortable fence-sitters, were fearful of what would happen if they did.

As the debates proceeded the delegates learned how different each colony was, and how difficult it would be to form a lasting alliance. Hitherto the colonies had been watchful, insular settlements looking homeward for protection and sustenance. Now Southerners met men who spoke of machines, ships, fish and lumber. Puritan New Englanders sat down with men whose wealth was in tobacco, sugar, rice and slaves. The conservatives from New York and Massachusetts feared that if authority broke down, the mobs might not confine themselves to destroying loyalist property but also turn on the wealthy. The Southerners, although grateful that in a slave-based society there were few poor whites to worry about, remained in constant fear of an African insurrection.

It had been decided early that each colony would have only one vote at Congress, which meant there were many backroom discussions within each delegation to decide the colony's reaction to any particular issue, followed by intense lobbying of the votes of other colonies. Mostly this was done over dinner and long drinking sessions at one of Philadelphia's one hundred and twenty taverns. The favorites were the City Tavern, the Black Horse and the Indian Queen.

These discussions were long and lavishly victualed, as John Adams diarized with enthusiasm: "A most sinful feast again! Everything which could delight the eye, or allure the taste, curds and creams, jellies, sweet meats of various sort, 20 sorts of tarts, fools, trifles, floating islands, whipped sillabuba[16], etc. etc.—parmesan cheese, punch, wine, porter beer etc., etc."

Such a diet, combined with the weight of his responsibilities, was too much for the portly Peyton Randolph; a month after Wythe's arrival at the Congress, he died of stroke. The erstwhile Speaker of the Virginia Assembly was taken ill during an extended dinner with other congressmen at the house of Henry Hill, a merchant of Philadelphia. According to a letter Richard Henry Lee wrote to Washington, "at 9 o'clock at night [he] died without a groan."

There was a solemn funeral, organized by a committee of the Congress and attended by most of its delegates. The Reverend Jacob Duche, assistant rector of Christ Church, and chaplain to Congress, delivered the address. Then followed a long procession to a burial ground where the coffin was stored until it could be taken to Virginia and interred in the chapel of William and Mary.

---

16   A dessert of whipped cream, sugar and brandy.

*

Wythe had thought he would be in Philadelphia for only a few months but, as the crisis with Britain worsened, he remained at his congressional duties for nine months—from September 1775 to June 1776, with a further session of three months the following year. Thus he was able to gauge the city in all seasons. In fall, thunderheads rolled up the Delaware lashing the city with squalls that smelt of the sea. In winter, Philadelphia was a city of moody monochrome, the river dimpled with rain, and the tenements made into white cubes by snow. Come spring, the trees turned green and flowers blossomed in the gardens. Summer in its turn brought stifling humidity, and plagues of flies and mosquitoes.

The far-famed John Adams resided in the same lodgings as Wythe, and the two men occasionally took morning walks together before the morning's business began. Adams, with all the prejudices of a New Englander, initially seemed surprised to find a well-read Southerner as his walking mate. He wrote a friend describing Wythe as "a lawyer of high rank at the bar, a great scholar, a most indefatigable man and a staunch Virginian."

It was an unusual friendship. Adams was a puffed-up pigeon of a man, balding, red-faced, opinionated and quick to judgment. Wythe was slender-limbed, pale, tall, poised and excessively considered. They were brought together by their regard for the law and a love of intellectual debate informed by a sound knowledge of the classics.

The Virginian, whose previous experience of a city was confined to Williamsburg and its two thousand souls, viewed Philadelphia with its population of 38,000 with awe. Manufactured items, which in Wythe's experience had to be imported from England, were here made locally. Down every street near the waterfront Adams and Wythe saw leather-aproned men and their black assistants laboring as ironmongers, rope makers, nailers, silversmiths, potters and wireworkers. As the two wanderers passed the dockyards on the Delaware River every few mornings, they took note of the steady progress shipwrights made in the intricate art of creating oceangoing vessels.

Philadelphia was the largest, and in every respect the most important city of the thirteen colonies. There seemed to be a church every few blocks, a public building facing every square, and a tavern on every corner. The more important thoroughfares were brick-paved, straight, and met at right angles. At night, the streets were lit by whale-oil lamps. And Philadelphians had a hospital for the poor, a college and a fine lending library, thanks to the enthusiasm of Benjamin Franklin.

Franklin, renowned inventor, drawer of thunderbolts from the heavens, diplomat and possessor of the best private library in America, was the elder statesman of the city. The son of a soap-boiler and candle-maker in Boston, Franklin had arrived in Philadelphia a youthful runaway carrying a loaf of bread and a lone Dutch dollar in his pocket. He obtained work in a printer's shop. After a period in England he returned to obtain fame as the owner of the *Pennsylvania Gazette.* He also wrote and published *Poor Richard's Almanac,* a volume of rustic wisdom and shrewd wit, loved for its aphorisms that have taken on the status of American proverbs.

He had helped to secure the repeal of the Stamp Act in 1766 by his direct representations in London. When he began to believe that war with Britain was possible, he returned to Philadelphia. Now aged sixty-nine, he was a citizen of the world and Pennsylvania's automatic choice as a delegate to Congress.

*

On their strolls Adams sometimes used Wythe as a sounding board for some of his private thoughts, secretly held. He was certainly a stimulating mixture. He reached out to the public for support yet he feared the multitude, which he regarded as turbulent and easily led. Nor did he trust the wellborn whom he thought ever grasped for power and were liable to corruption. This last barb particularly applied to the Southern elite, whom he disdainfully regarded as lords of a semi-feudal society of poor whites and blacks. He wanted rule by the people instead of a hereditary monarchy, yet he thought a good king was a godsend. And his belief in democratic forms did not stop him engaging in the most sinuous political intrigues to undermine them.

Wythe's fascination with John Adams never quite extended to undiluted admiration. From his own perspective as a Southerner, Adams seemed like most seaport traders from the north, blunt, cynical and quite devoid of common courtesies. Publicly, he was talkative, and his conversation was peppered with explosive chuckles which made him seem quaint and gnome-like; but this was most certainly not the whole man. Of Puritan stock, and perpetually pessimistic about the morality of his fellow men, Adams had rarely met an honest fellow, and as the Congress proceeded over the tiresome months into 1776, he saw Caesar in any opponent of talent.

He categorized all who attended the Congress as *independence men* (who might qualify as friends), *doubters* (who were to be courted) or *conciliation men* (who must be despised). He was guided by a firm conviction that he knew what was right, and unperturbed by those who disliked him. "I have constantly lived in an enemy's country," he once remarked. Fortunately, he did not regard the Virginia delegation as enemy country; and Wythe he counted as one of the "independence men."

One evening in January, 1776, while passing a few hours with Adams in his rooms, Wythe observed that the greatest obstacle in the way of a declaration of independence was the difficulty of agreeing on a form of government. Adams suggested that the colonies should begin to create free governments for themselves. When Wythe asked what form they should take, Adams confessed that he had not come to a concluded view. That night he ordered his thoughts and packaged them in a long letter to his Virginian colleague.

Adam's plan of an "empire of laws and not of men" envisaged a government comprised of an assembly, a small council and a governor. He argued against a single assembly as being "liable to all the vices, follies and frailties of an individual." The judiciary would be independent. But Adams was not in favor of giving everyone a vote. He planned an assembly chosen by property holders, balanced by a house of independent, virtuous gentlemen.

In one striking paragraph of his letter he revealed his excitement at the prospect of the two of them creating a new and ideal system of government:

You and I, my dear friend, have been sent into life at a time when the greatest lawgivers of antiquity would have wished to live. How few of the human race have ever enjoyed an opportunity of making an election of government for themselves or their children! When, before the present epoch, had three millions of people full power and a fair opportunity to form and establish the wisest and happiest government that human wisdom can contrive?

Adams sent copies of his letter to several others including Richard Henry Lee, who published it under the title *Thoughts on Government.* It was to prove extraordinarily influential as a guidebook to the writing of several state constitutions.

*

Those searching the journals of Congress will rarely find Wythe's name entered in the record, yet his contribution was significant. He was a backroom counsel, a sounding board for others' ideas, and a member of numerous committees helping to sort out the thousand and one complexities of a rebellion of colonies not yet to brave enough to declare their independence.

One committee on which Wythe served grappled with the falling value of the paper currency issued by the Continental Congress. In the absence of a power to tax individuals, Congress had to rely on the miserly contributions of thirteen colonies, while facing the enormous costs of conducting a war. Soon the Congressional printers were churning out notes by the bail load. The Continental currency rapidly depreciated and traders began to refuse to accept the new paper money. Joining Wythe on the Currency Committee were Sam Adams, Thomas Jefferson and Benjamin Franklin. Despite the combined power of these distinguished brains, the currency continued to slide. In desperation Congress passed a resolution that "whoever should refuse to receive payment in Continental bills, should be declared and treated as an enemy of his country." Threats made no difference; the currency fell to worthless—giving rise to the expression "not worth a continental" in American parlance.

On another committee, with Silas Deane and John Adams, Wythe chronicled enemy damage to property—so Congress could later send

Britain the bill! He also served on the Saltpeter Committee, whose job was to monitor supplies of a chemical that was an essential ingredient in gunpowder. On yet another committee with Benjamin Franklin and others, Wythe made suggestions on how to entice the American Indians to the patriot side. The committee proposed giving native Americans gunpowder and trade goods to secure their neutrality, and donating money to missionaries in the hope that, under the influence of the gospel, the Indians would remain peaceable.

Whenever a legal issue arose the Congress thought of Wythe. When Washington wrote asking for direction on what he should do with captured enemy ships, Congress turned to a committee comprising Wythe, John Adams, Benjamin Franklin and others to provide the answer. When loyalists were allowed to leave New York for England he was asked to comment on the oath they were supposed to swear. When a border dispute between Pennsylvania and Connecticut led to an inter-colonial skirmish the ever-reliable Wythe was asked to join a committee that brought the parties to a temporary resolution.

Wythe also served on a committee attempting to find the money to pay Washington's troops. This was the second time that he had been paymaster to Washington's forces. He had performed a similar role when in 1754 he was on a war budget committee of the Virginia House doling out funds for Colonel Washington's defense of the frontier against Indian attack.

When rumors convinced Congress that New Jersey was about to petition King George seeking reconciliation, the softly spoken Wythe was sent with John Jay and John Dickinson to Burlington to talk them out of it. After the three delegates had addressed the assembly for an hour on the need for the colonies to adopt a united front, New Jersey decided to stick with the other colonies.

Wythe was also on a committee with John Adams and Roger Sherman to write directives to a mission headed by Benjamin Franklin to entice Canada into rebellion. Franklin, by then aged seventy-one, journeyed north on an assignment doomed to failure. He traveled by sloop and rowboat up the Hudson, at times camping out in the snow. Little wonder that when he reached Albany, he wrote farewell letters to friends foreshadowing his likely demise. Farther north he encountered American troops starving, dispirited, and dying of smallpox. The Canadians he met responded to the American mission with indifference or hostility. When a British fleet arrived in Montreal with reinforcements, Franklin thought it prudent to return to Philadelphia.

Wythe made few speeches on the floor of Congress and then only when prompted by a matter of conviction. He rose to urge the creation of an American navy. "Why should not America have a navy?" he argued:

No maritime power near the seacoast can be safe without it. This is no Chimera. The Romans suddenly built one in their Carthaginian War. Why may we not lay a foundation for it? We abound with furs, firs, iron ore, tar, pitch, turpentine. We have all the materials for construction of a navy.

Going further, he joined with Richard Henry Lee to suggest that the navy's first assignment should be the arrest of Governor Dunmore, who was still stationed aboard a British man-of-war, patrolling Virginian rivers and stealing what he could. This plan was voted down by some delegates on the grounds that it was impracticable and by others because Dunmore was intimate with the royal family and his capture would provoke the British to even greater rage.

Some other delegates thought it would be better to delay until Congress received an answer to the Olive Branch Petition. This initiative was the brainchild of a Pennsylvanian, John Dickinson, who with a sword clutched in one hand and a white flag in the other, had early on convinced the Congress to petition George III for peace: all on the assumption that the monarch was an innocent upon whom evil ministers had worked their wiles. Upon reading the petition, the king would immediately put things right, Dickinson hypothesized. So, while colonial troops were taking potshots at the British in Boston, and New York patriots were constructing fortifications at the mouth of the Hudson, the Olive Branch Petition was dispatched to England, begging King George to protect American rights against the aggression of Parliament.

Wythe spoke against it, finding it illogical that Continental troops were in the field fighting the greatest empire on Earth so that Americans could remain part of that empire on terms its rulers would decide. He told the Congress:

> Our petition may be declared to be received graciously, and promised to be laid before Parliament, but we can expect no success from it. Have they ever condescended to take notice of you? Rapine, depopulation, burning, murder. Turn your eyes to Concord, Lexington, Charleston, Bristol, New York—there you see the character of the Ministry and Parliament.

His prediction was correct. The petition never received a formal reply. Instead, King George declared Congress illegal and said he would only respond to the colonies individually. Soon, he went even further. Early in November 1775 Americans received news that the king had issued a proclamation declaring the colonies in rebellion and calling on "obedient and loyal subjects" to suppress all "treasons and traitorous conspiracies."

But still Congress hesitated to declare independence.

If there was one thing Adams and Wythe agreed upon, it was that the opponents of independence were mired in an emotional veneration for how things had been previously and could never be again. It was wishful thinking to hope that if Congress waited a while longer, Mother Britain might relent and the colonies, after granting a few concessions, could run back to the empire's bosom. Did not the timid see that their talk of reconciliation was sapping the war effort? That recruitment was drying up because Congress could not explain what Americans were fighting for? In complaint, Wythe told Congress: "Why should we be so fond of calling ourselves dutiful subjects ... No we must declare ourselves a free people."

The journals of the Congress record that on May 29, 1776, it was resolved "that an animated address be published to impress the minds of the people with the necessity of their now stepping forward to save their country, their freedom and property." A committee of Thomas Jefferson, George Wythe, Sam Adams and Edward Rutledge was given the job of composing it. For some reason the address remained unpublished, but decades later a draft of Wythe's contribution was found among the papers of Thomas Jefferson. One can easily appreciate why Wythe's stodgy prose was not adopted as a propaganda tool, however sections are re-produced below to cast light on how a sincere, intelligent man came to overthrow a lifetime of obedience to the Crown. (The strikeouts appear on the original—by Jefferson or Wythe, it is impossible to say.)

There seems no reason now to expect an accommodation of the dispute between Great Britain and these colonies. All overtures toward it on our part have been ineffectual; and on the other hand no terms have been offered to us, but obedience to unconstitutional authority is required. Arms must decide, whether we shall be subject to laws made by men who are not appointed approved of or controllable by us, whose interest it is to oppress us, and whose pride and resentment will be gratified by humbling us; or whether shall be subject to laws made by men we ourselves choose and may change ...

If the enemy conquer, we must be wretched; if not, we may be happy; in either event, our posterity must be involved in our fate. Uniting closely firmly, resolving wisely, and acting vigorously, it is morally certain, we cannot be subdued. Those among us, if there be any, who will not join with us, it is hoped, are as contemptible for their numbers as for their baseness of soul. This is the season when others may prove that love for their country which they profess themselves to be inspired with, and shew that they are what they would appear to be.

There are none of us who cannot do some good service in this great conflict. The aged may supply their want of strength by counsel. The young will probably never meet with another opportunity to signal-ise [an illegible line] their valour so much to their honour. Whilst you are asserting the rights of mankind, and delivering your country from bondage, those who fall cannot die in a better cause, nor can those who survive with victory earn a nobler triumph. Vast indeed will be the expense of armaments we must for a time sustain: but what do men who know the value of liberty think too great a price to purchase it with! And what is property worth, or rather can we have property, if we enjoy not liberty.

While the delegates spent sleepless nights trying to convince themselves they were united Americans, a phenomenon to encourage nightmares burst upon them. During the first weeks of 1776 Philadelphians began to whisper about a political scandal sheet originating in their city. Written in the most extraordinary language and throwing aside all sense of moderation, it argued that the enemy was not the British Parliament, nor the British ministry, nor the royal advisers, but King George himself! It was monstrous, it was scurrilous, it was seditious—but written with such verve! Naturally, everyone wanted to read it. The few well-thumbed copies available were passed to friends on solemn promise to return them safely.

Then a box containing more of the pamphlets arrived from Boston where it had been republished. Inside was something called *Common Sense*, by someone called Thomas Paine. Argued in simple, direct language, the pamphlet was directed to the mind of the common man. Priced at two shillings and stitched together by twine, its pages announced that King George III was "the royal brute of Great Britain!" "A pretty business indeed," complained Paine, "for a man to be allowed eight hundred thousand pounds sterling a year … and worshiped into the bargain! Of more worth is one honest man to society, and in the sight of God, than all the crowned ruffians that ever lived." How could anyone believe in the Divine Right of Kings, Paine demanded, when the English royal line originated with a "French bastard with an armed banditti … establishing himself King of England against the consent of the natives?"

By making the king human, Paine stripped him of his royal mystique and turned him into a befuddled mortal of unrepentant wickedness. The genius of Paine's diatribe was that a fool would be so much easier to pull off the throne than a monarch. But what manner of man would dare write such an outrage? Paine was known to a few of the delegates as an Englishman who had arrived in Philadelphia just a year earlier with a recommendation from Benjamin Franklin. He was a common artisan, the son of a corset-maker, a drunkard, and an ungodly Deist to boot.

His assault on the empire was praised, condemned and ridiculed in turn. In the meantime, printers from New York to the Chesapeake kept churning out *Common Sense* by the cartload. Extracts were published in newspapers across the country. A translation was made for German-Americans. George Washington was so moved by its "sound doctrine and unanswerable reasoning" that he read passages to his troops. Before long every lounger in every tavern had a copy, and debates across the country now echoed with Paine's best lines: "The time hath found us." ... "Should an island govern a continent?" ..."Government of our own is our natural right" ... "'Tis not in numbers but in unity that our great strength lies."

10

Independence for Virginia

Dunmore frees the slaves—the Governor's Ethiopi-
an Regiment—that these United Colonies ought to
be free—Jefferson writes a constitution and gets a
Bill of Rights—Williamsburg reads the Declaration
of Independence—Wythe designs a seal

In November 1775 Lord Dunmore, after spending months commanding a small fleet cruising up and down the James River, issued a proclamation which sent a jolt of fear through Virginia. It declared freedom for the colony's slaves, if they joined the British. It was penned by the governor from the safety of the warship *William* on the James River, and printed in the loyalist settlement of Norfolk, in the Hampton Roads.

Despite the difficulties of finding Dunmore's fleet moving up and down the river, over the summer men and women, young and old—indeed, whole families of slaves—fled to the British forces. Some paddled on small boats, some walked, others swam out to British ships. Washington lost sixteen of his slaves. Twenty-two of Jefferson's workers were noted in his farm book as "joined enemy." A man named Neptune ran from Wythe, though he must have been recaptured, because his name appears in a list of those later held in jail.

By the end of November, Dunmore was pleased to report to London that "between two to three hundred [have] already come in." By

December, more than eight hundred slaves had joined him. Dunmore created from his imagination something called the Ethiopian Regiment, and handed his new soldiers jackets emblazoned with the words *Liberty to Slaves*. British officers began drilling them in musket shooting and formation marching.

With some 180,000 slaves in the colony, the governor's decision to arm those who fled to him cost him his last vestige of moral authority with white Virginia. By freeing slaves he had turned them into men, and now he was turning men into soldiers—and a symbol to slaves everywhere. Of course, he was not motivated by humanitarian scruples. Dunmore's proclamation welcomed only able-bodied males "appertaining to rebels." He did not free his own slaves, and after the War of Independence he was content to become governor of the slave colony of the Bahamas. His proclamation was a naked military tactic that probably did him more harm than good by turning wavering neutrals and loyalists into firm patriots. The wellborn William Byrd III and Robert Carter Nicholas who both owned hundred of slaves became revolutionaries overnight. Virginians might respect a man in a valiant fight, but not one who chose to ally himself with slaves in the murder of his own race and the rapine of white property. George Washington denounced him as an arch-traitor to the rights of humanity who must be crushed. Edmund Pendleton deplored his "base and insidious arts," while Patrick Henry claimed the proclamation proved the king was "a tyrant instead of the protector of the people." Later, Jefferson went so far to include in the Declaration of Independence the charge that the king that "has excited domestic insurrections amongst us."

The Virginian Convention hurriedly responded to Dunmore's challenge by declaring that slaves caught running to the British would suffer death without the benefit of clergy—but if they returned immediately they might be pardoned. The declaration concluded by asking "all humane and benevolent persons in this colony to explain and make known this our offer of mercy to those unfortunate people."

After a month of training and a successful scattering of patriots at Kemp's Landing, Dunmore was ready to pitch his Ethiopian Regiment directly into battle. For weeks, the rebels and the British had been sniping at each other over possession of a bridge across the Elizabeth River to the village of Norfolk. At one end of the bridge, the British were secure in a fort. At the other, a long causeway led through a swamp of mud and tangled vines to a rebel-occupied church and a few houses. Given the extent of the swamp and the narrowness of the causeway there was little real possibility of either side dislodging the other. Dunmore saw it otherwise. Irritated by the constant peppering of sharpshooters, he decided to test the mettle of his troops in a strategy of Napoleonic audacity.

On a morning early in December 1775 Dunmore watched from the fort as British regulars, a handful of loyal colonials and his Ethiopian Regiment marched onto the causeway to the beat of a drum. At the other end, the Virginia militia crouched behind a barricade. Dunmore gambled on the enemy fleeing at the sight of disciplined troops advancing steadily with fixed bayonets. But the enemy did not flee. Instead the farmers' militia readied to fire as Dunmore's troops marched toward them in parade order, six abreast on a path edged with water and no wider than a cart track.

The militia delayed until the enemy was almost upon them. They fired and the first line crumpled. They reloaded and fired again. The next line fell. They fired again. When the smoke cleared they cheered to see Dunmore's troops stumbling in disarray back across the causeway, leaving the soldiers of the Ethiopian Regiment and the Crown strewn before them.

That evening the Scottish lord abandoned the fort and retreated to a camp at Portsmouth. It was the beginning of the end. Several months later, smallpox ripped through his army, reducing it by half. He moved to Gwynn's Island in Chesapeake Bay where, in appalling conditions, nearly five hundred souls perished. Most were former slaves. The Ethiopian Regiment, destroyed by bullet and disease, was no more. In August 1776, Lord Dunmore sailed away to New York.

*

Although the specter of independence continued to haunt the deliberations of Congress, by mid-1776 the issue was coming to a head. Wythe was there on June 7, 1776, when Richard Henry Lee of Virginia got to his feet and in a voice of clear certainty put forward a resolution that some delegates had prayed they would never hear: "That these United Colonies are, and of right ought to be, free and independent States, and they are absolved from all allegiance to the British Crown."

An exultant John Adams seconded the motion, then in a fiery response a cabal of conservatives argued for delay—"until the voice of the people drove us to it!" The middle colonies were not "yet ripe for bidding adieu to [the] British connection," they claimed. "We must wait."

Some of the wavering delegates, uneasy at being rushed over the edge of the abyss, forced a postponement until early July so they could seek the views of their home colonies. In an adroit counter-maneuver, the radicals secured the appointment of a committee to draft a declaration of independence, ready to be signed should the decision swing in their favor. John Adams, Benjamin Franklin, Roger Sherman, Robert Livingston and Thomas Jefferson were assigned to the task.

At this crucial juncture, Wythe left Philadelphia and so was unable to witness the birth of the American nation. Duty took him away—duty, and his esteem for Thomas Jefferson, who in reputation and fame had now overtaken his former teacher.

The convention sitting in Williamsburg was about to create a new constitution for Virginia. But what sort of constitution? Jefferson discussed his fears with Wythe. Many of the delegates were veterans of the old House of Burgesses, and Jefferson did not trust them. Edmund Pendleton, cautious by nature, had been elected president. The erratic Henry would wield his influence. John Adam's *Thoughts on Government*, which would restrict franchise to men of property, was in the hands of many Virginian landowners. Men such as Carter Braxton, whose idea of a republic was to divvy up the powers of the monarch amongst the gentry, favored an upper house of life-tenured gentlemen, just like himself. Besides, Jefferson argued, the Virginia Convention had no authority to make a constitution. Only the people's representatives, especially elected by popular will, could do that.

Not a man to be overwhelmed by doubt or difficulty, Thomas Jefferson decided to write his own constitution. He labored through three drafts in thirteen days, creating his version of the ideal democracy. Then he called Wythe to his lodgings and presented him with the finished document. Jefferson could not leave Philadelphia to press his views on the Williamsburg forum, not when the task at hand was writing a declaration of independence. But Wythe could be spared. Wythe must be his emissary. He must hurry to the Williamsburg Convention before it was too late.

The document that Jefferson placed in Wythe's hands was his constitution for the State of Virginia. All the liberal thoughts of Jefferson's high intellect had been compressed into a dozen pages of precision and detail. He made the people the source of authority; set out a scheme for broad, property-based suffrage by giving land to the land-poor. He inserted controls over the military; sought equity for Indians; protected the independence of the judiciary; and prescribed freedom of religion and freedom of the press. Furthermore, there would be no further importation of slaves into Virginia "under any pretext whatever."

Under Jefferson's constitution, "public liberty" was not merely acknowledged—it was guaranteed by the printed letter of the law. "All persons shall have full and free liberty of religious opinion; nor shall any be compelled to frequent or maintain any religious institution," he wrote. "No person shall be debarred the use of arms (within his own land or tenements)." "There shall be no standing army but in time of actual war." "Printing presses shall be free, except so far as by commission of private injury cause may be given by private action."

On June 13, 1776, Elizabeth and George Wythe set out for Williamsburg, carrying with them Jefferson's draft constitution. Throughout the journey of some three hundred miles, Wythe worried that he would arrive too late. As soon as the coach pulled up at the Capitol building in Duke of Gloucester Street, he rushed inside to discover that the vote on the constitution had not been taken. Thus far the energy of the convention had been directed toward passing into law a Virginian Bill of Rights.

*

The opening article of the Bill of Rights read sweetly indeed (at least to white Virginians):

That all men are by nature equally free and independent, and have certain inherent rights, of which, when they enter into a state of society, they cannot, by any compact, deprive or divest their posterity, namely, the enjoyment of life and liberty, with the means of acquiring and possessing property, and pursuing and obtaining happiness and safety.

The bill went on to declare for religious freedom, a right to jury trials, protection against cruel and unusual punishment, freedom of speech, and the subordination of the military to the state.

Remarkably the gentlemen who readily agreed to this statement of philosophers' dreams were the elite of a slave-owning society familiar only with a system of royal paternalism and an established church. Seemingly they felt obliged to create a system based on how they would want to be treated by their equals. Thus they adopted a classic statement of individual rights cribbed from Locke's edicts on the social contract and the security of property, the Magna Carta, the Petition of Rights, the Acts of the Long Parliament and the settlement of the English Revolution of 1688.

The bill was largely the work of George Mason, a fourth-generation Virginian born to planter wealth. An ascetic and idiosyncratic intellectual, he was educated at home by private tutors and through his own prodigious reading. His bill was quickly understood to be a remarkable document; a luminous, precise statement of human rights imagined by liberal thinkers and philosophers over the centuries. Yet Mason was an insular and rather inconsistent man. He was firm in his opposition to slavery—even though at Gunston Hall, his family seat on the Potomac, he had two hundred slaves waiting on his beck and call, and he never freed any of them. Although outspoken in his support for religious freedom and critical of the privileged position of the Church of England, he served his local Anglican parish as a vestryman. A man of passionate political views, he was easily disturbed by the corruption of public life, and retired from public life at frequent intervals to nurse his chronic ill health.

The opening paragraph of the Bill of Rights is not as enlightened as it seems. The words "when they enter into a state of society" were not in the first draft. Some of the delegates to the convention were puzzled that Mason seemed intent on giving freed coloreds and slaves rights so precisely denied in practice. They were assured by other delegates that dark-skinned people were not Virginians, and as this was well understood, it need not be spelt out.

But Robert Carter Nicholas wanted something stronger. The crafty Edmund Pendleton made a suggestion that satisfied the doubters. So the phrase "when they enter into a state of society" was inserted on the unstated understanding that it excluded those of African descent from the rights enjoyed by everyone else.

Wythe no doubt hoped that with the glorious words of the Bill of Rights ringing fresh in their ears, the delegates would be open to Jefferson's draft constitution. Not so. Wythe thrust his friend's document into the hands of Pendleton and Henry who, after receiving it with ill-disguised exasperation, raised a fusillade of objections to even putting it before the assembly. With Mason and James Madison they had begun work on their own constitution, and it was almost agreed. Another version would throw the convention into confusion. The delegates had been in Williamsburg for six weeks and wanted to go home; it was hot, everyone was tired.

Anyway, that was what they told Wythe, who reported back to Jefferson: "Such was the impatience of sitting long enough to discuss several important points in which they differ, and so many other matters were necessarily to be dispatched before the adjournment that I was persuaded the revision of a subject the members seemed tired of would at that time have been unsuccessfully proposed."

Perhaps the truth was they did not want Jefferson's brand of democracy with its broad voting rights and reform of land rights. Practical republicanism of the Pendleton variety with its emphasis on leadership by those fixed by wealth was preferable to the Virginian elite. The power brokers in the Convention pasted Jefferson's indictments against George III to the front of the constitution, and adopted his suggestions for reform of the courts. The rest of his draft was discarded.

So instead of a House of Burgesses and a Council, Virginia got a House of Delegates and a Senate, but the rub was that only those qualified to vote for the old could vote for the new. The aristocratic elite remained firmly in power. Excluded from the vote were the unpropertied, colored men and all women, whether black or white. The Anglican Church remained the established religion supported by state taxes, and English feudal laws continued to apply to land tenures. Judges were appointed by the legislatures and not by voters.

It was left to Wythe to write Jefferson with the disappointing news. "The system agreed to in my opinion required reformation. In October you, I hope you will effect it."[17] Jefferson's reaction was thorough dismay. His hopes for a fair, free society for all Virginians had been dashed. The Tidewater gentry had triumphed. The cry of no taxation without representation seemed hollow when so many of Virginia's citizens had been denied a say in electing their representatives. In Jefferson's mind, what had transpired in the house was not a revolution of the system, but merely a transfer of power.

*

After forty weeks absence, George Wythe and Elizabeth were grateful to be back in their own beds in the house on Palace Green. Their nearest neighbor now was Patrick Henry, newly elected as governor—a little over a year earlier Lord Dunmore had declared him an outlaw. In the House of Delegates coonskin caps sat on the hat pegs and the fashion was for military uniforms, buckskin breeches and plain hunting jackets. Only the Tidewater elderly dressed in lace cuffs and frilled shirts.

Williamsburg, from the governor down, waited anxiously for news from Philadelphia.

*

In some cities, bonfires were lit, cannons fired, and royal statues toppled at reports of the final break from Britain. Not so in Williamsburg. On July 20, residents of the city awoke to read in the *Virginia Gazette* the Declaration of Independence printed in full. Citizens gathered in small groups in

---

17   Jefferson did return in October to Williamsburg to take his seat in the House of Delegates, though he failed to reform the constitution. Despite repeated attempts over the years he was rebuffed every time. The constitution remained virtually unchanged until after Jefferson's death.

the streets of the city as the literate read out the declaration for those who could not. A few days later the Attorney General Benjamin Waller stood on the courthouse steps, watched by a large crowd, and carefully read the declaration to the state troops lined before him.

The words he spoke to the assembled soldiers and citizens that day have become sacred to Americans. In the celebrated second paragraph, the principal author, Jefferson (assisted by John Adams and Benjamin Franklin), distilled the faith upon which the union of former colonies was to be built:

> We hold these truths to be self-evident, that all men are created equal, that they are endowed by their Creator with certain unalienable Rights, that among these are Life, Liberty and the pursuit of Happiness.

Somehow, Jefferson had tapped directly into the American soul. Perhaps his most surprising inspiration was the elevation of the pursuit of happiness as a natural right of mankind. Upon first reading the declaration, many Americans felt a tinge of embarrassment that such a childish desire as *happiness* should be included in a document declaring nationhood. Yet it is easy to believe that as it was read to the soldiers, farmers, women and children from the steps of the Williamsburg courthouse on that summer day in 1776 that the idea of the pursuit of happiness went to the core of their beliefs. Rather than a frippery, happiness was the bedrock of all that followed, because human happiness was only possible if life and liberty were secure. A right to happiness required government to do more than abstain from evil: to actively promote good for all its citizens. Whereas ancient charters such as Magna Carta were aimed at crimping tyranny, Jefferson's declaration spelt out the rights of the people and made it clear that they derived from their Creator, not a begrudging monarch.

Critics have said there is nothing in the Declaration of Independence that cannot be found in the works of Locke, Vattel and George Mason's Declaration of Rights. This was Jefferson's way. He was a habitual pickpocket of others' thought, but that should not deny him his due in converting their florid writing into plain, pithy, yet elevated phrases that have inspired a nation to this day. The genius of Jefferson was to synthesize and simplify, yet lose neither clarity nor purpose. Simple, well-understood words, ordered correctly in bold, natural language, gracefully conveyed their burden of great ideas.

*

In the fall of 1776, the former colony of Virginia sent Wythe back to the Philadelphia Congress where, as best he could, he assisted in the worrisome, complex task of running a country at war. Before returning, he had one last duty to perform. He was asked to join a committee chaired by George Mason to devise the official seal of the Commonwealth of Virginia. The colonial seal, which depicted a kneeling Indian presenting a sheaf of tobacco to a crowned monarch, was no longer acceptable. Wythe's design was chosen by the committee: it showed Virtue, a spear in one hand and a sword in the other, standing on the fallen figure of Tyranny.

The inscription underneath read *Sic semper tyrannis* ("Thus always to tyrants"). On the reverse side were the words *Deus nobis haecotia fecit*. Jefferson, writing from Philadelphia to his friend John Page, translated this to read "God give us this leisure," and dismissed it as "aenigmatical, since if it puzzles now, it will be absolutely insoluble fifty years hence." This rather hurt Wythe, who insisted the words meant "God gave us these retreats" and referred to the virtue and peace of the Virginian countryside. Jefferson ultimately prevailed. In 1779, as governor, he substituted *Perseverando,* which is clear enough although perhaps lacking gravitas. Apart from that alteration, the seal designed by Wythe is used to this day.

11

Reformers and Revisors

Wythe signs the Declaration of Independence, maybe—Washington crosses the Delaware—Jefferson and Wythe reform the law—Pendleton falls from a horse—freeing the slaves by degrees—Jefferson and Wythe's reforms falter—James Madison saves the day

It is generally assumed that George Wythe added his signature to the Declaration of Independence when he returned to Philadelphia in September 1776. The problem is that the signature attributed to him on the document looks nothing like his usual one. The name *George Wythe* appears at the head of the Virginia delegation in letters large enough to dwarf those that follow, whereas his normal mark was a reserved *G. Wythe*. It seems probable that someone else attached his name while Wythe was in Williamsburg.

In any event, after the king-killing task of ensuring his name was on the declaration, he took his place in the congress of a nation-state struggling with the enormous challenge of defending itself even as it was in the process of being born.

Congress had to safeguard a band of territory extending from the fields of New Hampshire to the sea island of Georgia—about 1,300 miles. An army had to be raised, paid, armed and fed—all while its masters attempted to agree on a working confederation of its constituent elements, and to establish a national administration. Amid all these difficulties, on September 9, 1776, Congress brought forth a defiant title for itself, the United States.

The assembly had more than its quota of lawyers, orators and misty-eyed visionaries, when what it needed was bankers, clerks, bookkeepers and administrators. Wythe contributed as best he could. He wrote instructions to the American commissioners to France, led by Benjamin Franklin, who were seeking official recognition of America's break from Britain. He made a sulfurous speech imploring German mercenaries employed by the British army to leave American shores (they did not).

He protested when some of the New England states decided to pay their soldiers more than the southern states could possibly match (they went ahead anyway), and he drafted a memorandum to the French leadership designed to lure them into the war on the side of the rebels (they joined a year later). He also wrote out an oath of allegiance to be taken by officers upon accepting their commission, and sat on a committee supervising the supply of camp utensils to Washington's soldiers.

As the afterglow of independence faded to the darkness of war, every dispatch from the front seemed to bring bad news. The British returned, as Americans knew they must. They sailed into New York with its harbor of islands in an armada of three hundred ships. Augmented by Hessians (Germans), they numbered thirty thousand men. Washington faced them with fewer than twenty thousand and a navy of longboats and privateers.

After a bitter defense of Brooklyn Heights, on Long Island, Washington's troops were forced to retreat into the fog and back across the East River to Manhattan. After more inconclusive fighting Washington abandoned Manhattan and slipped across to White Plains, where he lost another battle. Then, with the British in leisurely pursuit, he was rolled back all the way across the Delaware River and into Pennsylvania. By the time he arrived there, his straggling force, reduced by capture, death and desertion, numbered no more than three thousand.

These survivors had insufficient tents, blankets, uniforms, supplies, medicine, fieldpieces and powder. The men were badly paid, ill clad, poorly armed, and running out of ammunition. They knew the territory, but no rules of engagement; they abandoned towns and ports, continually losing ground, continually in retreat against an enemy they feared. The best Congress could hope was that with losses such as these Washington, over time, might out-endure the British until their former masters were defeated.

In those desperate days Washington counted it a success if he could merely keep his army going. He was not so much the commander of a single force, but the coordinator of federal forces and militiamen supplied by the former colonies. These militias were led by independently minded officers, and provisioned and paid for by the states with varying degrees of meanness. Many of Washington's soldiers were part-timers who had signed up for a term of months, and expected to be home in time for the next harvest.

*

In October 1776, Jefferson resigned his post in Congress to serve in the new House of Delegates in Williamsburg. Wythe offered his residence on Palace Green to his old student. "Make use of the house and furniture," he wrote. "I shall be happy if any thing of mine can contribute to make your and Mrs. Jefferson's residence in Williamsburg comfortable." A month later Wythe received a letter from Jefferson, saying he was embarking on a monumental project in the service of the Commonwealth of Virginia, and required Wythe's immediate assistance in Williamsburg.

Jefferson's constitution for Virginia had been rebuffed, and war was raging to the north, but Jefferson saw the revolution as more than a protest about taxes and autonomy. If Virginians were destined to spill much native blood, as now seemed certain, then the republic's aim should be the creation of a new state free of ancient divisions and religious intolerance. Jefferson regarded the archaic legal system inherited from the English as a manor house of privilege that should be rebuilt from the ground up.

This was a task dear to Wythe's heart. He immediately wrote back from Philadelphia: "Whenever you and the speaker think I should return to Virginia to engage in the part which shall be assigned to me in revising the laws, I shall attend you. As to the time and place of meeting and my share in this work, I can accommodate myself to the appointment, and be content with the allotment my colleagues shall make."

By early December, Wythe and Elizabeth were back in their own house in Williamsburg, and Thomas and Martha Jefferson removed to rented rooms in Pinckney's town house. Jefferson's account book shows that on his departure from Wythe House, he tipped the servants a generous fourteen shillings.

To undertake the mammoth task of revising all the state's laws, the Virginia Assembly elected a committee of five: Thomas Jefferson, Edmund Pendleton, George Mason, Thomas Ludwell Lee and George Wythe. Since the prime mover was Jefferson, he became chairman of the committee. He was the youngest, at thirty-three.

Even before the committee convened, he and Wythe met to discuss the scope of the mission ahead. There was much that was good in English law, they agreed, but much was bad. With decisive cuts, they would prune English law to its true essentials of justice. The thickets from which only the rich and their lawyers could emerge unscathed would be stripped bare. Equality for all would be the touchstone.

Thrown out (wrote Jefferson) would be statutes "which from their verbosity, their endless tautologies, their involutions of case within case, and parenthesis within parenthesis, and their multiplied efforts at certainty by *saids* and *aforesaids*, by *ors* and by *ands* … do really render them more perplexed and incomprehensible, not only to common readers, but to lawyers themselves."

The reformers faced immediate problems. They had grossly underestimated the enormity of the task. Perhaps they thought they could rewrite Virginia's laws in a mere six months, but it soon became apparent that it would take years, and many of them. Secondly, the members of the committee were bound to disagree. Pendleton's natural bent was caution and over-concern with the welfare of the wealthy. Mason was an angst-ridden eccentric, who favored reform as long as it did not affect planter rule. Lee, though inclined to think as a liberal, was at heart unadventurous.

Finally, even if their reforms were drafted and presented to the assembly, there was no guarantee that any of them would be enacted.

The committee held its first meeting in the second week of January 1777, in Fredericksburg. Each member carried with them to the meeting the glorious news that Washington's armies, after five months of retreat, had achieved a remarkable victory over a Hessian garrison at Trenton, New Jersey.

During Christmas night, in a blinding snowstorm, Washington had assembled his troops on the shores of the Delaware River. They stood shivering in threadbare clothing, many with only rags on their feet. The bulk of his troops had enlisted for a year, and on 31 December many of them would pack up for home. Washington had but a few days in which to strike at the enemy. Several days earlier, he had read to his men the famous opening words of a new pamphlet of Tom Paine:

These are the times that try men's souls. The summer soldier and the sunshine patriot will, in this crisis, shrink from the service of their country; but he that stands it now, deserves the love and thanks of man and woman. Tyranny, like hell, is not easily conquered; yet we have this consolation with us, that the harder the conflict, the more glorious the triumph.

Washington ferried his men across the ice-choked river in flat-bottomed boats. After a march of nine miles to Trenton, they surprised the Hessian mercenaries asleep after a Christmas carouse of schnapps and beer. With bayonet, sword and pike, the Americans overwhelmed the enemy in little over an hour. A thousand men were captured; importantly, so were their stores. This victory was followed ten days later by a running battle at Princeton, which forced the British from much of New Jersey. It was suddenly possible to believe that the revolution might succeed.

*

The first task of the Fredericksburg meeting of law reformers was to divide the workload between the three lawyers of the group: Jefferson, Wythe and Pendleton. It was agreed that Jefferson would redraft the ancient laws before colonial settlement, Wythe would rewrite British statutes made since the settlement of Virginia, and Pendleton the statutes made by the House of Burgesses. That settled, the members of the committee fell into dispute on the basic question of whether the committee should abolish the whole and start afresh like a latter-day Justinian, or reform the ignoble pile of imperial and colonial law piece by piece.

Pendleton proposed the committee start with a clean slate. Jefferson, Mason and Wythe disagreed. Apart from being a task so large as to be impossible, the new legislation would become "subject of question and chicanery until settled by repeated adjudication" (Jefferson's words). The majority prevailed, although it was never safe to assume that Pendleton gave up on anything. It was also agreed that the common law was not to be meddled with, except when alterations were clearly necessary.

It was all very well to say they were about to do the right thing "with a single eye to reason" (as Jefferson put it), but once the committee descended to detail, inevitably they clashed. Religious freedom, the structure of the courts, the law of inheritance and public education became their battlegrounds.

Just as Jefferson and Wythe were beginning to despair that the committee would agree on anything, the other three members of the committee departed the scene. Pendleton, riding his estate, was thrown from his horse and badly dislocated his hip. It refused to mend and he was bedridden for months. Mason, after dragging his gout-ridden body to Fredericksburg, announced that being no lawyer he was unsuited to the task, and resigned. Lee, with a wan eye, examined the mountain of papers he had to read, and died shortly thereafter of rheumatic fever. So there were two.

Wythe and Jefferson were in a position almost without precedent: two lawyers, quite undisturbed, given the task of rewriting society's laws from top to bottom. The Revisors, as they liked to call themselves, made law reform their occupation for the next two and a half years. They examined bundles of statutes and found needless complexities and anachronisms. They unearthed laws that lawyers had forgotten ever existed. They scratched their heads over laws that contradicted one another. They read definitions that defied meaning.

Within several months, Jefferson and Wythe knew what needed reforming, but drafting substitute laws proved difficult. Wythe would work for days on a topic, refining, condensing and turning it into simple English, but still ending up with pages of provisos and exceptions, all in the name of justice. He would then hand his composition to Jefferson who would return Wythe a document codifying the most complex of concepts in plain, unambiguous language and fluent logic. In ten days Jefferson rewrote the entire judicial system of the state, delineating courts in a hierarchy descending from Appeals through Chancery, General, Admiralty and County.

Both men were criticized for not doing more to assist in the war effort. Washington wrote plaintively to Benjamin Harrison "it appears as clear to me as ever the sun did in its meridian brightness, that America never stood in more eminent need of the wise, patriotic, and spirited exertions of her sons than at this period ... I cannot help asking: Where is Mason, Wythe, Jefferson, Nicholas, Pendleton, Nelson, and another I could name."

Washington was not the only one who asked why Jefferson was devoting himself to the puerile task of clearing cobwebs from statutes when the nation was soaking in the blood of young men. With deep sarcasm, Richard Henry Lee pictured Jefferson consulting ancient texts in Olympian isolation at Monticello: "It will not perhaps be disagreeable to you in your retirement, sometimes to hear the events of war, and how in other respects we proceed in the arduous business we are engaged in."

Jefferson, showing remarkable detachment, ignored the criticism. Reform was in the air and he had to act while the legislature was hot for change. It seems he felt a responsibility to those fighting in the field, to chronicle the freedoms and rights of Everyman so that every man could derive something lasting from personal sacrifice.

Their work caused Jefferson to miss most of 1778 session of the House of Delegates, but at least Wythe was able to make his contribution to the governance of the state. By May 1777 Pendleton, still hobbling on crutches around his country estate, was unable to continue as Speaker of the House of Delegates, and Wythe was elected in his stead.

Thus in addition to devoting himself to reform of the law, Wythe was now Speaker of a legislature charged with running a war. Said Jefferson of Wythe's appointment: "His pure integrity, judgment and reasoning powers gave him great weight." Sufficient weight that under his guidance Wythe was able to push Jefferson's reforms of the court system through the house. This was followed by a controversial act to draft men into the army, and to increase property taxes to pay them. Somehow, in his spare moments Wythe also found time to revise British statutes applicable to Virginia; most of his labor was mundane, but still necessary. He redrafted laws on the circulation of private bank notes, the procedure of impeachment, the speedy recovery of debts and the conduct of auctions.

*

In the new society that Thomas Jefferson wanted to create through his reforms, the doors of Virginia's schools and university would be thrown open to all white children of talent, regardless of wealth. In Jefferson's revelation Virginia's future rulers would be aristocrats of virtue and talent, rather than aristocrats of wealth. He envisaged "a system by which every fibre would be eradicated of ancient or future aristocracy; and a foundation laid for a government truly republican."

Education from youth to maturity fell under Jefferson's examination in his celebrated Bill for the More General Diffusion of Knowledge. It reflected his conviction that citizens who could make informed, rational and educated decisions were essential to a truly free society.

His revolutionary bill proposed a broad-based, three-tiered pyramid of secular public education. Those "whom nature hath endowed with genius and virtue," wrote Jefferson in the introduction to his bill, "should be called to that charge without regard to wealth, birth or other accidental conditions or circumstances." His plan required local authorities to provide instruction in reading, writing and arithmetic for "all free children, male and female" for three years. He did not envisage colored children attending these schools. For students showing ability, the state would build grammar schools, leaving parents to meet the running expenses. In a companion bill he proposed that children of impoverished parents should be admitted to the College of William and Mary by scholarships.

Jefferson also turned his capacious mind to matters of conscience. Mason's Bill of Rights had guaranteed the free exercise of religion, but Jefferson regarded this as a job only half done. His own bill on religious freedom was a broadside at state funding of the Church of England to the exclusion of all other religions. "Almighty God hath created the mind free and manifested his supreme will that free it shall remain by making it altogether insusceptible of restraint," wrote Jefferson in the preamble to his bill. "That to compel a man to furnish contributions of money for the propagation of opinions which he disbelieves and abhors, is sinful and tyrannical."

Jefferson devoted more time to reforming the criminal law than to any other field. Under colonial rule, Virginia had executed horse thieves, pirates, arsonists, heretics, sodomites and embezzlers. Jefferson proposed that the hangman's noose would not be ordered except for convictions for treason and murder (in which he included death by dueling). In a quirky afterthought he prescribed that convicted poisoners should be punished by taking poison themselves.

In the midst of his labors he wrote to Wythe:

I have got thro' the bill 'for proportioning crimes and punishment in cases heretofore capital,' and now inclose it to you with a request that you will be so good as scrupulously to examine and correct it, that it may be presented to our committee with as few defects as possible. In its style I have aimed as accuracy, brevity and simplicity ... And I must pray you to be as watchful over what I have not said as what is said.

Because Jefferson's draft had so curtailed the deterrent of capital punishment he resorted to the principle of *lex talionis* for lesser crimes. He proposed shockingly severe penalties, which would later cause him acute embarrassment in the salons of Paris: "Whosoever shall be guilty of rape, polygamy, or sodomy with man or woman shall be punished, if a man by castration, if a woman, by cutting thro' the cartilage of her nose a hole of one half inch diameter at the least."

Then there was the awful, unsolvable problem of what to do about slavery.

Jefferson and Wythe spent many hours debating this subject. They were agreed that slavery must end. It was against the law of nature for one half of the citizenry to trample on the rights of the other. Its existence shamed their commonwealth. It was degrading to the moral character of masters. It nursed children in the daily exercise of tyranny. And the day must surely come when the oppressed would shake off their chains in violent insurrection.

All this was understood.

Yet practical men could see that even if the legislature was inclined to free the slaves, it was not possible. It would be the ruination of Virginia's economy. A moralist who tried to farm without slaves would go broke. Any politician who spoke against slavery would face oblivion at the ballot.

Even the most impassioned advocate of emancipation would acknowledge the folly of Virginia letting loose its 180,000 slaves in the midst of a desperate war. Even to foreshadow their freedom would be disastrous because, as Dunmore had shown, it was delusional to believe Virginia's slaves were so devoted to their masters that they would not take up arms against them.

Still Jefferson and Wythe persevered. They drew up a plan for the gradual elimination of slavery, which envisaged that all slaves born after the passage of their legislation (they hoped for 1779) would be bound to their master until the age of eighteen, if they were female, and twenty-one if they were male. Thereafter they would be free. During bondage they would be trained at public expense to learn tillage, arts and sciences.

Jefferson did not contemplate that these former slaves would remain in Virginia; his desire to rid the new commonwealth of slavery extended to clearing the land of black people as well. Freed slaves would be banished to virgin lands, perhaps in Africa or some emptiness beyond the Mississippi. Under his legislation, the state would supply these exiles with arms, implements and useful domestic animals, in order to assist them to establish an independent and liberated community.

But if Virginia expelled its black-skinned residents, who would pick Virginia tobacco? Who would tend the gardens, churn the butter, make beds and bring the horses from the stable when the master wanted to ride? Jefferson's answer was that ships would be sent "to other parts of the world to bring back an equal number of white indentured servants." He could only have meant from teeming Europe.

In his *Notes on the State of Virginia* Jefferson rationalized his scheme:

It will probably be asked, Why not retain and incorporate the blacks into the state, and thus save the expense of supplying, by importation of white settlers, the vacancies they will leave? Deep rooted prejudices entertained by the whites; ten thousand recollections, by the blacks, of the injuries they have sustained; new provocations; the real distinctions which nature has made; and many other circumstances, will divide us into parties, and produce convulsions which will probably never end but in the extermination of the one or the other race.

This plan of a white Virginia was entirely consistent with Jefferson's vision of the great American landscape being a quilt of medium-sized farms occupied by white families living virtuously in bucolic prosperity and tranquility. He regarded small farmers (whom he dubbed husbandmen) as the bedrock of a sound and self-perpetuating republic:

Those who labor in the earth are the chosen people of God, if ever he had a chosen people ... [G]enerally speaking, the proportion which the aggregate of the other classes of citizens bears in any state to that of its husbandmen, is the proportion of its unsound to its healthy parts, and is a good-enough barometer whereby to measure its degree of corruption.

In the Jefferson ideal, cities and manufacturing industry were undesirable, governments should be lean and unobtrusive, and banks were odious. "I sincerely believe ... that banking establishments are more dangerous than standing armies," he wrote in 1816, "and that the principle of spending money to be paid by posterity under the name of funding is but swindling futurity on a large scale."

Undoubtedly, Wythe and Jefferson saw their gradualist plan to eradicate slavery and replace it with a white workforce as a worthwhile reform, although it would entrench slavery in Virginia for at least another seventy to eighty years, and the cost would be horrendous. In any case, it was certain to be rejected by the legislature. Jefferson and Wythe's draft laws on education, inheritance and religion were radical enough without proposing to members of the house that they give away their wealth as well. The rumblings from their fellow legislators against the plan grew so intense that Wythe and Jefferson scrapped the whole idea. Their bill was never put to the house and in their report to the assembly they said nothing about the emancipation of slaves. No copy of the plan has ever been found—its existence is known because Jefferson summarized its terms in his *Notes on the State of Virginia* (1782) and his autobiography (1821).

If the Revisors could not bring themselves to ban slavery, the least they could do, for humanity's sake, was to reform its worst excesses. Virginia, after more than one hundred and fifty years of experience of black bondage, had accumulated a myriad of laws controlling slaves, known colloquially as the Black Code. They were a hodgepodge of domination, brutality, discrimination and petty interference. They covered matters such as night walking, being at large without a pass, carrying arms, rebellion, miscegenation, owning a horse, running away, resisting a master and administering medicine. The prescribed penalties for breaches of the code ranged from whipping, cutting off ears, and castration to branding with a hot iron and hanging.

In Jefferson's reforms, he substituted generalities for some of the hideous punishments of the colonial code. Instead of prescribing a specific punishment for a particular offence, magistrates were given discretion to be as merciful or as brutal with the whip as they thought fit. He confidently believed Virginians, freed of British rule, would be more enlightened and likely to temper sentences with clemency.

Yet Jefferson did not tamper with the code's underlying prohibitions and philosophy. He had a stated abhorrence for interracial sex, which led him to write a provision that was later rejected by the legislature as being too harsh:

> If any white woman shall have a child by a negro or mulatto, she and her child shall depart the commonwealth within one year thereafter. If they fail so to do, the woman shall be out of the protection of the laws, and the child shall be bound out by the Alderman of the county.

In the spring of 1778, the Assembly considered a momentous bill drafted by Jefferson to end the slave trade into Virginia. The legislation, as finally passed that year, declared that in future all slaves imported into the state would become free. Although the legislation did not of itself liberate one slave, its effect was to slam the gate on their further introduction. Jefferson's bill met an open door from the legislators because the plantocracy in the house had a motive for doing good. The captive women of Virginia were so fruitful that the slave quarters were well stocked with African children, and the planters could see the price of their possessions rising if imports ceased. Whatever their reasons, Wythe and Jefferson could rejoice that the ban was passed. Never again would they see Africans bearing tribal scars, wild-eyed with fear, shuffling in chains from the wharf on the James River to Williamsburg's auction block.

In November 1776, Jefferson had guided a bill through the House of Delegates eliminating entails.[18] Now he proposed the legislators take a hatchet to the spreading branches of the great families of Virginia by abolishing the feudal law of primogeniture. This plan had Wythe's enthusiastic support. As a second son, he had watched as Chesterville was handed to his elder brother.

Pendleton thought differently. He had argued that the great Tidewater estates (which he saw as the pride of all Virginians) required protection from subdivision when the head of the family died. Faced with the determination of Wythe and Jefferson to abolish primogeniture, he suggested the compromise of giving a double portion to the eldest male. To this Jefferson testily observed "that if the eldest son could eat twice as much, or do double work, it might be a natural evidence of his right to a double portion."

*

---

18   An entail allowed a property owner to write a will restricting possession to the heirs of his body, or if he was so minded, limited to the male or female line. An entail could tie up landed estates and property in slaves for generations, causing much ill will among family members.

After two and a half years of unrelenting labor the two Revisors were approaching the end of their task. Jefferson had carried the major burden, including the more contentious bills such as those on education and crime. Pendleton had worked alone in Caroline on his portion, the laws of colonial Virginia. When Jefferson and Wythe finally viewed his contribution they were horrified. All he had done was alter a passage here and there, and delete what he disapproved of. The result was brief and quite incoherent.

Jefferson and Wythe had to rewrite his bills. The Revisors assembled in Williamsburg in February 1779, where by Jefferson's account "meeting day by day, we critically examined our several parts, sentence by sentence, scrutinizing and amending until we had agreed on the whole." There are conflicting reports on whether Pendleton attended this meeting.

In May and June, the work was concluded, and Jefferson and Wythe gingerly placed one hundred and twenty-six bills before the Virginia Assembly. That wily dissembler Edmund Pendleton did not sign off on them. The assembly reacted with a morning of puzzlement, a few days of stony silence then postponement to the next session. Then followed weeks of opposition and finally indifference.

The bill on religious freedom provoked only a brief uproar—brief because the house quickly moved to defer further consideration. The proposal to do away with capital punishment except for murder and treason was thrown out on the desire of the delegates to hang horse thieves as well. Jefferson's *Bill for a More General Diffusion of Knowledge* was rejected three times over the next six years. On the last occasion, in 1785, Jefferson was in Paris. He wrote in a fury to Wythe: "Let our countrymen know ... that the tax which will be paid for this purpose is not more than the thousandth part of what will be paid to kings, priests, and nobles who will rise up amongst us if we leave the people in ignorance."

What was well understood by opponents was that the reforms were meant to burrow beneath the foundations of the established order. By amending the inheritance laws Jefferson and Wythe intended to break up the large estates, with their laws on freedom of religion they hoped to crush the privileges of the Anglican Church, and their bill for general education would allow the masses' voice to be heard in a republican government.

The house's offhand rejection of two and a half years of unrelenting toil devastated Wythe and Jefferson. Perhaps they should not have been surprised. What sort of dreamy radicals would submit during a time of war a bill for the expenditure of a sultan's fortune (uncosted by the Revisors or anyone else) for the free education of children? And what would the delegates have thought of their plan to build a public library lined with books and adorned with paintings and statues, brought forth at a time when American troops had no shoes?

One of the few supporters of the reforms was James Madison, one of the youngest delegates, and the son of Orange County's leading planter, James Madison senior, who owned four thousand acres worked by one hundred slaves. A delicate little man and a prissy dresser, James Madison junior sometimes appeared in the house dressed in a trim-fitting suit of buff and blue with ruffles at his bosom and wrist, which led his detractors to quip that he resembled a cake of ribboned French soap. His voice was no bigger than his frame, and his speeches, although usually sound, were dull and frequently interrupted by calls from the hard-of-hearing to speak louder. Yet, he carried an indefinable authority that caused listeners to want to hear what he had to say. Perhaps it was his humorless persistence, his aura of implacable honesty, or his tense devotion to the written word: in any case, he was better researched than anyone else. An earnest Christian first, later a Deist, in the House of Delegates he fervently championed religious freedom.

A radical who knew how to create a compromise, Madison was born to the intrigue of politics. At the precocious age of twenty-five he had already become a broker of other men's ideas. Jefferson and Madison, being from similar backgrounds, introspective in thought and of radical dispositions, became natural allies, co-contrivers of reform and perpetual correspondents on matters both trivial and great.

It was at Madison's insistence that five hundred copies of Jefferson and Wythe's reform bills were printed at public expense in 1784. He regarded the Revisors' bills as "a mine of legislative wealth," and from time to time he lovingly lifted one from its pile, dusted it down and re-submitted it to the house. In this way, Jefferson's criminal law reforms passed in 1797, but only after severe modification.

In 1785, while Jefferson was in France, Madison took up the task of enshrining religious freedom in law and ending taxpayers' support of the Anglican Church. Swept along by a mountainous petition organized by the busy Baptists and Presbyterians, and supported by Virginia's multiplicity of sects, he presented the Revisors' statute for religious freedom to the House of Delegates. Predictably, it was opposed by the Tidewater gentry, and the Anglican clergy roaring to high heaven of rampant heresy if Dissenters were given their heads.

Madison had his allies, and sometimes in surprising places. They included that upright moralist and keen Anglican George Mason. A number of notable Virginians such as Patrick Henry, John Marshall, Richard Henry Lee and George Washington rallied behind a compromise plan of state funding of all Christian denominations. Madison and Mason were having none of it. After a rancorous debate, Madison's bill passed. Mason declared jubilantly: "I flatter myself [I] have in this country extinguished forever the ambitious hope of making laws for the human mind."

Without state financial support Anglican clerics, never comfortable in selling their beliefs in the market place of religious ideas, were out-pilgrimed by Dissenting preachers, revivalists and tent-show evangelists. Across Virginia, many Anglican churches closed their doors and were abandoned to nature. Roofs fell in, foundations crumbled and sacristies became havens for pigeons and foxes.

In the same year Madison, to the delight of Jefferson and Wythe, also persuaded the legislature to abolish primogeniture. In 1786 and 1787, largely at Madison's urging, other bills were lifted from the Revisors' pile of un-enacted legislation for further consideration by a committee comprising Pendleton, Wythe and John Blair. Thus it was that over the decades, piece by piece, about a third to a half of the code was accepted into Virginian law. A much watered-down version of Jefferson's code for education was passed in 1797.

12

"Hither You Shall Go, But No Further!"

The British in Philadelphia—Wythe becomes a judge in Chancery—Jefferson becomes governor and reforms William and Mary—Wythe, Professor of Law and Police—John Marshall neglects his studies—Wythe upholds the constitution

In the fall of 1777, the war was going badly for American patriots. The British, in an armada of two hundred and sixty ships, landed seventeen thousand men near the mouth of Elk River on Chesapeake Bay, about fifty miles from Philadelphia. After scattering Washington's forces in the Battle of Brandywine Creek, General Sir William Howe and his army entered Philadelphia to be feted by loyalists there as saviors. The royal invaders spent the winter snug in the occupied city while Washington retreated to the bleak hills above the Schuylkill River at Valley Forge. There several thousand bitter-enders, starving, perpetually cold and teetering on rebellion sat out a miserable winter, waiting until they could attempt to recapture the city that had become a symbol for Congress.

Amid the gloom, Washington received wonderful news from the north. American forces had thwarted a British attempt to descend from Canada and invade the Hudson River Valley. General Horatio Gates and the dashing Benedict Arnold had won a series of battles in the deep forests of

Upper New York, forcing the enemy to surrender more than five thousand men at Saratoga.

It was a major turning point in the revolutionary war, for this unexpected victory persuaded the French (with a touch of Yankee salesmanship from Benjamin Franklin, on diplomatic duty at the French Court) that a rabble of freemen might just defeat the British. Louis XVI had such a craving for revenge that he ignored the inconsistency of coming to the aid of a king-defying republic, and sent a French fleet bristling with munitions and troops to the New World. Soon after Spain joined in, and Britain found itself involved in a growing international conflict. In London, Lord North began to consider the peace option. In June 1778, the British, concerned about the French involvement in the war, quietly departed from Philadelphia. Yet the war still had five years to run.

*

The legislative career of George Wythe in the House of Delegates came to an end in 1778 when he resigned after both houses of the Virginia Assembly unanimously elected him judge of the High Court of Chancery. Governor Patrick Henry swore him into office on April 6. Edmund Pendleton, standing on crutches besides Wythe, was also sworn in as a judge of Chancery. Wythe was fifty-two, Pendleton five years his senior. Even on the bench the pair were destined to spend the next quarter of a century sparring with each other. To Wythe's dismay, Pendleton gained precedence over him later that year when he was promoted to chief justice of the Court of Appeals.

There were other changes afoot. Patrick Henry, who by the constitution of Virginia could not continue in office for more than three terms, retired in 1779. He departed with two counties named after him: Patrick County in the southwest of the state, and its neighbor Henry County. Henry settled in the county of his surname, on ten thousand acres worked by seventy-five slaves. A decade later, the Virginia Assembly honored Wythe by naming a county after him. It may be found on maps to this day: Wythe County, sitting amicably near Patrick County and Henry County. There is no evidence that Wythe ever visited there.

Thomas Jefferson, now aged thirty-six, was narrowly elected Henry's successor as governor. In June, he moved into the palace, where seventeen years earlier he had played fiddle in Fauquier's quartet. He would discover, as his predecessors had, that the governorship was a position of little power and much blame.

Nevertheless, as governor he turned his attention to a task dear to his heart—an attack on the clerics' hold on the College of William and Mary. This was an idea he had savored from the days when, as a student of the fiery Scots professor William Small, he had observed firsthand the clergy's assumption that religion was the foundation of knowledge. As Jefferson once famously declared: "I have sworn on the alter of god eternal hostility against every form of tyranny over the mind of man."

Just a few months before Jefferson became governor, he and Wythe had presented a bill to the legislature to reform the college: it was indulgently read then ignored. But now Jefferson was presented with rare opportunity to convert William and Mary from an institution structured to train priests into a university for the citizens of the state.

Presumably, Jefferson discussed the project with Wythe, who had been on the Board of Visitors of the college since 1758. One imagines Jefferson inviting Wythe to dinner at the palace—and delving further into possibilities, over an enjoyable vegetarian meal (since both invariably avoided eating meat).

In the latter months of 1779, the governor was ready to commence his assault on the college. He and eight like minds gained control of the Board of Visitors, and Jefferson made himself rector. Many of the college's loyalist professors had fled to England. The former college president, the Reverend John Camm, held on grimly to office until 1777. He was remembered with odium as the priest who, behind Governor Fauquier's back, had gone to London in 1758 to complain of the Two Penny Act. Then in 1769 he had shocked the worthies of Williamsburg by taking as his wife a fifteen-year-old girl (whom the easily disturbed said he had first seen naked when he baptized her). The distraction of marriage seemed to lessen Camm's combativeness, and when the Board of Visitors removed him and two other professors for loyalist sympathies, he went quietly. He retreated to a priest's living in York County, where he and his young wife raised five children.

Camm's replacement as president of the college was a school friend of Jefferson's, the Reverend James Madison, second cousin of the future president of the same name. Although Anglican, he was strongly republican and distinctly amenable to the governor's new order.

In Jefferson's plan for William and Mary there would be five schools: Natural Philosophy and Mathematics, Moral Philosophy, Anatomy and Medicine, Modern Languages, and Law and Police.[19] The new professors would be chosen purely on their academic credentials. Before Jefferson went to work there were two professors of theology, one who taught Hebrew and the testaments, while the other taught divinity and controversies with the heretics. Jefferson abolished both positions. There was also a grammar school for boys conducted in the grounds of the college. Boisterous children were not compatible with the Jeffersonian notion of scholarship amid tranquility, so the governor closed it down and dismissed the professor in charge.

The school for Indians, which had stood in the grounds of the college for eighty years, suffered the same fate. It had been established in 1698 through an endowment from the Anglo-Irish scientist Robert Boyle (famous for his law describing the action of gas under pressure). The school's mission was to convert Indian boys to the way of Jesus so that after they returned to their people they would live like Englishmen: pick up the plow instead of the hunting bow, wear modest clothing, and spread the word of an Anglican God. None of these aims were achieved. The boys had been taken more or less forcibly from neighboring tribes and clothed in ill-fitting cast-offs from charities. Subjected to a regime of Christian disciple and rote learning of the catechism, few thrived. Although they were supposed to mix with the rest of the student body, in fact they were shunned. They fell easy victim to European diseases such as measles, whooping cough and smallpox, with the result that during the 1770s there were rarely more than a half-dozen boys in attendance.

The school would have shut down years before, had not Boyle's estate in Yorkshire sent money as regularly as clockwork—at least until the

---

19   Police: at that time meaning the maintenance of society through laws and the court system.

Declaration of Independence. Jefferson said that instead of the Indian school, he would send a missionary among the tribes to investigate the culture, laws, customs and religions of a benighted race. It was not something he got around to doing.

After Jefferson had transformed William and Mary into a seminary for republican citizens, he appointed George Wythe the Professor of Law and Police, a post his friend accepted, while remaining a judge. Thus in December 1779, Wythe became the first law professor in the United States, and, after Oxford, the second in the English-speaking world.

Dr. James McClurg became the professor of anatomy and medicine. Robert Andrews was appointed the professor of moral philosophy. Signor Carlo Bellini became professor of modern languages. This was quite an elevation, for Bellini had first arrived from Florence in 1733 as a viniculturist for Jefferson. The college president, James Madison, taught natural philosophy and mathematics. It was a thorough clearing-out of the old order. Every professor including Reverend Madison had supported the revolution, and for the first time in the history of the college none had been born in Britain.

The doors of the reconstituted William and Mary opened in January 1780 with an enrolment of about eighty students. The old rules regulating matters of dress, morals, physical exercise and scholarship were gone. Under the new administration, students were regarded as scholars and gentlemen of honor who had no need of regulation or surveillance. Attendance at chapel became voluntary. The corridors resounded to talk of the new society to be created after the British were expelled. One enthusiastic student, Isaac A. Coles wrote to a friend:

> The spirit of skepticism which so much prevailed & which every student acquired as soon as he touched the threshold of the college is certainly the first step toward knowledge; it puts the mind in a proper state not only to receive, but also to receive correctly. That it leads to Deism, atheism etc I will acknowledge, but on the same grounds we may object to reason. Skepticism indeed only gives it the reins.[20]

---

20   Isaac A. Coles later served as Jefferson's private secretary from 1805 to 1809.

Jubilantly, Jefferson wrote to his political ally, James Madison, in July 1780:

> Our new institution at the college has had a success which has gained it universal applause. Wythe's school is numerous. They hold weekly courts and assemblies in the capitol. The professors join in it; and the young men dispute with elegance, method and learning. This single school by throwing from time to time new hands well principled and well informed into the legislature will be of infinite value.

This letter rather minimized the difficulties the college was experiencing. Even the simplest things such as paper and ink, and oil for lamps, were in short supply. Students frequently abandoned their studies to hasten to the battlefield. In an attempt to hold them on campus Reverend Madison formed a company of scholars and drilled them on the college green.

Faced with falling enrolments and the drying up of endowments from Britain, the college sold several parcels of land and some of its slaves. As a further economy measure, the professors had to accept payment in tobacco, rather than currency. Each professor was paid an annuity of eight hogsheads of tobacco plus a head of tobacco for each student enrolled. Students who paid one thousand pounds of tobacco were entitled to attend the lectures of two professors, and for one-and-a half thousand pounds they could attend any three. There was of course rivalry among the professors to keep numbers up, though Wythe won that contest hands down, with as many as forty students attending his lectures. He taught law as a branch of the history of mankind, and many days he would have the irregulars (as students from other faculties were called) standing several deep at the back of his class.

All this learning went on among constant reminders of war and almost daily rumors of the arrival of the British army. Williamsburg had taken on the air of a military encampment. Soldiers marched through the streets, men who had never borne arms in public now carried them off the shoulder, and wagons full of armaments rumbled along the roadways.

April '79 saw two weary armies staggering into the fourth summer of an inconclusive struggle. In New Jersey, Washington's attack on the British at Monmouth Courthouse had been costly, ill disciplined, and finally indecisive. He returned to conducting a defensive war, a war of holding out. He yielded much ground and lost many battles, but his army survived. The dreadful wilderness, the vastness of territory, and the extremes of weather were his allies. He never had the troops, stores or armaments Congress promised him, and a growing disenchantment with the war took a toll on recruitment.

Despite everything, admiration for Washington spread through the ranks. The men did not think him invincible or even a brilliant strategist, but they knew he would stand resolutely with them so long as he drew breath. He continually walked among them, and obviously cared for their wellbeing.

He was the unifying symbol for men from colonies that had never before thought of themselves as united states. They accepted the possibility of death, endured awful terror and committed unspeakable cruelties only because they believed in a vague notion of a better future where, even if they did not survive to see it, their new nation would be run by people like them.

The British were also tiring. They were far from home, and forced to hug the seacoast for supplies. Yet somehow they were supposed to hold a huge territory with few decent roads, and few significant cities to occupy, all the while coping with a climate ranging from sweltering to frigid. Trained to march into battle across open ground to the relentless tap of a drum, the redcoats found themselves searching the undergrowth for an elusive enemy that refused to play by the rules.

An advance of many days, conquering miles of territory, gave them nothing more than possession of a wilderness bristling with sharpshooters. Each town captured meant another place to defend. The hard lesson learned over and over was that overrunning a country was not the same as conquering it. At the end of 1778, in an attempt to break the stalemate the British invaded the South, gaining control of the cities of Georgia and the Carolinas, but never the rural areas.

With Spain allied with France in war against its old enemy, Britain found itself fighting in Europe, the Caribbean, Africa and India, while the home island also had to be protected. The thousands of troops necessary to quell the rebellion in North America could hardly be spared. Britain's Lord North offered peace talks but not independence. The war continued.

In Virginia, Governor Jefferson worried that Williamsburg was a plum ripe for the picking. Royal ships controlled the Hampton Roads and sailed at will up and down the James and York Rivers. British troops could be landed anywhere along the peninsula. At Jefferson's urging, the House of Delegates agreed to move the legislature, along with its archives, servants and voluminous paraphernalia of government, upriver to Richmond. The assembly met there for the first time in the spring of 1780.

With its removal, the folk of Williamsburg had little idea of what was happening twenty miles away, let alone in New York or in the Carolinas. The only certainty was that eventually the British would attack—and that Washington's ragged, starving army, quartered well to the north, would not save them. Lack of information bred fantastic rumors, and fear led to the thought that they may be true. Morning's gospel that a British armada was in Chesapeake Bay would oft be replaced by afternoon's news that British general Charles Cornwallis had marched up from North Carolina and was in Portsmouth! And then the rumor, thanks be to God, that a French fleet had been seen in the James River—except by the next day it had mysteriously disappeared. Meantime, the city's only defense, a farmers' militia, practiced its drill of prime, load and fire, every third day on the market green.

*

One of Wythe's law students was John Marshall, later fourth chief justice of the United States Supreme Court. After serving with Washington at Brandywine Creek, Monmouth and Valley Forge, Captain Marshall spent the spring and summer of 1780 studying at William and Mary. At twenty-six, he was older than most of the other students.

He was remembered as an indifferent scholar, given to dining, drinking and carousing, and covering his lecture notes with dreamy missives to a young woman, Polly Ambler. Despite this, he had sufficient native intelligence to keep up with the other students—he was, after all, related through his mother to the intellectual stock of the Jeffersons and the Randolphs. As a matter of historical trivia, the Polly who distracted Marshall in Wythe's classes was the daughter of Rebecca Burwell, who, in spurning Jefferson seventeen years earlier, had sent his studies awry. She had married Jaquelin Ambler, now state treasurer of Virginia.

Marshall left Wythe's classes at mid-year to go to Richmond, where he pulled his well-connected strings to have Jefferson sign his admission papers. By year's end, he was a lawyer. His two terms at William and Mary were the only formal legal education he knew.

Within a few years, Marshall was one of the leaders of the Richmond bar. He married Polly Ambler, and much later became a commissioner to France. Upon his return he served in the House of Representatives, until President Adams appointed him secretary of state. Then, in 1801, in the shadow of the Jefferson presidency, Adams named him chief of the Supreme Court.

Marshall was an annoyance to Jefferson throughout his time as president. Before Marshall's arrival, the Supreme Court was such an ineffectual institution that when the Capitol was completed in Washington in 1800 it was discovered that the architect had forgotten to provide for the court's existence. So it was obliged to sit in a pokey downstairs committee room of the Senate.

Soon after being installed as chief justice, Marshall penned a decision that lifted the status of his court for all time and profoundly altered the political landscape of America. *Marbury v. Madison* (1803) acquainted American citizens with the surprising news that the Supreme Court was the self-appointed guardian of the U.S. Constitution, and if any of the nation's assemblies passed laws that violated its sacred text, his court would strike them down.

With that one decision Marshall blew wind into his court's sails, and set it scudding against the tyrannies of the legislature. Jefferson was horrified, of course. In a single leap, the judiciary had elevated itself above the other two branches of government. Unelected appointees for life could now interfere with the say-so of the nation's representatives. This strained every fiber of Jefferson's political philosophy. He worried that, unrestrained, the Supreme Court would whittle away at the rights of the people by giving expansive powers to the federal government. That was not the Jeffersonian ideal of common-man democracy.

Nonetheless, Marshall was not the first judge to proclaim the right of a court to uphold the word of the constitution against the predations of politicians. Almost twenty years earlier, in 1782, Wythe had spelt out the selfsame principle in a celebrated judgment, which Marshall, then a young lawyer practicing in Richmond, would certainly have read. Wythe's case concerned the necks of three loyalists, John Caton, Joshua Hopkins and John Lamb, who had rushed to aid Governor Dunmore in his marine attacks on Virginia.

They were eventually captured, tried at the General Court and sentenced to hang. The three threw themselves on the mercy of the House of Delegates. The house granted them a pardon under the Treason Act. The only problem was that the Senate failed to concur and the Treason Act appeared to be contradicted by Virginia's constitution. The hangman, uncertain whether to obey the Delegates, the Senate or the constitution, asked the state's attorney general, Edmund Randolph, for advice. He referred the matter to the Court of Appeals where Wythe sat with seven other judges.

Wythe had no wish to see three men hang for misguided loyalties, but to his mind the more important issue was the integrity of the constitution. Most of the other judges, including Pendleton, sidestepped the issue by declaring that the Treason Act was not at variance with the constitution but the concurrence of the Senate was required; therefore, the pardons were invalid. But Wythe went to the heart of the issue in a dramatic statement supporting the primacy of the constitution:

and, to the usurping branch of the legislature, you attempt worse than a vain thing; for, although you cannot succeed, you set an example, which may convulse society to its center. Nay more, if the whole legislature, an event to be deprecated, should attempt to overleap the bounds, prescribed to them by the people, I, in administering the public justice of the country, will meet the united powers at my seat in this tribunal; and, pointing to the constitution, will say to them, here is the limit of your authority; and; hither shall you go, but no further.

Ultimately, Caton and his co-conspirators did not hang. Another petition was prepared by their lawyers, and this time both chambers agreed to a pardon on condition Canton serve a term in the army and Hopkins and Lamb leave the state. It was a satisfactory outcome for Wythe, who would not have wished a constitutional principle to require a triple hanging to prove it.

13

Yorktown

Jefferson has a bad war—Benedict Arnold turns traitor and ravages Virginia—Cornwallis in Williamsburg—Washington hurries south—siege of Yorktown—Chesterville for sale—Jefferson writes a book—William and Mary reopens—Wythe educates Peter Carr

The spring and fall of 1780 turned to a bitter winter of suffering. The British were firmly established in New York. After a six-week siege of heavy bombardment, five-and-a-half thousand Americans troops surrendered at Charleston. General Gates was routed in Camden leaving behind baggage, artillery and a field strewn with the corpses of Virginia's finest. In the north, some regiments of Washington's army of pinched bellies mutinied in protest against lack of pay and provisions. Then to American horror it was learned that Benedict Arnold had turned traitor. This was the most grievous blow of all.

It was bad enough to admit that loyalist spies and saboteurs lurked everywhere, but how could the American hero of Saratoga bargain to betray the Hudson's defenses at West Point? The story emerged that he was led into debt by a beautiful wife from a royalist family, and believing that he had been slighted by jealous superiors he sold out to the British for a fat purse and the pitiful rank of brigadier general. His personal tragedy was that if he had remained true to the revolution he would have been re-membered as a great patriot, whereas his eventual fate was to die indebted and unnoticed in London, a detested traitor to Americans.

*

A few days into the new year of 1781, riders galloping along the peninsula from the Virginia Capes electrified the population with the news that American's most hated renegade, Benedict Arnold, was coming up the James River. His troops were plundering plantations and homes, and sweeping up deserting slaves. This was no rumor, and within days classes at William and Mary were suspended, and the students packed up and left their studies behind.

Governor Jefferson descended from Monticello to organize the de-fense of his state. Few books on military tactics had ever decorated Jefferson's shelves; he had no experience of the art of warfare and limited knowledge of the administration of government. A woeful delegator, Jef-ferson assumed the role of recruitment officer, quartermaster, chief of intelligence and military strategist. The result was ignominy.

Jefferson believed Arnold would proceed upriver to land his troops on the shores of the lower James. Instead, Arnold took the winds upstream, past Williamsburg to Westover, within striking distance of Richmond, where the legislature was meeting in a mood of nervous indecision. Jef-ferson, not wishing to panic the population, delayed calling out the militia for two days while Arnold landed one-and-a-half thousand troops. As the arch-traitor plundered and burnt his way toward the capital, Jefferson dithered, eventually fleeing Richmond with the remnants of the Virginia Assembly.

Arnold's forces brushed aside two hundred Virginian defenders and entered the city. According to Isaac (one of Jefferson's slaves left behind): "In ten minutes not a white man was to be seen in Richmond." Quite un-opposed, British troops proceeded to burn the capital's mills, foundries, stores of tobacco and government records.

A few months later, on a delightful spring day, Benedict Arnold's forces pranced through the streets of Williamsburg without a shot being fired in opposition. Arnold raised the British flag over the former capitol, made an insolent speech to the curious, was cheered by a few loyalists and, finding nothing of strategic value in a university town, departed two days later.

In Jefferson's defense it must be said it would have taken a Fabius or an Alexander the Great to protect Virginia. Much larger than the British Isles, its coastline was indented with navigable rivers and harbors wide open to invasion. Because many of Virginia's regular troops were serving in defense of South Carolina, Jefferson was left with a badly armed, ill-disciplined militia, likely at one moment to fight to the death and at another to break ranks and run. He was also caught in the intrigue of a disordered assembly that complained about rocketing inflation, an empty treasury and a lack of weapons, but took no decisive action to provide a remedy. Jefferson, a man for reasoned debate, and with an abhorrence of arbitrary rule, was not the man for the moment.

In alarm, he wrote to Washington asking for help. The commander in chief responded by sending twelve hundred troops led by a youthful Frenchman, the Marquis de Lafayette, to his rescue. Meanwhile one of Britain's generals, Lieutenant General Charles Cornwallis, fresh from occupying the Carolinas, began to march northward. Perceiving Virginia to be virtually defenseless he sent units of light horsemen riding rough-shod over the dominion, seizing animals and provisions and destroying magazines and stores at will. While the dashing Lafayette stood firm to save Richmond from a second plundering, Jefferson and a handful of his legislators retreated again, this time to Charlottesville.

But not for long. A British raiding party charged inland toward the town hoping to capture Jefferson and the rump of the Virginia Assembly. In total disarray, the assemblymen scrambled over the mountains for safety. Jefferson returned briefly to Monticello, before fleeing over Carter's Mountain. As he left his scattered administration behind him, his term as governor expired. He decided this was no time to offer himself for reelection.

A handful of the assembly, their nerves severely jangled by the ease with which their state had been conquered, crossed the sheltering Blue Ridge and met in the hamlet of Staunton. Jefferson was not with them; he had joined his family at one of his remoter plantations, at Poplar Forest. It was unwise of him not to attend, for his reputation was subjected to a sustained attack. Although not recorded in the minutes, and ever since shrouded by evasion and denial, it seems a motion was put forward to install a dictator to save Virginia—and the man in mind was Patrick Henry (or so Jefferson believed). The story went that Henry himself seconded the motion.[21] It was lost by six votes. Instead, they elected as governor General Thomas Nelson Jnr., a Yorktown merchant who had proved to be a competent commander of the militia. The assembly, still smoldering at Jefferson's deficiencies, ordered an enquiry into "the conduct of executive of this State for the last twelve months."

*

On June 25, 1781, Cornwallis's forces marched into Williamsburg. The general took over the College of William and Mary, made the college president's house his headquarters, and lodged his officers in classrooms. Several thousand of his soldiers camped around the town, and busied themselves by plundering stores of corn, bacon and rum and herding off every cow and sheep within twenty miles.

It is not known where George and Elizabeth Wythe resided during the occupation. Most likely they remained behind locked doors in their house on Palace Green. As one of the signatories of the Declaration of Independence Wythe perhaps feared for his life, although there is no evidence that the British had among their aims the capture of a fifty-five-year-old professor of law.

After ten days in occupation Cornwallis departed Williamsburg, leaving the city infected with smallpox. He had received orders from his superior in New York, Sir Henry Clinton, to set up a defensive base on Chesapeake Bay. The moment Cornwallis's troops left, Lafayette's shadowing dragoons rode in.

---

21   This event, recounted with great bitterness by Jefferson in his *Notes on the State of Virginia* (1780–82), accused many in the Staunton Assembly of voting to be 'laid prostate at the feet of a single man.' He did not mention Henry by name, though there can be no doubt to whom he was referring. Others have a different recall: that the names mentioned as possible dictators were Washington or General Greene.

After considering alternatives, Cornwallis made his base at Yorktown, a village a few miles up the York River. Although aware that it could not be readily defended, he believed that so long as the British controlled the Chesapeake he was safe. Besides, being a deepwater port, supply ships could have safe access to its wharfs. For his was an army desperately in need of supplies. Cornwallis had been fighting and marching through Georgia, the Carolinas and now Virginia for a year. His men were full of fever, ill fed and poorly clothed. Although Cornwallis's raids across Virginia had been terrifying to the inhabitants, he had conquered nothing and achieved nothing. As the British marched to Yorktown they were reduced to scrambling, shameful raids, taking hogs, slitting the throats of horses, stealing slaves and burning barns. Although Williamsburg's citizens did not realize it at the time this was an army bleeding toward defeat.

To the north on the Hudson, Washington received news that a formidable French fleet was entering American waters. For five years he had been fighting a patient war of survival, but now circumstances were combining to give him the chance of trapping Cornwallis on a peninsula with its surrounding waters patrolled by the French Navy.

He assembled his troops and made a dash of five hundred miles to the south. While he was traveling south, Admiral de Grasse of the French Navy entered the James River and landed three thousand soldiers a few miles from Williamsburg.

About four o'clock on the afternoon of September 14, Washington rode into Williamsburg without pomp or parade, attended by the French commander Count Rochambeau and a handful of French and Continental officers. His first wish was to inspect his troops. Word had spread through the camp that the commander in chief, after an absence of six years, had returned to his home state. The Americans hurriedly donned their best uniforms and, with fixed arms, stood to attention, awaiting his arrival. In the fading light, Washington rode slowly between the lines. He showed no emotion, but his eyes were everywhere, assessing with quiet satisfaction that these men, buoyed by the possibility of victory over an enemy that had run them ragged for months, stood ready to fight.

The next day Wythe sent his former client a note offering him the use of his house. Washington moved in immediately. He turned the house into

his operations center, and on Wythe's dining table he, the Marquis de Lafayette and the French general, Count Rochambeau, planned the attack on
Yorktown.

*

On September 28, at five in the morning, the French and Americans filed
out of Williamsburg for the half-day march to Yorktown. Quickly they
took up their positions and besieged the town. They faced a force of British and Hessians troops of seven thousand, seven hundred, augmented by
four thousand to five thousand black recruits, mostly runaway slaves. For
over a month Cornwallis had been building high defensive earthworks
spiked with sharp-pointed logs around the village. So desperate was his
position that he ordered work to proceed under lantern light, long into the
night.

If Cornwallis looked seaward over the walls of the fortified town, he
could see the iron-grey waters of the York River and beyond that, in Chesapeake Bay, thirty-six French warships of the line, no doubt bristling with
cannon. If he turned to look inland he could see surrounding marshlands
and lines of trenches containing a combined American and French force
of eighteen thousand, backed up by an array of artillery.

When the siege was several days old, crowds of curious onlookers rode
the twelve miles from Williamsburg to witness the slow strangulation of
the British. Wythe may have been one of the spectators, standing on one of
the abandoned enemy redoubts, watching in awe when eleven days after
the siege had begun, the battery sites were readied and the cannon's thunder commenced. Within hours, the Allied gunners had found their range
and could drop their shells on any target they chose. The American and
French guns pounded the British day and night.

The buildings of Yorktown began to crumble. At night the glowing
tails of red-hot cannonballs blazed through the darkness. The shuddering
booms, the cracking of timbers and the screams of pain and terror carried
clear to the spectators. Meanwhile, under the cover of timber and brush
screens, the Americans dug zigzagged trenches ever closer to the British
fortifications.

By the second week the besieged were running out of ammunition, and rarely returned fire. Then on October 14 with provisions low and starvation looming, Cornwallis ordered the expulsion of some of the former slaves. At dusk, pushed ahead at bayonet point, about one thousand pitiful figures including children clutching at their mothers' dresses came staggering toward the American lines. Many were disfigured by the smallpox raging through the British encampment. Some, half-naked, terrified and starving, refused to return to slavery, and hid between the lines. Johann Ewald, a Hessian officer, was troubled by what he saw:

We drove back to the enemy all of our black friends ... We had used them to good advantage and set them free, and now, with fear and trembling, they had to face the reward of their cruel masters. Last night I had to make a sneak patrol, during which I came across a great number of these unfortunates. In their hunger, they lay between two fires, they had to be driven out by force. This harsh act had to be carried out, however, because of the scarcity of provisions, but we should have thought about their deliverance at this time.

A few nights later under the cover of a swirling fog, French and American forces led by Washington's trusted offsider, Alexander Hamilton, crept out of their trenches carrying muskets with bayonets fixed. Their instructions were to move stealthily and kill silently. By the time the British defenders discovered the attackers it was too late. Both fortifications were overrun in minutes.

The besieging forces immediately brought their guns up to the captured redoubts, and began to shell the British at point-blank range. A few nights later, Cornwallis's forces made a desperate attempt to escape across the York River in longboats. After one successful crossing, a violent storm sent his boats scudding downstream. His forces were now divided and vulnerable, so the following morning he ferried his troops back again. The deadly bombardment continued. All prospect of escape had gone.

The very next day, the siege's twentieth, after a morning's barrage the American and French gunners halted fire in order to assess the damage. There was no return salvo. In eerie silence, a lone drummer boy stepped through swirling smoke onto one of the ramparts. The little soldier began to play a slow tattoo on his drum. The smoke parted to reveal a blindfolded redcoat standing next to him. He held aloft a white flag. A hush settled over the battlefield. The Americans and their allies watched in awe as the soldier stumbled forward holding an envelope in his outstretched hand.

After forty-eight hours of negotiations the terms of capitulation were agreed. An audience of several thousand gathered to watch the ceremony. Some six thousand British and Hessians, wearing in full uniform, holding their standards furled, marched out of their crumbling fortifications. Watched by the American and French forces lined up in military order, the defeated troops solemnly stacked their arms in a pyramid, and then to the rat-tat of a slow drum marched off to captivity.[22] Cornwallis said he was too ill to attend, instead sending a deputy, so Washington reciprocated the slight by having one of his generals accept the sword of surrender. It was October 19, 1781.

The British still occupied New York and Charlestown, and it took another two years to negotiate peace, but for Virginia the war was over. The state was now in charge of its own destiny. Life could return to normal.

*

When Wythe next visited Chesterville he found a few ancient slaves sitting in the sun on the verandah. The others had run away during the hostilities, and were unlikely ever to be recovered. The house was empty, and no tobacco had been planted in the fields.

Wythe's manager at Chesterville, Hamilton Usher St. George, had also fled. He had collaborated with the British from the moment Lord Dunmore departed the governor's palace in 1775. Initially, he had advised Dunmore where marines might profitably raid his neighbors' stores and animals. A number of patriots, suspecting St. George of

---

22   The story that the British played the tune *The World Turned Upside Down* as they surrendered, first appeared in print in 1828. Most historians regard the claim as doubtful.

treachery, had raided his plantation on Hog Island, burning his house, plundering property and running off with slaves.

St. George subsequently faced court on a charge of aiding the enemy, but was acquitted due to lack of evidence. Thereafter he laid low at Chesterville, protesting his innocence, until Cornwallis arrived in 1781. Again, he offered his services. Making free with Wythe's possessions, St. George gave the enemy livestock and sacks of produce. Just before the French bottled up the waters surrounding Yorktown, St. George fled to a British ship bound for New York, leaving his wife and five children behind. From New York, he returned to England.

Back in London St. George made a claim to the Office of American Claims, a government body set up to compensate loyalists who had suffered losses by supporting the Crown. Mrs. St. George, who had followed her husband to New York with their children, added her side of the story, describing Wythe's meanness to her: "Immediately after the surrender of York Mr. Wythe took possession of Chesterville, where he has chiefly resided ever since; and obliged us to move off, at an unseasonable time of the year (for I could not possibly get away till 20th December) without any stock which he would allow no part of; without any provision not even bread for the people."

Upon his return to Williamsburg from Chesterville, Wythe found a letter awaiting him from Jefferson, inviting him to spend some time at Monticello until William and Mary recommenced classes. With much regret, he declined:

> I know not a place, at which my time would pass so happily as Monticello, if my presence at Chesterville were not indispensably necessary to adjust my affairs left there by the manager who hath lately eloped. I can therefore only thank you for your friendly invitation and offer.

Jefferson also asked his friend to look out for several runaways. The obliging Wythe replied: "Send me a description of the other servants belonging to you, whom you suspect to be in the lower part of the country. I have heard of several lurking there, supposed to be slaves."

The incident of "the manager who hath lately eloped" convinced Wythe it was time to sell the family plantation. He knew this would not be easy. The years following the victory over the British were marked by economic depression, and no one wanted a ruined plantation saddled with the burden of supporting half a dozen slaves who were too old to run away when they had had the chance.

Chesterville was on the market for a decade, before Wythe sold it in 1792 to a fellow lawyer, Daniel L. Hylton, for about half what it was worth before the revolution. Even so, Wythe had to give him years to pay. Hylton was unable to keep up payments, and the property went back on the market in a forced sale in 1801. There were no bidders, so like an unwanted dog Chesterville returned to its original owner. Wythe was not able to find a buyer for a further year.

*

If Wythe had accepted the invitation to visit Monticello he would have found the ex-governor working on a book later to be called *Notes on the State of Virginia*. Jefferson had begun writing the *Notes* in response to a request from the secretary of the French legation in Philadelphia for information about the former colony. In his response, Jefferson took the opportunity to meander over the hills and vales of his home state, not forgetting to explore its laws, its economy and the recesses of its citizens' minds.

The result, arranged under twenty-three headings, was part guidebook, part manual for the conduct of life, and part political polemic. With poetic grandeur, its author described mountains, rivers, plants, animals, Native Americans and seaports, before passing on to an outline of his political philosophy, views on religion and public education, and in a paragraph five pages long his stark thoughts on the tragedy of American slavery.

When Jefferson wrote his *Notes* under the columns of Monticello and in the gardens at Poplar Forest he was retired from public life, and did not expect to offer himself to the American people again, much less as their president. Even so, he wrote with such compelling frankness that he hesitated to put his volume before American eyes until 1785. By then he was

in Paris on diplomatic service and far from the turmoil of domestic politics; at that distance, he thought an honest guide to his home state would
not hurt.

Unadorned honesty is rarely a qualification for political life however,
and when Jefferson appeared on the national stage in 1790 his political
opponents seized handfuls of honesty from the *Notes* and began throwing
them at him—particularly his remarks on religion. Viewed properly, his
arguments on the relationship between church and state were an unexceptional blend of natural rights, reason and the delineation of limits to the
authority of the clergy. He argued that rulers can only make laws in respect of such natural rights as the people submit to them—but this could
not include rights over conscience for in that domain people are answer-
able only to God. If Jefferson had left it there he might have escaped the
ire of clerics, but he could not:

> Millions of innocent men, women and children since the introduc-
> tion of Christianity have been burnt, tortured, fined, imprisoned; yet
> we have not advanced one inch toward uniformity. What has been
> the effect of coercion? To make one half the world fools, and the oth-
> er half hypocrites. To support roguery and error all over the world.

His critics responded that he was godless.

It was also in the *Notes* that his forthright and famous words on slavery
appeared. The whole relationship between master and slave was a "perpetual exercise of the most boisterous passions," he wrote, the "most
unremitting despotism" on one side, and "degrading submissions on the
other":

> Our children see this, and learn to imitate it; for man is an imitative
> animal . . . The parent storms, the child looks on, catches the linea-
> ments of wrath, puts on the same airs in the circle of smaller slaves,
> gives a loose to his worst of passions, and thus nursed, educated, and
> daily exercised in tyranny, cannot but be stamped by it with odious
> peculiarities. The man must be a prodigy who can retain his manners
> and morals undepraved by such circumstances . . . For in a warm

climate, no man will labour for himself who can make another labour for him. This is so true, that of the proprietors of slaves a very
small proportion indeed are ever seen to labour. And can the liberties of a nation be thought secure when we have removed their only
firm basis, a conviction in the minds of the people that these liberties are of the gift of God? That they are not to be violated but with
his wrath? Indeed I tremble for my country when reflect that God is
just: that his justice cannot sleep for ever.

*

In December 1781, Jefferson rode to Richmond to face the Virginia
Assembly inquiring into the conduct of the war. Just as Yorktown saved
Virginia, it also saved Jefferson. The enemy had been routed, there was
peace in the Old Dominion and it was a time for celebration, not for an
examination of failings. After Jefferson provided perfunctory answers to
a number of pernickety queries, the House of Delegates passed a half-
hearted resolution of gratitude for his services, and Jefferson rode away
dissatisfied.

Deeply hurt, Jefferson returned to his shining palace on a mountain
and noted in his garden book when the almond and peach trees came into
bloom. These were dark days for Jefferson. He fell badly from his horse,
broke his wrist and was immobilized for weeks. His beloved wife Martha
remained weak after the birth of her sixth child, and for months hovered
between life and death. Jefferson was never out of range of her call as, almost imperceptibly, she drifted away.

Moments before her death, her distraught man was led outside by
friends, only to faint when informed she had left him forever. It had been
a blessed marriage and its tragic end devastated Jefferson. He retired to
his room for several weeks. Unable to sleep, he paced incessantly day and
night around his room. Enticed out of doors by his ten-year-old daughter,
Patsy, they took long, melancholic rides together along the least frequen-
ted roads and woods surrounding their home.

*

Immediately after the victory at Yorktown, French troops took over the College of William and Mary as a barracks and hospital. The only faculty member who seemed to enjoy the military's occupation was Professor Bellini, who was forever chatting in a range of foreign tongues with the French officers, and conducting tours of the university with all the verve of a college president.

The upper floor of the Wren Building became an infirmary for wounded soldiers, while its library became a surgery. Becoming alarmed at the wear and tear caused by the French, Wythe wrote to Washington:

> There are, in one apartment of the college, a costly library, in another, a valuable apparatus for making philosophical experiments.[23] I beg your Excellency to signify to the Count de Rochambeau that you will take it kindly if the officers who have charge of the soldiers to be lodged in the college, be desired to prevent any injury to those articles, and the places in which they are deposited. I am persuaded you will pardon my freedom and earnestness in this business, because I think you will attribute them to the true motive.

The damage continued, and Reverend Madison and Wythe waited on General Washington with the request that troops vacate the college "as soon as it could be done conveniently." In a letter to Jefferson, Wythe explained that Washington "was very civil, and gave a kind answer." But no satisfaction it seems, because within a few weeks the French had inflicted more punishment on the college buildings than Cornwallis's occupation had earlier in the year. During some bacchanalian celebration at Reverend Madison's residence, the French burnt it to a pile of ashen bricks. A few nights later the Americans wounded, who were lodged in the governor's palace, set this building alight as well. Embers flew to the houses along Palace Green; at one

---

23 Probably an electricity generator made of a large glass globe filled with lead shot that revolved to produce sparks and shocks. Students observing this miracle were led to consider questions such as: was this the same force as lightning? as fired the stars? as moved magnets?

stage Wythe feared his own house would be destroyed. It took most of the night to bring the palace fire under control.

In 1784, the French government paid for the rebuilding of the college president's house. Two years later King Louis XVI presented two hundred "well-chosen" volumes to the college library in further compensation.

*

In July 1782, the French vacated. The college president's house was a ruin, the lecture rooms and dormitories badly damaged, the gardens and grounds were in a shambles, and the entire faculty comprised just four professors: Madison, Bellini, McClurg and Wythe. The coffers were empty, and the college was forced to sell more land and slaves merely to pay for food and heating. Despite the difficulties, classes recommenced in October.

Wythe served as the professor of law at William and Mary for the next seven years in parallel with his duties as a judge in Chancery. That Jefferson's reforms had begun to bear fruit is apparent from archives which show that Adam Smith's *Wealth of Nation* had became a prescribed text, along with Emmerich de Vattel's *The Law of Nations*. When Ralph Izard sought advice about his son's further education, Jefferson had no hesitation in recommending William and Mary:

> The professor of Mathematics and Natural Philosophy there (Mr. Madison, cousin of him whom you know), is a man of great abilities, and their apparatus is a very fine one. Mr. Bellini, professor of Modern Languages, is also an excellent one. But the pride of the institution is Mr. Wythe, one of the Chancellors of the State, and professor of law in the College. He is one of the greatest men of the age, having held, without competition the first place at the bar of our general court for twenty-five years, and always distinguished by the most spotless virtue. He gives lectures regularly, and holds moot courts and parliaments wherein he presides, and the young men debate regularly in law and legislation, learn the rules of parliamentary proceeding, and acquire the habit of public speaking . . . I know

no place in the world, while the present professors remain, where I would so soon place a son.

During these years Wythe, as well as being a judge and a professor at law, tutored a number of private students in classical education, always without charge. Among his private students was Jefferson's favorite nephew, Peter Carr, a student at William and Mary. In December 1786, Wythe reported to his old friend, by then based in Paris as the U.S. Minister to France: "Peter Carr . . . with me reads Aeschylus and Horace, one day, and Herodotus and Cicero's orations the next; and moreover applies to arithmetic. The pleasure, which he gives me, will be greater, if you approve of the courses, or will recommend another. I think him sensible and discreet, and in a fair way of being learned."

Wythe's letter delighted Jefferson:

I return you a thousand thousand thanks for your goodness to my nephew. After my debt to you for whatever I am myself, it is increasing it too much to interest yourself for his future fortune. But I know that, to you, a consciousness of doing good is a luxury ineffable. You have enjoyed it already beyond all human measure, and that you may long live to enjoy it and to bless your country and friends is the sincere prayer of him who is with every possible sentiment of esteem and respect, dear Sir, your most obedient & most humble servant, Th. Jefferson.

Wythe also wrote to the youth's uncle asking him to obtain the coat of arms of Elizabeth's family, the Taliaferros. Wythe wanted a copy engraved on a small copper plate. Jefferson enquired in Florence, and being successful, wrote back in August: "You do not mention the size of the plate, but presuming it is intended for labels for the inside of books, I shall have it made of the proper size for that."

*

To the relief of those who feared that Washington might be tempted to become a usurping Caesar or Cromwell, he resigned as commander in chief, bade farewell to his army and announced he was now a private citizen. When in December 1783 Washington addressed Congress in a farewell speech, a member wrote home to his wife "there was hardly a member of Congress who did not drop tears." Washington's troops would have followed him anywhere, even to batter down the doors of Congress and make him monarch if he had allowed. It is said that when that other George, "the royal brute of Great Britain," asked what Washington would do now, he expressed astonishment when told he would return to his farm. "If he does that," said the king, "he will be the greatest man in the world."

Washington retired to Mount Vernon, where he divided his time between planning the construction of a mansion on his estate, land speculation, agriculture and responding to a bulging mailbag. He showed no interest in Virginian politics though he could have become governor merely by asking. He had served the nation for eight years and was spiritually and emotionally exhausted. He was also deeply in debt.

Nor was he alone in being in straitened circumstances. The fight for independence had been costly. Virginia was sitting on a massive stockpile of tobacco but had lost the guarantee of a British market. The administration was bankrupt and its currency worthless. Distress and discontent were everywhere.

The finances of the national administration were equally parlous. Congress had funded the war by priming the printing presses and deluging the nation with paper money, now deemed good for wallpaper and little else. Soldiers saw their promised pensions dwindle to almost nothing. Disabled soldiers and widows of the slain demanded support from the government, but were told to speak to the states. The states cried poor and began to tax each other's goods while bickering over boundaries, trade and debt. To many it seemed that patching the states into a workable union might be more difficult than the decision to break from Britain.

14

Constitution

*Wythe called to Philadelphia—Shays' rebellion
—Madison arrives early—Franklin in Philad-
elphia—Washington warns the delegates—Wythe
writes the rules—the imponderable Alexander
Hamilton—Edmund Randolph presents the Virginia
Resolves—kingly worries—Madison takes notes
—Wythe's farewell to Philadelphia—death of
Elizabeth Wythe—Wythe frees his slaves—the draft
is signed*

Travel, they say, broadens the mind. Wythe's several journeys back-
ward and forward to Congress in 1775–76 had broadened his mind
sufficiently to admit a resolve to never travel again—yet here he was
in May 1787, bucking along terrible rutted roads in a coach winding
its way inland to Philadelphia. He traveled alone this time, as Elizabeth had been suffering a prolonged illness, and was advised to rest at
home.

The call to Philadelphia was to discuss the Articles of Confederation
cobbled together by the Continental Congress in 1777 and subsequently
ratified by all thirteen states. The crisis of war had bound the states but
peace had loosened the bands; the union was beginning to fall apart. The
problem was provincial rights.

The articles guaranteed each state's "sovereignty, freedom and independence"—words well remembered, and much repeated by those protective of their own welfare. All too often the deliberations of Congress resembled an assembly where diplomats from an array of nation states came to advance their own narrow interests. Congress might pass all the laws it liked but it had no means of enforcing them. It could not speak for the states in negotiating international alliances, or regulate the economy, or prevent trade wars. It could raise money only by begging at the counting houses of the states. There were no national American coins, and shopkeepers had to reckon up a confusing array of foreign currency or local coins, often of dubious value. Some states insisted on issuing their own currency, much to the irritation of Jefferson, who argued for a national coinage with decimal divisions valued on the Spanish milled dollar.

Because Congress so distrusted a monarchical model of government it had not appointed a national leader, in case he attempted to turn himself into a king. The question was becoming urgent: was the new country intending to remain a confederation of states held loosely together by treaty or firmly united in a national government?

The problems of this ragged union were on show during Congress's incoherent response to an uprising of impoverished farmers in western Massachusetts. Its leader, the outspoken Captain Daniel Shays, was a revolutionary hero to whom the Marquis Lafayette had presented a sword for bravery. At war's end, Shays found himself deeply in debt and hounded by tax collectors. A natural demagogue, at town meetings he made much of the fact that he had to sell Lafayette's sword just to feed his family.

In the fall of 1786, he called upon distressed farmers to put aside their plows and pick up their pitchforks and guns and march against the symbol of oppression nearest at hand—the courts where, at every sitting, impoverished veterans were imprisoned for debt or failure to pay taxes. Shays' fifteen hundred rebels freed prisoners from jails, sent magistrates fleeing from their benches, and lawyers running for their lives. Emboldened by popular support, his army attempted a raid on the federal arsenal at Springfield, and came a hair's breath from success, until it was repulsed by a local militia loyal to the authorities.

Under the old regime, it would have been the duty of the royal governor to call out the militia and crush the rebellion, but now most of the militia had joined the Shays-ites and the republic was the symbolic enemy. Congress, now sitting in New York, and lacking an adequate army, dithered over its role in a state matter. As the disorder extended into winter the governor of Massachusetts assembled an army, funded by Boston's bankers and merchants alarmed by the Shaysites' call to banish lawyers from the courts, abolish debt and redistribute property. After a number of running battles, Shays' ragtag force was finally scattered to the uplands from whence it came. The rebellion had shaken the New England establishment to the core, while emphatically demonstrating that Congress was powerless. How would America survive an attack by Britain or Spain if it was not capable of quashing a revolt by several hundred of its own people?

Before setting out for Philadelphia Wythe wrote to Jefferson, asking him for his "thoughts on the american confederation of the states." His correspondent was touring southern France and Italy, and did not reply until September:

> It is now too late to answer the question, and it would always have been presumption in me to have done it ... My own general idea was that the states should severally preserve their sovereignty in whatever concerns themselves alone, and that whatever may concern another state, or any foreign nation, should be made a part of the federal sovereignty. That the exercise of the federal sovereignty should be divided among three several bodies, legislative, executive, and judiciary as the state sovereignties are; and that some peaceable means should be contrived for the federal head to enforce compliance on the part of the states.

This answer was remarkably similar to the solution that finally prevailed after long debate.

Jefferson with typical generosity placed this letter in a box containing one hundred and twenty nine books for Wythe to distribute to friends, including twenty-six books for Wythe himself. Among the volumes were multiple copies of Jefferson's own *Notes on Virginia*, of which thirty-seven were "for such gentlemen of the college as Mr. Wythe from time to time shall think proper, taking one or more for the college library."

*

Arriving in Philadelphia a few days earlier than was necessary, Wythe was surprised to discover that James Madison had been there for more than a week already. Madison, not a naturally outgoing man, had been calling on delegates as they arrived, to urge them to strengthen the American union by giving sweeping powers to a federal government. What the delegates made of the intense little Virginian, one can only imagine. Before the convention he had written to friends begging them to attend, and had even helped persuade George Washington to come as leader of the Virginia delegation.

No delegate was more committed than Madison. No delegate was better prepared. And none was more aware of the fate of the republics that had flourished in classical Greece and Rome, and medieval Florence and Venice, but which were ultimately destroyed by internal squabbles and civil war, leading to harsh and tragic dominance by despots. He had spent months studying comparable constitutions and had enlisted Jefferson, in Paris, to source for him volumes on Greek democratic theory, the structure of the United Netherlands, the Swiss Confederation and the Delian League. Madison had studied them all.

The convention was supposed to commence on May 14, yet on the appointed day the only delegates present were from Virginia and Pennsylvania. It was dispiriting. From his experiences of 1775–76 Wythe anticipated that when debate began it would continue for months, and although he was paid a small allowance by Virginia, he knew living expenses would be a constant drain on his pocket. Most of the delegates were in this position; some were given a pittance by their states, others were completely without public support, and had borrowed from relatives or friends. Yet others, wealthy delegates such as Alexander Hamilton and Charles Pinckney, lived in style.

Wythe settled into his lodgings and waited.

Washington arrived the day before the scheduled opening to be met by three generals, two colonels, a bevy of lesser officers and a parade of troops of the light horse—all from his old command. Wythe had not seen the nation's military hero since Yorktown. His complexion had ruddied, his stride was slowed by rheumatism and he had taken on some weight, though he had the height and bearing to carry it.

Virginia was the best represented of the states, in terms of both numbers and quality. Aside from the demigod, Washington, there was Wythe, Edmund Randolph (now state governor), John Blair, James Madison, James McClurg (a physician, and Wythe's colleague on the faculty of William and Mary) and George Mason, the revered author of the Virginian Declaration of Rights. Though Mason was aged in his early sixties, it was the first time he had traveled beyond his familiar world of the Tidewater. Patrick Henry had declined to be part of the delegation. He was not in good health, but stayed away because (as he said) he "smelt a rat"—meaning he feared an attack on states' rights.

Other states took the convention less seriously than Virginia. Three weeks after the convention was due to commence many delegates were still missing, blaming bogged roads, sick wives or the poverty of the state treasuries. Rhode Island, hogtied by an agrarian party that wanted nothing to do with centralization, did not attend at any stage. The New Hampshire delegates arrived nine weeks after the convention had commenced, and for most of the summer a lone delegate represented Georgia. New York was unrepresented for weeks at a time. John and Samuel Adams, of Massachusetts, did not attend, the first because he was on diplomatic service in London, the second because he agreed with Patrick Henry.

While the Virginian delegation, snug in rooms in the Indian Queen on Fourth and Chestnut Streets, waited for other states' representatives to arrive, they occupied themselves by plotting a sweeping reconsideration of the way Americans governed themselves. Wythe's experiences at the Continental Congress had convinced him that if the states were allowed to veto or ignore decisions on international affairs, interstate trade, defense and the raising of money for national purposes the union would become unworkable. The other five (absent Washington, who remained aloof in his lodgings) agreed.

After the Virginian delegates arrived at a broad consensus, Madison and Randolph retired to a back room to draft what became to be known as the Virginian Resolves. Not for these hearty federalists a mere tinkering with the Articles of Confederation. They were beyond repair. Virginia would propose a radical new system. There would be a national executive and a national judiciary, under the supervision of two legislative houses. A new Congress would have the power to tax and would assume responsibility for "common defense, security of liberty and general welfare." A republican form of government would be guaranteed. And provision made for the admission of new states as the nation spread west.

During the last weeks of May more delegates arrived. Some carried riding instructions from their states to resist change at any cost, while others clutched grand speeches they had prepared which had to be delivered whether enlightening or not. Over the ensuring months several delegates said not a word while others expressed an opinion on everything. Some, like Alexander Hamilton of New York, became more cantankerous the longer the convention continued. Others, like Gouverneur Morris of Pennsylvania, mellowed.

At last a quorum was filled, eleven days late, on May 25, 1787. Only seven states were represented when some thirty men gathered in the Pennsylvania State House (the venue where the Declaration of Independence had been signed). Most of the delegates were old warriors of their state legislatures, or had been to an earlier Congress. Wythe renewed acquaintances with men he had not seen for a decade. Others were strangers to him, known only by reputation or as the author of a pamphlet arguing this way or that. As the convention proceeded, some men who had loomed large and wise in print showed themselves to be small and petty in the flesh, while others previously unknown grew in reputation and influence.

On that first morning, several members mentioned how different it had been in '76. Then the nervous excitement of what lay ahead had made them feel bold at heart. Now they were burdened by gnawing anxiety that although they had been able to stand together in war, unity in peace might be beyond them.

As the first item of business, the assembly unanimously elected Washington president of the convention. The general, who as a rule held that politicians were self-serving and untrustworthy, found himself in a hall full of politicians who admired him so much that they fell to a respectful silence whenever he spoke. His words of acceptance, as reported by Gouverneur Morris, were a sober assessment of the task ahead, and perhaps a mirror of what most of the delegates thought:

> It is too probable that no plan we propose will be adopted. Perhaps another dreadful conflict is to be sustained. If to please the people, we offer what we ourselves disapprove, how can we afterwards defend our work? Let us raise the standard to which the wise and honest can repair. The event is in the hands of God.

Wythe, who was now aged sixty, was respected as a judicious and learned elder, although among luminaries such as Franklin and Washington, and accomplished orators such as Morris, Pinckney of South Carolina and William Patterson of New Jersey, he understood that his main contribution would be in side-room discussions where logic and calm reasoning might be given a hearing. Accordingly, on the opening day he was given the prosy task of drafting the rules of conduct for the convention. The other drafters were Pinckney and Alexander Hamilton, and they given but Saturday and Sunday to complete the task.

Given Congress's urgent need for procedural rules, Wythe recalled those he had set for his law students when conducting moots at the College of William and Mary. His colleagues were content to go along with his idea of adapting them to the assembly's need. They were a list of common courtesies really. Members should rise to speak, and while they were on their feet, none other should speak, pass paper or hold discourse with another. Nor should they read a book, pamphlet or paper, printed or manuscript. A member should not speak oftener than twice without special leave on the same question, and not speak again before every other who had been silent. Everyone who chose to speak on a subject should be heard. And when the house adjourned, every member should stand in his place until the president pass him.

Serving on the rules committee gave Wythe an opportunity to observe Hamilton closely. What an imponderable the delegate from New York was! Handsome, elegant, confident and admired, yet he seemed to have many enemies and few friends. His revolutionary credentials surpassed those of most men at the convention. During the war he had served with distinction in the battles of Long Island and White Plains, then as aide and secretary to Washington, and was one of the Yorktown heroes.

His admirers spoke of his industry, intelligence and commitment to the ideal of united states. Those he offended with his acute sarcasm delighted in the gossipy gibe that he had risen above his lowly beginnings as the bastard child of a West Indies planter only by marrying into a moneyed New York family. All were taken aback by his frank admiration of a hereditary monarchy and his contention that the rich and wellborn, rather than the ignorant and resentful masses, should have the guiding role in government.

From the outset Hamilton made it clear he was there to create a binding covenant between the states with power concentrated at the center—which, as events later confirmed, he hoped to inhabit. Much to his irritation, he was frequently outvoted by anti-federalists in his own delegation and at times he barely knew how to contain his quick-fire intellect at the ponderous nature of the convention's deliberations. Eventually he went home in dismay. He returned several times during the summer and finally to place his signature on the final draft. This took great courage, as he was the only New York delegate to do so.

*

When the convention resumed on Monday, Franklin, who was absent on the first day through gout and errant stones, created a sensation by his manner of arrival. Four jogging prisoners from the Walnut Street Jail carried the great man to the State House in a glass-windowed sedan chair. Beaming with delight as he was conveyed up the stairs at a clip, he waved to the astounded delegates as if he were royalty.

Franklin had been seventy when he signed the Declaration of Independence; now, at eighty-one, he was ready to serve again. Outside the convention, he held court in the Indian Queen, chortling over a beverage and surrounded by admirers hoping to savor his puckish wit. He had become a caricature of himself: truncated, rosy with fine living, un-wigged, bespectacled, and clad in the plain dress favored by Quakers.

On Monday May 29, Wythe read his rules to the assembled delegates. They did not seem to object to being treated like college students, for the rules were passed with only a few amendments. One was that a majority of those states represented on any given day would be sufficient to decide an issue. This measure was necessary, most agreed, if they were to avoid the convention's atrophy.

The next day Wythe presented a further rule, again adopted: that proceedings should be held behind closed doors. Outside publication of debate was barred, and delegates sworn to confidence. Not surprisingly, the "rule of secrecy", as it became known, was attacked in the press as being undemocratic. Jefferson on hearing of the secrecy agreement expressed sorrow that "they began their deliberations by so abominable a precedent as that of tying up the tongues of their members."

Many delegates, however, including Wythe, believed it would ask too much of human nature to expect delegates to set aside local patriotism, personal prejudice or appeals to popularity, were the torch of public opinion brought to bear on every vote. Confidentiality meant that, as the debate proceeded, opinions could change, bargains could be struck, arguments win converts, and members give ground. Within the protection of privacy, the timid could hide within the votes of all. The secrecy rule meant the convention's deliberations were akin to the efforts of the portrait painter who refuses to show their work in progress to their sitter, lest the first impression be thought too crude and unpromising.

Surprisingly, the pact to keep proceedings confidential held. Perhaps it had something to do with the awe in which the delegates held the president. At the close of one particularly vexing day of breathing air that had been breathed many times before, Washington, who had not spoken so far, broke his silence:

Gentlemen! I am sorry to find that some one member of this body has been so neglectful of the secrets of the convention as to drop in the State House a copy of their proceedings, which by accident was picked up and delivered to me this morning. I must entreat gentlemen to be more careful, lest our transactions get into the newspapers and disturb the public repose by premature speculations. I know not whose paper it is... . Let him who owns it take it.

With an expression of great severity, he dropped the notes on a table and departed, while everyone anxiously checked their pockets. No one owned up: the notes were never collected.

*

On May 29, after the Convention dealt with Wythe's rules, Edmund Randolph rose to present the Virginia Resolves. On his feet for half a day, he expounded on the legitimate aims of government, the defects of the present confederation and how the remedy lay in a strong national legislature. When he finished there was an uncertain silence, soon to be replaced by a buzz of opinion, both doubtful and supportive. Many of the delegates had attended the convention in the belief they were to have a general chinwag about the union's problems—at most to make recommendations to Congress on improving the Articles of Confederation. Yet here was Virginia, at the very outset, announcing a plan to throw out the confederation and replace it by an entirely new form of government, in the process trampling states' rights. Consternation bubbled away but as the hour was late, the peacemakers suggested an adjournment to ten o'clock on the morrow.

The next day, after some preliminary wordplay, the convention moved to the core of the Virginia Resolves. Randolph had worked on amendments overnight, the third one of which read: "That a national government ought to be established consisting of a supreme legislature, judiciary and executive." The word *supreme* was whispered around the hall. *Supreme*! He had said it! He intended the national government to have supremacy over the states. While delegates gathered their wits, Wythe asked to be heard. He stood, bowed to Washington, and said: "From the silence of the House, I presume that gentlemen are prepared to pass the resolution?"

The house came alive in uproar. No, they were not prepared to pass anything! In fact there was opposition, strenuous opposition. Did the

Virginian delegates intend to abolish the states altogether? asked Charles Pinckney. For days, the delegates wiggled and squirmed around Virginia's proposal, irked by the idea that they might surrender their hard-won independence to a central authority. Even supporters gnawed at the bone of contention. Virginian George Mason threw up a conundrum, asking whether, if a state did not wish to accept federal supremacy, it could be brought to subservience by force? Surely, that would mean war!

Yet in their hearts most delegates understood that merely revising the Articles of Confederation would not be enough—there *had* to be a new constitution. The present system was not working. Still state loyalties tugged at them. Their concerns were put in various ways: They were part of a confederation and would not be inferiors in a union. They would not surrender both the sword and the purse to the same body. It was essential for the parts to rule the center, not the center to rule the parts. Never would they accept a federal army flying a federal flag in their territory.

On Friday June 1, the delegates reassembled to contemplate the nature of the executive. Who should administer the United States day to day? One man or a committee? How should he or they be chosen? For how long? The word *president* was not yet used in the debate, but the concept was there, and it filled the delegates with apprehension. If there was a one-man executive would he not be a king by another name? Even if they created an elected king for a fixed term, did not history show that autocrats spawn their own dynasties? How easy would it be to slip from a popular leader to an emperor!

*

The State House was ill-suited to June's heat. It had high slatted windows, and by eleven o'clock the temperature climbed to the uncomfortable, and remained that way all morning. Nor could the delegates look forward to a cooling afternoon breeze because Washington had ordered the doors closed to secure confidentiality and had placed sentries on duty to keep the curious away. While the delegates suffered in the heat, James Madison, without any sign of weariness, sat like a perched bird in a place he claimed for himself in front of the president's chair. He busily took notes of everything uttered (finishing up with a record of one thousand pages), while his ears remained pricked for signs a speaker might eventually be shepherded into a group seeking a strong central government.

In early June, Wythe received a letter from Elizabeth saying she was seriously ill and asking him to return. Wythe had been absent for barely a month, yet he understood she would not have asked him to come home to her without good reason. On June 4, 1787, he reluctantly left the humidity, heat, flies, mosquitoes and bed bugs of Philadelphia and began the long journey back to Williamsburg. On his final day, Wythe handed over the balance of his allowance from treasury funds, fifty pounds, "to be distributed to such of his colleagues as should require it." In a journal note marking his departure, Madison recorded Wythe as being in favor of a single executive.

He left a convention agreeing on generalities but squabbling like seagulls over details. It was true that the delegates had reached a majority view in favor of a national legislature of two branches, including a popularly elected federal house (whatever that meant) with authority over some state laws (unspecified). It was apparent also that they were inching toward a "national executive to consist of a single person." But huge issues remained for the convention to resolve. Should each state have an equal number of members elected to the national legislature, regardless of size or population? What funds should each state contribute to the national government? Which powers should be given to the national government, and which to the states? Would someone have the power of veto? Should everyone be allowed to vote and to hold office, regardless of position or wealth? Should there be a religious test for holding office? Should trade between the states be free? What powers should the judiciary have? And a topic which had been hardly mentioned: should slaves be counted in determining representation and revenue?

Any one of these perplexities could cause the convention to falter, yet Wythe rode home with a measure of optimism, based on the surprising unity of purpose which had accompanied the deliberations. There were disagreements aplenty, but anger and petulance were infrequent. To a large degree this might be put this down to two men who, by their presence, decreed calm consideration of the issues rather than personal abuse.

The good Dr. Franklin spoke but rarely, but when he did the delegates leaned forward to catch his bourgeois common sense. Peering over his famous double spectacles, he was most political when he was at his most philosophical. On compromise: "When a broad table is to be made and the edges of planks do not fit, the artist takes a little from both, and makes a good joint." On voting rights between states: "When a ship has many owners they decide on her expedition in proportion to their contributions." On his objection to salarying congressmen: "Place before the eyes of such men a post of honor that shall at the same time be a place of profit, and they will move heaven and earth to obtain it."

The other force outlawing petulance was the convention's president. Like a broad river running silently toward its destination, Washington faithfully attended every day's discussion, presiding on a raised platform in a carved, high-backed chair. But although he occasionally voted, he took no part in the debate until the last day, when he spoke in favor of setting the ratio of representation in the lower house to one member for every thirty thousand citizens. Not a man known to suffer fools, for hours on end he listened to every delegate who claimed the right to speak. Just occasionally, he allowed his exasperation at a tiresome orator to be known, by cocking his eye as if he was a blackbird examining a worm. It was assumed by all that if only the states could agree on a constitution, the chief magistracy of the new government would be his.

*

Upon his return to Williamsburg, Wythe was shocked to see how poorly Elizabeth had become during his absence. She was in the grip of a wasting disease that left her in dreadful suffering. Within days Wythe wrote a letter of resignation to Edmund Randolph at Philadelphia:

> Mrs. W's state of health is so low and she is so emaciated, that my apprehensions are not a little afflicted, and, if the worst should not befall, she must linger, i fear, a long time. In no other circumstances would i withdraw from the employment, to which i had the honor to be appointed. But, as probably i shall not return to Philadelphia, if,

sir, to appoint one in my room be judged advisable, i hereby author-
ize you to consider this letter as a resignation.

The weeks at the constitutional convention, combined with the expense of doctors' fees, had left Wythe in straitened circumstances, so
even while Elizabeth faded Wythe advertised in the *Virginia Gazette*
his willingness to accept students in classical languages, English poetry
and arithmetic. Ever since Jefferson had replaced Latin and Greek with
modern languages at William and Mary, there had been few places in Williamsburg to study the ancients. And perhaps he hoped that listening to
youngsters stumbling over Horace and Herodotus would momentarily distance his thoughts from the tragedy of Elizabeth's slow decline.

His wife lingered through the summer months, panting in agony for
breath as both she and her husband lost faith in her survival and the skill
of the attending doctors. Doctors Galt and Barraud called at the house almost daily. They proposed bleeding. Wythe agreed. They showed Wythe
a beaker of blood that they said was dark with disease. More had to be
taken. Over several weeks they drained her away.

An entry in the *Virginia Gazette and Weekly Advertiser* of August 23,
1787, noted:

On Saturday the 18th instant departed this life in the 48th year of her
age Mrs. Elizabeth Wythe, spouse of the Hon. George Wythe, Esq.,
of the city of Williamsburg, after a very long and lingering sickness
which she bore with the patience of a true Christian.

The couple had been married thirty-two years, and had together survived the grief of losing their only child in infancy. Elizabeth was buried
not in Bruton Churchyard close by Wythe House in Williamsburg, but in
the Taliaferro family plot at Powhatan in James County, where her father
had been laid to rest eight years before.

Nothing more is known of Elizabeth Wythe. No description of her has
emerged from letters, or an anecdote to illustrate her character. No draw-
ings or paintings of her have survived. She appears to have been one of
those gentle souls who passed through the world in harmony with those

around her, contributing silently to the happiness of her husband by her very presence.

*

A month after the death of his wife Wythe transferred sixteen slaves to various members of the Taliaferro family, and freed those that remained with him.[24] He had decided to cease being the owner of other humans. Henceforth, his simple needs would be attended by ex-slaves he employed as domestic servants. One of then was Lydia Broadnax, who had probably come to the Wythe household with Elizabeth, as one of her possessions. Lydia served Wythe up to the time of his death. Another was a man named Benjamin (no second name recorded), who appears in the archives because, in 1788, he received medical attention to his injured finger from the same doctors who had treated Elizabeth.

Wythe may have had the power to change Lydia from a chattel into a housekeeper, but nothing he could do would make her equal to a white person in the eyes of the law. As a freed black citizen, she was immediately enveloped by a blizzard of state legislation that set her caste and limited her freedoms. She had to register every three years with the county, and purchase a certificate saying she was free. Nor could she travel far from home without carrying her freedom papers. She had to pay a special black tax and if she failed, she could be arrested by the sheriff and hired out to the highest bidder. She could not vote or hold office. She was segregated in theatres, taverns and churches. Free blacks could not keep firearms unless they owned a house. They could not give evidence in court against white people, be jurors or hold public office; the law also said that insolence to a white person warranted whipping.

*

---

24 Whereas in 1768 the law of Virginia prohibited Governor Fauquier from freeing his slaves despite wishing to, in 1782 the law was altered to allow masters' manumission.

Week after week, through the summer of 1787, the debate dragged on in Philadelphia. The nation's taverns and parlors buzzed with rumor and speculation. Surely the science of government was not so difficult that it took months for the country's best minds to arrive at a plan for the administration of the United States? In the steam of the hottest August in Philadelphia's memory it was said the delegates planned to ask the second son of George III to become king. Philadelphia issued a statement of denial, only for another rumor to circulate that the convention had collapsed and the delegates were about to come home.

But the assembly did not break up. Instead, reports of arguments, threats and disagreements within the convention circulated freely. The *Pennsylvania Packet* slyly commented: "So great is the unanimity, we hear, that prevails in the Convention upon all great federal subjects, that it has been proposed to call the room in which they assemble—Unanimity Hall." The stories of disputation gave rise to another rumor, that it was proposed to partition the country into two nations of North and South.

Then in the second week of September, America received the dramatic news that after four months of secret negotiations the delegates had agreed upon the draft of a new constitution.

*

The radical nature of the very first words of the draft strike readers even today: *We, the People of the United States, in order to form a more perfect union ...*

This was unashamedly a proclamation of national authority, garnered not from the states but from the people united. Accepting the frailty of human nature, the Philadelphia Convention had invented an administration of co-dependent and separate legislative, executive and judicial branches, each acting as a check and balance on the other. The delegates had created an indirectly elected head of state who would be known by the title of president, a role restricted by limited tenure via the ballot box and the requirement to obtain finance from the nation's elected representatives for any project that involved expenditure.

The military would be kept under civil control, with the president assuming the role of commander in chief. God was not to be found in the American constitution, for the delegates had emphatically separated church and state with a prohibition on a religious test for public office. There were no property qualifications for senators, judges or the president. Legislators were to be paid from the national purse. To be valid, treaties had to be passed by a two-to-one majority in the Senate. Members of the House of Representatives would be voted in by the people on a numerical basis, while in the Senate each state would supply two members, elected by the state legislature. Then there was a Supreme Court, whose functions and powers were as yet masterfully unshaped.

Something of a miracle had occurred. Philadelphia had produced a clipped yet comprehensive document which could be easily read in half an hour. When he perused it, Wythe saw that this was a document capable of binding the states. It was not perfect, but then what document could emerge from the hand of man that was. Perhaps its greatest strength was its elegant espousal of principles without descending to detail, which meant that it could attract warm support from people who held opposing views on its meaning. As Wythe saw the issue, Americans either accepted the constitution with all its faults or the union would fail. It was the only constitution on offer and it had to be supported.

The draft did not refer directly to slavery: it would have been too shameful for the national design for liberty to be reduced by a confession that many would be held in bondage. Yet they were there, shackled securely to their masters, in coded words all Americans understood: "person held to service," the "importation of such persons as any states now existing shall think proper" and "person held to service or labor."

If the compact to bind the states required one soul in six to remain in chains, this was a price the delegates in Philadelphia were prepared to pay. Indeed, there could be no other way: if slavery was not protected there would be no union. The southern states would fly to their own confederacy, and perhaps even to align with a foreign ally. So slave owners had their rights of ownership recognized, with a constitutional guarantee that there would be no interference with slave imports for at least twenty years. Further, slaves would be counted at three-fifths of a white person for purposes of direct taxation and representation in the House of Representatives—although, of course, the slaves themselves were neither represented nor taxed.

Thirty-eight members of the convention, representing twelve of the thirteen states,[25] had signed the draft constitution, along with George Washington as the convention's president. Only John Blair and James Madison signed for Virginia. Wythe and McClurg were absent. Surprisingly, Edmund Randolph declined to sign. After presenting the Virginia Resolves to the convention and participating in the drafting committee, Randolph objected to concessions given the smaller states, and to making one man president. When he could not obtain agreement to delay until a second convention might be held, he disowned the document he had helped create.

George Mason also refused to sign. This was less of a surprise as he had long made known his objection to the constitution's continuance of the slave trade and the absence of a bill of rights. This large, rotund man with hair whitened by age and body weakened by gout burned with fire against the further importation of slaves, calling it an "infernal traffic" and "diabolical in itself and a disgrace to mankind."Despite deploring the whole institution of slavery, he accepted that the best he could hope for from this convention was for it to follow Virginia's ban on importation. The delegates listened politely to him because they respected the man, but then ignored his pleas. His parting sally (as noted by the indefatigable Madison) was to tell the convention that "he would sooner chop off his right hand than put it to the constitution as it now stands."

Thus it was that amid considerable contention the draft went forward for ratification. Before it officially became the Constitution of the United States, its terms would have to be ratified by at least nine states. Until that was achieved, it was no more than a shaky scaffolding for a new nation.

---

25   Rhode Island, as previously stated, did not attend the convention.

15

Ratification

Five states to go—Wythe is surprised to become a delegate—James Monroe against ratification—Henry in opposition—Randolph changes his mind—Mason protests—Madison argues—the vote is taken—a Bill of Rights—President George Washington—Jefferson returns from France—Jefferson ponders parliamentary procedures

By the time the Virginia Ratifying Convention met in Richmond in June 1788 no other state had rejected the draft constitution, and eight had agreed to it, namely Delaware, Pennsylvania, New Jersey, Georgia, Connecticut, Massachusetts, Maryland and South Carolina.

Another acceptance would create a binding compact between those states and the center, yet the matter was still nicely balanced, for there was intense opposition in New York. If either that state or Virginia said no, it was thought likely North Carolina and Rhode Island would follow suit. Meanwhile New Hampshire continued to adjourn its convention to allow further public debate. Virginia, as the largest and most influential state, held the key.

The adversaries lined up. George Mason and Patrick Henry were early opponents of ratification. Henry was the more influential of the two. Among Virginians, the former governor was regarded almost as highly as Washington, and without doubt he would be the outstanding orator of the convention. Mason had left Philadelphia with all the bitterness of a slighted elder statesman. Although he understood himself to be the conscience of the convention, he had been unable to convince the delegates to include a bill of rights or to begin the tortuous task of dismantling the slave trade.

From Paris, Thomas Jefferson wrote to friends criticizing the proposed constitution. He was concerned at the lack of a bill of rights, the unlimited tenure of the president if he was repeatedly reelected, the failure to guarantee the freedom of the press and the absence of a list of things Congress could not do, including create a standing army. Yet, apart from advising Madison that "I am not a friend to a very energetic government. It is always oppressive," he did not enter the fray.

But Mason and Henry found a keen ally in Edmund Randolph, then governor of Virginia, who published an open *Letter on the Federal Constitution*, explaining in detail why he had not signed the document, emphasizing his concerns over the powers given the president. Other influential opponents hovered behind them. Always quotable, Richard Henry Lee wrote an open letter opposing ratification: "for to say, as many do, that a bad government must be established, for fear of anarchy, is really saying, that we must kill ourselves for fear of dying." Despite this dash, he decided not to attend the convention, saying Richmond made him sick.

The delegates opposed to ratification—the "anti-rats" as their opponents disparaged them—were supported at the Virginian convention by an unlikely union of states rights champions and frontiersmen out in Kentucky (then part of Virginia) who were convinced a federal government would cede the Mississippi to the Spanish.

The firm friends of the constitution were few: Edmund Pendleton, James Madison, George Nicholas, "Light-horse Harry" Lee (a distant cousin of Richard Henry Lee, who had earned his nickname as a cavalry officer in the Continental Army), John Marshall and George Wythe. Washington, wearied by the effort of presiding at the Philadelphia convention, declined to attend, much to the regret of the constitution's supporters.

In the months leading up to the convention, the question of whether or not to ratify galvanized Virginians. They filled the newspapers with their arguments, and handed out pamphlets on street corners. Copies of the Federalist essays penned by Madison, Alexander Hamilton and jurist John Jay were shipped down from New York, to supply much needed ammunition against Patrick and the opponents of ratification. William Wirt remembered the passions unleashed:

> the rostrum, the pulpit, the field, and the forest, rung with declamations and discussions of the most animated character. Every assemblage of people, for whatsoever purpose met, either for court or church, muster or barbacue, presented an arena for the political combatants; and in some quarters of the union, such was the public anxiety of the occasion, that gentlemen in the habit of public speaking, converted themselves into a sort of itinerant preachers, going from county to county, and from state to state, collecting the people by distant appointments, and challenging all adversaries to meet and dispute with them.

The sweeping changes envisaged by the draft constitution had caught the public by surprise, which gave those opposed to ratification the opportunity to discover a nest of snakes on every page. A federal standing army might turn on the states, they said. The northern states would dominate. The president was nothing more than the old king writ large. The planned seat of the federal government, designated in the constitution as "ten miles square," would be an empire intent on dominating a helpless population. Faceless men seeking bloated rewards would flock there in an unholy conclave to plot and plunder the rest of the nation. Federal laws made by a federal legislature would be enforced by federal courts and the states, being disunited and distant from each other, would be unable to resist.

It seemed the vote was doomed. Most citizens could not see how Virginians, ever a proud and independent people, would vote to be hogtied by a central government.

Wythe had intended to stay away from the convention. Newly widowed, and now aged sixty-two, he was adjusting as best he could to a life without Elizabeth. He believed that whatever talents he possessed were not likely to prevail in a raucous shouting match with Patrick Henry in a public hall. But others thought differently. York County had the right to send two delegates and the election to select them proceeded on a sunny morning in front of the local courthouse. Two candidates stood up and declared that if given the voters' trust they would vote the constitution out, while two others declared they would vote it in. Just before the poll was about to take place, an old-timer of the county, Charles Lewis, asked to be heard. In a voice tremulous with emotion, he said that although he had studied the constitution up hill and down dale and inside out he was still uncertain of what was for the best.

He asked the candidates to excuse him for not voting for any of them, and said he would rather deputize men who were better qualified to render a judgment based on wisdom and experience. Those he had in mind were George Wythe and John Blair, both distinguished patriots and men of great learning. Lewis's speech caught the mood of the audience. They began shouting for Wythe and Blair, only to discover that they were not present. A dozen or so stout-hearted men led by General Nelson jumped on their horses, declaring they would ride to Williamsburg and inform the two of their election.

A young student, Littleton Tazewell, was reciting Greek to Wythe when there came a knock on the door. Wythe peered out the window and was alarmed to see a number of riders on sweat-flanked horses trampling on his flower beds and calling his name. It took many minutes to comprehend that they meant him no harm. As he stood on the front step of his house, he was greeted with the call: "Will you serve? Will you serve?" Wythe, touched to the point of tears, whispered his agreement. "He will serve!" shouted Nelson to the crowd. "The Chancellor will serve!" A roar of approval arose. Wythe was so overcome with emotion it was all he could do to bow repeatedly. Each of the horsemen came forward to shake his hand and expressed their gratitude. Then they mounted and rode off to inform Mr. Blair of the honor they had bestowed on him. "The experience had been a most exhausting one for an old man," wrote Tazewell, "and Wythe immediately retired to his bedroom and was seen no more that day."

*

The Virginia convention was held in the Academy Building on Broad Street, Shockoe Hill, near the center of Richmond. At that time, the new state capital was still a village of fewer than three hundred houses and Jefferson's elegant capitol building had yet to be completed.

As Patrick Henry entered the hall all eyes were on him, the crucial opponent of the draft. With him was a young man Wythe had not seen for many years. Wythe remembered James Monroe as a raw-boned, rather solemn student who had attended a few of his law lectures at William and Mary in 1780. At that time Monroe, though just twenty-one, was already a battle-hardened veteran holding the rank of colonel. As a raw recruit of seventeen, he had taken part in the surprise slaughter of the Hessians at the Battle of Trenton, incurring a severe shoulder laceration. Then he had wintered with Washington at Valley Forge, before recovering to fight at the indecisive and bloody battle of Monmouth. After studying with Wythe, Monroe qualified as a lawyer and opened an office in Fredericksburg. Thereafter his career was one of steady progress. He became a member of the Virginia Assembly, U.S. senator, minister to France and Great Britain, governor of Virginia, secretary of war and then was twice president of the United States. At this moment, however, it seemed that he was Henry's newest recruit in the fight against ratification of the American constitution.

On the opening day of the convention, Edmund Pendleton, still stiff-limbed from his riding injury, was elected president, and Wythe was appointed to preside over the Committee of the Whole. This was the more difficult job as it required the man in the chair to guide stormy debates according to parliamentary rules. Wythe performed this duty for all twenty-two sitting days, except once when he sought permission to speak on his own behalf.

After two days of preliminaries, George Mason got down to the main business at hand by asking that the draft constitution be taken up clause by clause. This was as the supporters of the draft would have desired, because if there was one thing they feared it was Patrick Henry ranging free in an attack on the generality of the constitution without being tethered to its detail.

After Mason had finished, all eyes turned to Henry. Quite ignoring the resolution for speakers to deal with the constitution article by article, he stood as an indignant metronome ceaselessly beating the death out of the document entire. Who authorized the men in Philadelphia to speak the language of *We, the People*, instead of *We, the states*, he demanded to know. Surely these words set the scene for the national government to ride roughshod over the thirteen former colonies. Plainly, that secret convention in Philadelphia had exceeded its powers.

Randolph also rose to speak on the side of those opposed to the constitution—or so everyone expected. Yet he was not the confident, self-assured governor known by all. With much nervous verbosity he explained he had originally intended to object to the constitution, and outline why it required amendment. But (in a mechanical gesture, he raised his arm)—but he would rather assent to the lopping off of his limb before he assented to the dissolution of the union. Everyone in the hall pricked up their ears. What was the man now saying? He went on. Because eight of the states had ratified, the issue now became simply union or no union—and his sense of nationalism would lead him to vote for the union.

It was not until he had taken his seat that the audience grasped fully that they had just witnessed an abrupt about-face. He was now for the constitution! Henry and Mason looked at him in open-mouthed astonishment. "He's a young Arnold, a young Arnold," hissed Mason in a voice loud enough for all to hear.

*

Several times each day Henry spoke; one day, he spoke eight times. Once he spoke for seven hours. Not the least reticent in using repetition as a weapon, he hammered his points home as if they were recalcitrant nails. Despite being in ill health and stoop-shouldered, he continued in full voice, setting forth his terrible vision of what would happen if the constitution was ratified.

To Henry, the central government was in effect a foreign power. Better the union break up on the shoals of dissent than suffer the evil of this document, he roared. Eight states may have adopted the plan, he shouted; even if twelve and a half states had adopted it, he would still reject it! The central government was a monstrous creation lodged in the heart of the nation. It would have free rein to tax and enslave the people. He would never support this constitution. It was a document so dangerous to the liberties of the people of Virginia, that even before it was considered, it must contain a bill of rights.

For a man who had once proclaimed *I am not a Virginian but an American,* he was at core the most devoted Virginian of all.

While Henry dazzled the convention with his verbal pyrotechnics, Mason, ever a confirmed oppositionist, became a complainer as well. "Is the state of Virginia to be brought to the bar of justice like a delinquent individual?" Mason demanded to know. "Is the sovereignty of the state to be arraigned like a culprit, or a private offender? Will the states undergo this mortification?"

They were a formidable combination, Henry speaking in high hyperbole and Mason in slow, calm, reasoned fear.

On June 7, Henry launched a blistering attack on Randolph for abruptly supporting the constitution after being one of its staunchest critics. He insinuated that the turncoat had been bribed by the offer of an important post in the federal government. Randolph responded angrily, and for a moment it seemed that they were preparing to settle their difference at dawn on a field of honor. Fortunately, overnight their seconds arrived at a peaceful settlement.

When the convention resumed, other speakers opposed to ratification set to work creating a world of hobgoblins for the delegates to worry about. They declared this constitution would create a consolidated government reaching its tentacles into every nook and cranny of citizens' affairs. Taxation would be collected by bayonet and sword. One spoke with horror of the day when ships passing up the James River might carry a flag other than Virginia's.

Those supporting the constitution were no match in eloquence or theatrics. Madison, standing on tiptoes to be seen, and holding his notes in his hat, gave the assembly the benefit of his well-considered views in a barely audible voice. George Nicholas, blunt and as immovable as a boulder, declared for the constitution and demanded Henry name the men he believed would seize power under the guise of federalism (Henry ignored him). Madison and Marshall queried why federal politicians should be more corrupt, more tyrannical or more aloof than state politicians. Why fear them when the constitution contained checks and balances, and voters had the choice whether to reelect them?

Wythe listened to men who had been his students over the years, proclaiming the arguments for and against with far more persuasive power than he could ever muster. John Marshall, who could never bring himself to pay attention to Wythe in class, now held everyone's attention as he explained there was nothing to fear from the federal courts as they would be staffed by Americans elected by Americans and beholden to Congress. James Monroe, a nervous stutterer in Wythe's law classes, now spoke fluently in allying himself with Henry by suggesting that under a new constitution Congress might surrender the Mississippi to Spain.

In a fug of repetition, article by article, section by section, the delegates debated day by day, until, finally, at the end of June the end was near. On the day preceding the final vote Wythe stepped down from the chair. He was bone-weary after enduring three weeks of debate, and according to the Virginian scholar Hugh Grigsby looked "pale and fatigued . . . so great was his agitation that he had uttered several sentences before he was distinctly heard by those who sat near him."

Recovering his equilibrium, Wythe described the faults of the existing system, and then admitted the "imperfection" of the proposed constitution. "But," he urged, "it had virtues which could not be denied by its opponents." He then argued that "from the dangers of the crisis, it would be safer to adopt the Constitution as it is, and that it would be easy to obtain all needful amendments afterwards." This was Wythe's compromise: that the convention should proceed to ratify with the rider that reforming amendments would be compiled and sent to the first Congress to meet under the new constitution.

The next day Henry asked to be allowed to speak one last time. Like a roaring Moses beating back the waves, he stood at the podium pointing out the calamity that would befall all if Virginia voted to support the constitution. He shrugged his shoulders, he slumped, he stood proud. He raised his eyebrows, pinched his nose, pursed his lips, and pulled his wig from his head in exasperation. At times he stood glaring at his audience with his coat up around his ears, his forefinger raised: "I see the awful immensity of dangers with which it is pregnant. I see it. I feel it."

In the final moment of his speech, the sky grew dark. A chill gripped the air. The windows of the Academy rattled. There was a thunderous clap and flashes of electrics shimmered across the room. A lesser orator might have made some facile comment about Nature or the gods warning of the danger ahead, but not Henry. He continued on his set path, merely repeating his sentence each time his voice was drowned out by a roll of thunder. Eventually the storm became so ferocious and the noise so loud the session had to be adjourned, not by any formal motion, but by the tempest overpowering any chance of debate.

The next day Pendleton rose on his crutches, and ordered that the motion be put. Overnight Henry had been counting the numbers. He feared the worst. In a quiet, sad voice, he begged the pardon of the house for having taken up more time than came to his share, and to thank it for the patience and polite attention with which he had been heard. "If I shall be in the minority," he added,

I shall have those painful sensations which arise from a conviction of being overpowered in a good cause. Yet I will be a peaceable citizen . . . I wish not to go to violence, but will await with hopes that the spirit which predominated in the revolution is not yet gone, nor the cause of those who are attached to the revolution yet lost. I shall therefore patiently wait in expectation of seeing that government changed, so as to be compatible with the safety, liberty, and happiness of the people.

The vote was taken. Although many were uncomfortable about turning against a man whom, despite his irritating certainty, they greatly admired, Henry was voted him down by eighty-nine to seventy-nine. Virginia had joined the United States.

As a concession to his opponents, Wythe remained at the convention to chair a meeting that proposed amendments and a bill of rights, to be enacted at some future time. He then rode back to Williamsburg in a daze of exhaustion, sustained by the thought that Virginia's ratification had saved the nation from crumbling into dissension and dissolution.

While Wythe slept the sleep of the weary, riders hurrying north with news of Virginia's decision were met by messengers hastening south with news of New Hampshire's ratification a few days earlier. Everyone's attention now turned to New York. Whatever the emotional opposition, few believed that great city of commerce and trade would be so foolish as to stand outside the union—and so it proved to be, albeit by the narrow margin of thirty to twenty-seven. For this victory, most of the credit must go to the persuasive powers of Alexander Hamilton, who swung an antagonistic New York Convention to his view. North Carolina and Rhode Island hesitated a little longer but eventually climbed on board.

In 1791, the Bill of Rights was added. Drafted by Madison and propelled by his advocacy, it passed through Congress with few objections and was ratified by the states. At first the bill's significance in protecting civil and personal freedoms was not appreciated—that would not happen until the twentieth century.

In a real sense, the Bill of Rights was a child of the obstinacy of anti-federalists like Patrick Henry and George Mason. Such men had challenged Americans at every turn in their opposition to ratification and forced them to reconsider, revise and finally to accept the need for a statement of individual rights.

So the United States had its constitution entire, containing freedoms and privileges for the ordinary man. America was blazing a trail into an epoch of untried rights and protections that hitherto had only been dreamed of. Authority was no longer the prerogative of kings and the powerful: a trust had been placed by citizens in its representatives. A trust circumscribed by the written word, and subject to recall by the people.

*

Early the following year, George Washington was confirmed in the role of the new nation's president by a unanimous vote of the Electoral College. His journey to New York City from Mount Vernon turned into a triumphal parade taking eight days. At every town citizens, city elders and children waited for hours to cheer him on, veterans who had served under him formed his escort, and he was regaled by mayors, bands, cannon fire and extravagant newspaper tributes. In Philadelphia, almost the entire population lined the streets. When he finally arrived in New York, thirteen oarsmen rowed him across the harbor in a ceremonial barge, and upon landing he rode a white horse through a joyful crowd to his residence.

He was the only man sound enough to inhabit the new office, and the only one acceptable to both North and South. Only Washington, it seemed, could be trusted not to turn into a dictator.

Before his inauguration, Washington found those around him debating how he should be addressed. Vice-President John Adams believed pomp and circumstance were necessary to earn popular reverence: he proposed that Washington take the title *His Highness* or *His Mightiness* or some such encumbrance. This idea was seriously considered by some, but Jefferson denounced Adams's posturing as "superlatively ridiculous." In the end, egalitarian minds settled on the title referred to in the constitution. Thus, Washington was referred to as *President of the United States of America,* while portly Adams earned the nickname of *Your Rotundity.*

*

In December 1789, after five years in France, Jefferson sailed for Virginia for a brief visit to put his personal affairs in order. He planned to return to his diplomatic mission in Europe, but these plans faded when, after landing at Norfolk Harbor, he picked up a newspaper to read that Washington had named him secretary of state. In case he had thoughts of backing out, he had already been confirmed in the role by the Senate.

Accompanying Jefferson were some eighty crates containing fine French furniture, exotic plants, ceramics, crystal, oil paintings, sculptures and wines to be housed in his half-completed miracle of radiance, elegance and proportion at Monticello. Eventually he had to sell fifty slaves to pay for these treasures. He also returned with a young girl named Sally Hemings, whom in 1787 he had sent from Monticello to accompany his youngest daughter to France. She was a pretty, honey-colored slave of barely seventeen years. She was also large with child.

After decking out Monticello with his European riches, Jefferson set off to the temporary federal capital of New York where the humble monarch ruled over an administration of intrigue. Washington had invited the best talent he could find to serve on his executive, regardless of political allegiances. As well as appointing Virginians to key positions (in addition to Jefferson's presence in Cabinet, Edmund Randolph was attorney general), Washington wisely maintained a degree of northern balance by making Henry Knox of Massachusetts secretary of war and Alexander Hamilton secretary of the Treasury.

Perhaps Washington expected his team to work in harmony, much like junior officers in the army. As it turned out, Hamilton, Adams and Jefferson clashed over almost everything, be it duties on imports, the establishment of a national bank, war debts, foreign affairs—even the extent of Washington's authority under the constitution.

Hamilton believed the viability of the new nation, and its liberty and wealth, depended on the exercise of federal power; Jefferson believed excessive use of federal power was the enemy of liberty. As their arguments over policy turned to personal dislike, both men stooped to anonymous attacks on each other in newspapers.

Jefferson saw Hamilton as the head of a faction of monocrats intent on undermining the protections of the constitution so they could imitate the class privileges of Britain. Hamilton described Jefferson as a poisonous snake, a contemptible hypocrite and a voluptuary under the plain garb of Quaker simplicity. Even Washington was caught up in the free-for-all. In bewilderment, he confessed he did not believe it possible he would ever be attacked in "indecent terms as could scarcely be applied to a Nero, a notorious defaulter, or even a common pickpocket."

Homesick for Mount Vernon, and weary and dismayed by his warring executive, Washington nevertheless answered the nation's need. He ran for a second term in 1793 rather than leave the country to the bickering Jefferson, Hamilton and Adams. Once again he was the unanimous choice of the Electoral College, with John Adams retained as vice-president.

Jefferson, disillusioned by his failure to neutralize Hamilton and his centralist policies, left Washington's cabinet at the end of that year. He returned to Monticello where he directed one hundred slaves in planting a thousand peach trees and row upon row of experimental plantings of Indian peas, grapes, buckwheat and Irish potatoes. Soon after, he threw himself into rebuilding the pillared porticoes of Monticello—at a time when he was so deeply in debt he had to mortgage slaves to raise the money.

Ever a lover of gadgets, he crammed his house with a writing instrument, automatic doors, a device for measuring human strength, a newfangled swivel chair and a dumbwaiter. He constructed a factory at the bottom of his garden where black children, working on a production line, made ten thousand nails a day. It was quite a moneymaking venture until English imports badly undercut his prices.

Declaring he would rather be in his grave than in the splendid misery of the presidency, the ageing Washington refused a third term. He was worn out by a vicious press, incessant intrigue within his administration, and by Secretary Hamilton, who apparently believed that as the national paymaster he ran the government, and that the president should be content to solidify into a figurehead.

Jefferson, who had written to friends many times assuring them he had given up on politics, returned to stand for president. It seems there was only so much intellectual stimulation to be harvested from raising peas and making nails. After a campaign in which neither he nor Adams made a single speech, Jefferson ended up being elected vice-president to John Adams.

Washington left a nation more or less united, almost out of debt, and stronger and more prosperous than when he first took the oath of office. During his tenure, three new states—Tennessee, Kentucky and Vermont—had been created. He had one remaining gift for the nation—the orderly handover of power to a new administration. As the three founding fathers, Washington, Jefferson and Adams, walked to an outside dais after the swearing-in ceremony, there was a moment of stuttering courtesy as they decided who should have the honor of bathing first in the adulation of the crowd. Washington, with a decisive thrust of his hand, pushed Adams forward, then Jefferson, while he followed in the rear. It was seen as a sign to the world that it was possible to transfer political power true to a constitution and free from violence.

*

Before taking office, the vice-president wrote to Wythe confessing he was "entirely rusty in the Parliamentary rules of procedure." He composed a series of questions, provided the answers, and asked Wythe to comment on his understandings. Jefferson told Wythe, "I know they have been more studied and are better known by you than by any man in America, perhaps by any man living."

Wythe found little to correct, as these examples from the many show:

Jefferson: When a member calls for the execution of an order of the house, as for clearing galleries et cetera, it must be carried into execution by the Speaker without putting any question on it. But when an order of the day is called for, I believe a question is put "Whether the house will now proceed to whatever the order of the day is?" Is it so?

Wythe: I agree, in believing with you.

Jefferson: When a motion is made to strike out a paragraph, section, or even the whole bill from the word "Whereas", have not the friends of the paragraph a right to have all their amendments to it proposed, before the question is put for striking out?

Wythe: I think the amendments should all be proposed before the question for leaving out is put.

Jefferson sought similar advice from Edmund Pendleton, and incorporated their wisdom into the *Manual on Parliamentary Practice for the Use of the Senate* (printed 1801), which became a valuable guide for decades to come to those presiding over the Senate and other legislative bodies.

16

The House on Shockoe Hill

Wythe devises a seal—over with William and Mary—Wythe moves to Richmond—the household at Shockoe Hill—without a kinsman in the world—Chancellor Wythe's domain—the fate of Sisamnes—Wythe's last battle with Pendleton

In January 1791 Wythe wrote from Williamsburg to Secretary of State Thomas Jefferson: "When you can attend to trifles, tell me your opinion, in general, of the drawing inclosed with this; particularly, should not parties appear before the judge?"

The enclosed drawing, sketched with the assistance of artist Benjamin West, was of Wythe's proposed seal for the High Court of Chancery. It depicted the grisly fate of Sisamnes, a judge of Ancient Persia. He was slain by the king for showing favoritism to his friends, his skin flayed, cured and stretched in strips across the judicial throne. The king then appointed the Sisamnes' son in his stead and bade him remember the fate of his father whenever he sat in judgment.

The drawing of Wythe's seal is now lost, but according to Wythe's letter it depicted litigants, a judge and Sisamnes' chair. Jefferson approved, replying: "I think the allusion to the story of Sisamnes in Mr. West's design is a happy one: and, were it not presumptuous for me to judge him, I should suppose that parties pleading before a judge must animate the scene greatly."

In September of 1789, at the age of sixty-three, Wythe resigned his professorship at William and Mary for reasons that are somewhat obscure. He must have discussed the matter with Jefferson, because the latter wrote to a friend: "Mr. Wythe has abandoned the college of Wm. & Mary, disgusted with some conduct of the professors, and particularly of the ex-professor Bracken, and perhaps too with himself for having suffered himself to be too much irritated with that. The Visitors ... will press him to return: otherwise it is over with the college."

How the professors disgusted Wythe is not known, although it may have had something to do with Bracken's dismissal, and his subsequent legal action against the college seeking reinstatement. In any case, as Jefferson had foretold, by the end of the spring term 1790, Wythe was "over with the college."

However the instruction of young minds remained his delight, and he continued to accept private students. One was Littleton Waller Tazewell, who became a governor of Virginia. Tazewell once explained how he became one of Wythe's pupils: the chancellor "accosted" the boy in the street then took him to his house and tested him on "an ode of Horace and some lines of Homer." Tazewell did not do well. Thereafter, he went daily to Wythe's house for instruction and for some time lived with him. Wythe imposed a rigorous regime of instruction:

I attended him every morning very early, and always found him waiting for me in his study by sunrise. When I entered the room he immediately took from his well stored library some Greek book . . . This was opened at random and I was bid to recite the first passage that caught his eye . . . This exercise continued until breakfast time when I left him and returned home. I returned again about noon and always found him in his study as before. We then took some Latin author and continued our Latin studies in the manner I have above described as to the Greek until about two o'clock when I again went home. In the afternoon I again came back about four o'clock and we amused ourselves until dark in working algebraic equations or demonstrating mathematical problems.

"For this he would receive no compensation," wrote Tazewell, "and could expect no satisfaction but that springing from the consciousness of performing a good action."

Another of Wythe's students was William Green Munford, whom Wythe began teaching in April 1791, when the boy was fifteen. Munford's father had died, leaving an embarrassing number of debts, and it seemed that he would have to give up his studies. Taking pity on him, Wythe offered him accommodation. Munford wrote to a young friend, John Coalter:

> I arrived yesterday and am now settled more advantageously than ever I have been hitherto, for thro' the surprising friendship and generosity of Mr. Wythe, I live in his house, and board at his table, at the same time enjoying the benefit of his instructions without paying a farthing. My esteem for this man, together with my love, increases every day, and tho' I can never make an adequate return for the favors which he bestows on me, yet I will do all I can, by scrupulously complying with his direction, and endeavoring constantly to please him. In this happy situation, tomorrow I begin the study of law, in which under such a tutor I hope to make some progress.

Young Munford was surprised to learn that he was not Wythe's only student. "Would you believe it," he wrote to Coalter, "he has begun to teach Jimmy, his servant to write? Nevertheless, it is true, and is only one more example of that benignity, granted by heaven to the minds of a few." Records show that several years later, in 1797, after arming Jimmy with an education, Wythe released him from slavery.

*

Virginia's High Court of Chancery had followed the Virginian legislature to the new state capital. If Wythe wished to remain a judge (and he certainly did), he would have to travel there each law term. It was a journey of two days by boat or horse. Wythe kept up this grueling routine for almost ten years, until in 1791, at the approach of his sixty-fifth year, he sorted through the possessions of a lifetime and throwing out little, and retaining much, left Williamsburg forever. It had become too exhausting to travel to Richmond for each sitting, and he had decided to relocate there.

Although he had lived in the same house for almost forty years, it was perhaps not difficult for him to sever his connection with the city, for everything there had changed. Since it had lost its leading role, the place had shrunk to be little more than a sleepy market town enhanced by a provincial college. Friends seldom called on Wythe anymore, and there was little opportunity to make new ones. He sensed it was time to move on. Richmond was the center of state political power—at least he could wander down to the House of Delegates every now and then and see what its members were up to.

In truth, Williamsburg was coping badly with its decline, and regarded each departure as a betrayal. No dinners were held for Wythe's farewell. No speeches were made. On an fall day, he simply sat in an oxcart loaded with his possessions and headed down to the James River for the passage upriver to Richmond. Behind him on carts were seated Jimmy and his two freed servants, Lydia Broadnax and Ben. His student, William Green Munford, who had been ill with ague, was bidden to follow when he recovered.

When Wythe moved to Richmond it was a bustling port city of about five thousand people, of whom about one third were slaves. The streets were unpaved, corroded tracks, the houses mostly wooden and cattle and pigs roamed the town. Whip-cracking wagoners, after weeks on upcounty roads lumbered into town bringing furs, wheat, tobacco and timber down to the wharves. The Capitol building, designed by Jefferson, was recently completed although not covered in white stucco as it is today. Instead its brick walls were on show.

The year after his arrival, Wythe sold his house in Williamsburg and purchased a yellow hip-roofed house shaded by a giant tulip-poplar, near the top of Shockoe Hill. His garden, half a city block in size, ran beside the house through to Franklin Street. When Wythe purchased this house, an oak and pine forest surrounded his yard. From his upstairs bedroom Wythe could see the bridge across the James River, and its famous falls tumbling through rocks, islands and clumps of trees to the calm waters below.

As Richmond awakened to its status as the capital of Virginia, houses began to be built flush beside his house, and the roads carried horses, ox-carts and pedestrians from early morning to dusk. Despite the increase in traffic, Wythe still insisted on bathing in the yard. Each morning, in all seasons, even if snow swirled around his head, he would rise early, don a wrapper around his body and go to the well out back. There he would draw up several buckets from the depths, fill a reservoir over his head, stand below, then pull a rope, releasing the water. "Many a time have I heard him catching his breath and almost shouting with the shock," reported one of his students. "When he entered the breakfast room his face would be in a glow, and all his nerves fully braced."

In Richmond Wythe began to take weekly lessons in Hebrew from a young rabbi, Isaac Benjamin Seixas of Congregation Beth Shalome, so he could read the Bible in its original form. Munford's son George recounts that Wythe "preferred to read it for himself, untrammeled by commentators or disputants over its translation. When a difficulty arose in his mind he investigated the matter by the original Hebrew, examined it in connection with the Greek, weighed the evidence for and against, as he would in a difficult case before him in court."

Wythe, the Deist, also relished his discussions with Parson Blair and Parson Buchanan under the blossoms of the tulip tree in his front yard. The two parsons were firm friends, although rivals in faith, for Buchanan was an Episcopalian and Blair a Presbyterian. George Munford wrote of the three scholars spending "many happy hours together, sometimes sitting in the yard under the shade of the spreading tree, reading the Greek and Latin poets together in the originals, and at other times discussing questions suggested by Eurypides, Sophocles or Homer."

*

As Wythe grew old, his writing hand was periodically rendered mute by arthritis. Fortunately a lad of sixteen who showed reasonable penmanship had begun to work in Richmond's Chancery as a filing clerk. Wythe made him his private secretary and copyist. His name was Henry Clay, a gangling six-foot youth with a sunny disposition, a garrulous mouth, and abundant intelligence despite having no appreciable education.

The son of a Baptist clergyman from Hanover County, his family had fallen on hard times after the death of his father when Henry was just four. His mother remarried and went to Tennessee to open a tavern, leaving Henry in Richmond, working as an errand boy in a drugstore. Clay's lucky break, setting his destiny in the law, came when Peter Tinsley, the clerk of Chancery, secured him employment in Wythe's office.

In quickness of mind, Clay reminded Wythe of Jefferson, his student of previous years, though Clay's upbringing meant he had had no chance to master classical languages, nor was he widely read. This meant that whenever the Chancellor fortified his decision with references from the ancients, Clay had to painstakingly copy them into the dissertation. "I remember that it cost me a great deal of labor," wrote Clay, "not understanding a single Greek character, to write some citations from Greek authors, which he wished inserted in copies of his reports sent to Mr. Jefferson, Mr. Samuel Adams, of Boston, and to one or two other persons. I copied them by imitating each character as I found them in the original works."

Henry Clay worked in Wythe's office for four years, until he was twenty-one, when the chancellor arranged for Clay to round out his legal experience in the office of the attorney general. He was admitted to practice a year later. In 1797, after perceiving Richmond to be top-heavy with lawyers, Clay took his long prairie bones over the mountains to Kentucky, where he quickly became one of the leading jury lawyers of that state. He entered Congress in 1806 where he became known as the 'the Great Compromiser' by persuading Congress to admit Missouri as a slave state, on the understanding that those states north of the parallel of 36 degrees and 30 minutes should come in free. He stood unsuccessful for the presidency in 1824, 1832 and 1844, famously declaring, "I would rather be right than President"—the voters agreeing with him every time.

Clay was obviously fond of his old employer, for he later wrote an affectionate portrait of the Chancellor:

> Mr. Wythe's personal appearance and his personal habits were plain, simple and unostentatious. His countenance was full of blandness and benevolence, and I think he made, in his salutations of others,

the most graceful bow that I ever witnessed. A little bent by age, he generally wore a grey coating, and when walking carried a cane . . . During my whole acquaintance with him he constantly abstained from the use of all animal food.

Wythe's courtly bow also served the purpose of warding off unwelcome visitors to his home, as B. B. Minor, a lawyer at the Richmond Bar, recalled: "He sometimes politely bowed in persons calling on business, attended to it and then politely bowed them out of the house without speaking a word. He was in the habit of going very early, rather in *dishabille*, to a neighboring bakery to buy his own bread; and for days successfully put down his money, and took his loaf without uttering a word."

Judge Beverly Tucker related two amusing stories of Wythe's legendary reticence, dating back to when he lived in Williamsburg. "Mr. W. visited nobody but his relation, Mrs. Taliaferro, who lived four miles from Williamsburg; and being a great walker always went on foot, sometimes taking young Munford with him. One evening, as they set out together, M. said on leaving the door, "A fine evening, sir." To which, as they entered Mrs. T's house, the old man replied "Yes, a very fine evening."

Then there was Tucker's story of Wythe's daily visits to a nearby coffee shop. The judge's avoidance of chitchat fascinated the other customers:

"Here comes Mr. Wythe," said one, "I wonder if he will talk this evening." Some said yes, some no. "I'll make him talk," said a saucy negro boy, who being always about the house had become a sort of licensed pet of the customers. The old man entered, walked in silence to the fire, and turning his back to it, stood with his hands behind him. The boy put the hot poker in his hand. "What did you do that for?" was all he said.

Judge Tucker put Wythe's avoidance of conversation down to melancholy:

As he descended into the vale of years, childless, and almost without a kinsman in the world, a morbid sadness came over him, which disqualified him for social enjoyment. He was not gloomy, nor morose, but silent and grave; his whole air and manner betokening a gentle sadness, which commanded the sympathy of those who knew nothing of its cause. And this sympathy was not misplaced; for though he moved through the world as if unconscious of all that passed around, yet there was that about him which showed that he had a heart to sympathize with others.

Tucker continued:

The writer remembers once . . . when a child . . . the feeling of awe, mingled with pleased surprise, when accosted by the venerable, attenuated, ascetic old man, with his thin, pale face, and his clear, mild eyes, and his sad smile; and how he held out his long, lean finger to the little urchin, and led him into his house, and up stairs, and into his bed-chamber, and held him up in his feeble arms to the window to show him the working of the bees, in a hive attached to one of the panes.

In 1793, Wythe's student, William Munford, left Richmond to complete his law studies at William and Mary. He went on to become a poet, lawyer and legislator at the Virginia House of Delegates. As a tribute to his old tutor he christened his son George Wythe Munford.

Upon Munford's departure he was replaced in Wythe's house by another student, William Cabell. Cabell was licensed to practice law in Richmond in 1794, and went on to become a member of the Virginia House of Delegates, and state governor from 1805 to 1808. Wythe's niece, a Miss Nelson, also lodged with him for several years during his early period in Richmond. After her departure, as the new century approached, the old chancellor withdrew into himself, the law and the languages of antiquity to occupy his mind—and for company, a mixed-race youth named Michael Brown, and two former slaves, Lydia Broadnax and Ben.

*

Wythe was the sole judge in the Richmond Chancery Court for close on fifteen years. On court days he would set off a little after nine o'clock on his accustomed ten-minute walk to the court, located in the Capitol. To discourage familiarity, he walked in a steady, stooped perambulation with his eyes fixed on the path ahead. The people of Richmond learned to leave him unmolested.

His dress remained that of a past generation, that is to say a white cravat folded behind, a single-breasted gray coat cut in the Quaker style with large pocket flaps, silk stockings, silver buckled shoes and knee breeches. He despised the fashion for wearing trousers which had swept America following the French Revolution and which aped the style of the Jacobins of the Bastille.

At the courthouse door, Chancellor Wythe was met by his clerk, Tinsley. Bowing respectfully to the judge, Tinsley would escort the old man to his chambers, and hand him the day's dockets bound in red tape. An African servant puffed up the cushions on his chair, topped up the inkwell on his desk, and positioned several sharpened quills ready for use, while Wythe read the day's law list.

His court was in the basement of the Capitol building. The sun angled in from high windows, and on fine days, the courtroom was bathed in light the color of dark honey. On grey days, it was imperfectly lit by flickering lamps. All year round, it was cold and musty, no matter the weather.

The chancellor took the bench promptly at ten, and dealt first with urgency motions moved on behalf of clients who (according to their lawyers' rhetoric) were certain to face ruin unless the chancellor immediately intervened on the side of equity. On a typical morning, he might order a search for a will thought to be secreted in a house where the plaintiff's brother ruled with a shotgun, or prohibit a hopelessly indebted shopkeeper from moving goods interstate, or command a bookkeeper who was accused of milking an aged widow's trust estate to come to court and explain himself. After these applications were dealt with, he heard matters set down for argument, usually until four in the afternoon, when the court would rise for the day.

The Chancery Court was Wythe's small domain. Everything happened at his chosen pace. He took the bench when he was ready and closed the court when he decided. Servants and clerks awaited his call and lawyers came to plead before him. His courtroom, with its whiff of dry rot, the smell of smoke from the oil lamps and the scent of bees wax in the floorboards, was to him a sanctuary, his world complete.

Above Wythe's court, on the first floor of the Capitol, sat the Court of Appeals. Its superior location was a harsh reminder of its dominance over the Chancery Court, for Wythe was the most overturned judge in the legal history of Virginia. In a thirteen-year period, appeals were taken against one hundred and fifty of his decisions—close on half the decisions the chancellor ever wrote—and almost all resulted in reversals in whole or part. Wythe did not accept correction mildly. At each reversal, his resentment and anger bubbled to a greater pitch.

Bitter battles between judges over abstruse points of law were of little interest to the population at large; but not so the *British Debts Case* of 1793 that concerned the purses of thousands of Virginians. Many of them felt that independence from Britain also meant freedom from British debts. Unfortunately, the Peace Treaty of 1783 between the United States and Great Britain obliged American debtors to honor pre-revolutionary borrowings. "If we have to pay our debts to the British what have we been fighting for?" Virginians asked indignantly. Particularly as Britain had failed to pay compensation for slaves it had carried away.

The Virginia legislature, in a neat maneuver to get around the treaty, extended a wartime provision saying that British debts could be satisfied by lodging with a Virginia loan office the equivalent in state paper—a currency so devalued by inflation as to be of little value. A number of British creditors took their objections to the High Court of Chancery in Richmond.

Wythe, in his comments on the case, began by strenuously rejecting the suggestion that he should lean toward the interests of American debtors. "A judge," he said, "should not be susceptible to national antipathy, more than of malice toward individuals—whilst executing his office, he should be not more affected by patriotic considerations, than an insulated subject is affected by the electric fluid . . . What is just in this hall is just in Westminster."

He added rather piously that those who urged otherwise "would, perhaps, deserve the punishment related by Herodotus to have been inflicted on the corrupt Sisamnes."

Wythe rejected the argument that he should find that the treaty "hath been rendered invalid, by the failure of the british king to perform the articles." He declared that "this court hath no more power to declare [this] than it hath to declare the british king and the united states of America to be in a state of war." (The lack of capitalization is Wythe's doing.)

With that, the chancellor decreed that payments to the state loan office did not discharge the debts to British debtors.

This was one decision not appealed against. Wythe had ascended the high moral ground, but his ruling made him exceedingly unpopular, especially among those most heavily in debt, the members of leading families. And they never forgave him.

*

Although Chief Justice Edmund Pendleton was only one of several judges on the Appeals bench, he became the main target of Wythe's indignation over his treatment by the higher court. Possibly this attitude was justified, because such was Pendleton's dominance that Judge St. George Tucker once observed: "If he went wrong they all went wrong together, for without him they could not go at all."

At last, smitten with resentment, Wythe decided to write a book acquainting his fellow Virginians with how erratic and muddled their appellate court had become. It would be a task requiring a great deal of research, for his counterblast would only succeed if he presented arguments of impeccable authority and logical persuasion. His assistant in skewering Pendleton was Henry Clay, who sat close by as the old man dictated to his copyist his attack on those who presumed to lecture him on the law.

Wythe's book of one hundred and sixty pages, *Decision of Cases in Virginia,* appeared in 1795. In format, the reader first saw Wythe's opinion, then the Court of Appeals in overruling him, followed by the author's acerbic comments on the superior court's lamentable efforts. In a few cases, Wythe completely rewrote his earlier opinions so he could better explain why he was right and the Court of Appeals was wrong. He did not hold back. A spiteful work, some called his book; completely lacking in restraint, said others.

In *Hill v. Braxton*, Wythe was particularly offended by Pendleton's misuse of the evidence of witness Carter Braxton. Heavy in sarcasm, Wythe wrote: "Algebraists indeed, in resolving problems by equations, frequently use zero or nothing, and are much assisted by it ... but, according to this decree, Carter Braxton's undisclosed intention, which of itself doth not produce a certain effect, combined with zero, doth produce that effect."

Wythe wrote in *Maze v. Hamilton* that illogical reasoning left him feeling "something like the poignancy which Galileo suffered when, having maintained the truth of the copernican in opposition to the ptolemaic system, he was compelled by those who could compel him to abjure heresy."

In *Burnside v. Reid*, Wythe admitted that his original decree was erroneous, but said he knew that when he wrote it. In fact he "declared, at the time, that it did not accord with his own opinion"—his judgment had merely followed an earlier ruling of the Court of Appeals. Now, Wythe complained, the Court of Appeals, in reversing him, in utter confusion, had reversed itself.

Wythe was particularly upset when Pendleton's court overruled him in *Hylton v. Hamilton* without the courtesy of reasons. Satirically, he considered the advantages of such an approach:

1. It is economical, for by it are saved the expenses of time and labour required, in a dialectic investigation, which is sometimes perplexed with stubborn difficulties. 2. It is a safe mode; for fallacy, if it exists in the refutation, cannot be detected. 3. It prevents unimportant discussion; for a detection of fallacy would be nugatory, the doom of judges in appeal being fate.

The crux of Wythe's attack on Pendleton and his court was its inclination to suppose that justice was best served by ignoring ancient precedent and devising solutions suitable for each case. Pendleton, in particular, regarded the law not as an exact science, but as a means by which he could mold society to the requirements of a Virginia plantation economy. Wythe, on the other hand, believed his Chancery Court was there to apply remedies for restoring rights and repairing wrongs according to precedent—not according to what judges fancied the law ought to be.

A famous Virginian statesman and commentator, John Randolph of Roanoke, once said that "when Mr. Wythe went into his court, it was as if Astræa had descended from the skies to administer justice amongst men":

He knew no one. The parties—their wealth—their reputation—their position in society, were all unknown to him. All who came to him for justice came on a footing of perfect equality. John Doe was the only plaintiff—Richard Roe the only defendant.

In true republican spirit, Wythe saw the law as belonging to the people—and if the people wished to change the law that was the province of the elected representatives and not self-indulgent men in wigs, appointed for life.

As he advanced in years, his written opinions were increasingly buttressed by analogies drawn from the recesses of his wide reading, especially from Greek and Roman antiquity. Thus, along the way to his final conclusion, one might read what the ambassadors from Troy said to Tiberius Caesar, or the condolences made on the death of Hector, or the plans of Themistocles before the battle of Salamis. These Wythe often rendered in the original Greek or Latin. No wonder that Pendleton, who understood English and nothing else, was irritated by Wythe's frequent resort to classical quotation in his argument.

No doubt Pendleton and many in the law would have loved to see Wythe retire. Unfortunately for them, he had no intention of doing so. The law was his life; he was nothing if not a judge. He was determined to sit so long as he could draw breath! Nor dare they dismiss him—not a hero of the revolution, a signer of the Declaration of Independence and a friend of presidents.

So, instead, judges and politicians combined to reduce Wythe's influence. When he was first appointed chancellor he had statewide jurisdiction in the Chancery Court and the right to sit on the Court of Appeals, but his scope was gradually reduced. Under a restructure given effect in 1789, he was denied a seat on the Court of Appeals. Then, in 1801–02, the Virginia legislature split Chancery into the three districts of Richmond, Staunton and Williamsburg. In his final days, Wythe was the chancellor for the Richmond district only.

Pendleton, furious at Wythe's book traducing his court, was preparing to take pen to paper in refutation, when someone whispered to him that only twenty copies of Wythe's book had been sold. Pendleton decided to ignore it. Wythe had expected his broadside to find a place in the libraries of most lawyers in Virginia, but it seemed he had not even enough friends to sell fifty copies. In the end, it was the attack of a bumblebee on the hide of an elephant.

*

Wythe's last battle with Edmund Pendleton, as bitter as any fought, took place in 1803, when Wythe was seventy-seven and his adversary eighty-two. It concerned religion, property and the Virginia constitution—more than enough to set two old men rubbing each other raw.

In 1796 the Virginia Assembly, under the sway of Dissenters, passed laws attacking the wealth of the Episcopal Church (which had prudently jettisoned its title of the Anglican Church and forgotten it had ever been the Church of England). Further legislation in 1802 said that a minister who possessed glebe land[26] could hold it during his lifetime, but thereafter it would be sold for the benefit of the poor of the parish. The church called this law theft; the legislature said they were returning property to "the good people of this commonwealth." When the overseer of the poor for the parish of Manchester attempted a forced sale of the glebe following the death of the incumbent, the churchwardens filed objections in the High Court of Chancery.

Wythe dismissed the claims of the churchwardens on two grounds: that they could not show title to the land and, in any case, his court did not have jurisdiction. This was only a minor setback, for the churchwardens

---

26   Glebe: in Virginia, a substantial area of land (100 to 400 acres) set aside in each parish since earliest colonial times to be farmed as part of a clergyman's living.

immediately filed in the Court of Appeals, where they expected that Pendleton, a devoted vestryman, might convince the other judges to his way of thinking.

The matter was heard before five judges during the spring term of 1803. After hearing argument over four days, the court adjourned, promising to have their opinions available in the fall session. At that stage Pendleton, believing the 1802 law was unconstitutional, had carried two others with him. A fourth judge disqualified himself because of a conflict of interest, so the majority, by three to one, had decided to overturn Wythe's decision.

But then fate intervened. On the day appointed for delivery of judgment, Pendleton did not come to court. The next day a message arrived, that he was seriously ill at his home several days' ride away. For two weeks the court waited for him, until they could wait no more. The judges announced that they would reconvene on October 26, when no doubt Pendleton would be well enough to join them.

In late October Pendleton, determined to swing the decision in favor of the church, rose from his bed. Racked with pain, and still desperately ill, he took a carriage to Richmond. The judges assembled the next morning but, again, Pendleton did not appear. Instead, the landlord of the Swan Tavern stood in the body of the court and announced that just a few hours earlier servants had found the body of the chief justice lying at peace in his bed. Later that day Pendleton's opinion, neatly written in his own hand, was found in a bedside table at the hotel. It would have given victory to the church. But it was too late.

The case was re-argued in the spring of 1804. With a new bench of four equally divided, Wythe's decision stripping the glebes from the Episcopal Churches of Virginia remained undisturbed.

17

Slavery

Hinde v. Pendleton—a case of manumission—the uprising of 1800—Washington's passing—President Jefferson—James Callender in Charlottesville—Sally Hemings—the wealth and status of Lydia Broadnax—the origins of Michael Brown

That was not the only time Wythe had a victory over the chief justice. In 1791, Edmund Pendleton appeared in court as the executor of the will of John Robinson, the disgraced Speaker of the House of Burgesses who died in 1766. So complicated was the task of collecting the "loans" Robinson had made to his friends from the state coffers that fourteen years later Pendleton was still at work. Around 1790 he discovered a hidden asset, namely a slave woman and her four children. In order to convert them into cash he arranged for them to be put up for sale at public auction.

As the auction day approached Pendleton learned that the women and her children had lived for most of their lives with Mr. and Mrs. Hinde, and that Mrs. Hinde, a compassionate woman, was determined to obtain them at any price so she could ensure the children would not be parted from their mother. All this was common knowledge, and Pendleton, fearing neighbors may not bid against the Hindes, told the auctioneer not to let them be sold under value. The auctioneer put the slaves up in separate lots and engaged a stranger to bid. The plan worked a treat and poor Mr. Hinde ended up paying an exorbitant fifty-two thousand pounds of tobacco to keep the family intact. Upon learning of Pendleton's deviousness, Mr. Hinde was outraged, and came to Wythe's court seeking to set the auction aside for fraud.

Wythe obliged. Triumphantly he declared it was a case of *dolus malus* (literally, bad deceit). Needling further, he wrote: "The by-bidder instead of being a buyer as he pretended to be was in reality the seller disguised, lending his own person to the seller; his office was dramatic no less than an actor in a theatrical exhibition; and the object of both was to deceive. However they differ thus: they use their art to persuade, one that he is, the other that he is not, whom he personates."

Then after describing Pendleton as the by-bidder's "prompter", Wythe ordered the tobacco be returned to Mr. Hinde, minus a fair assessment of the price of the woman and her children.

In his continuing war with his betters on the Court of Appeals, Wythe published a supplement to his book in 1799 and of course included *Hinde v. Pendleton*, even though in this case there was no appeal.

*

In *Pleasants v. Pleasants*, Wythe launched an attack on the rights of slave owners.

John Pleasants, a substantial slaveholder, was blessed with a Quaker's conscience. In 1771, he penned a will freeing all his slaves when they reached the age of thirty. However, at the time of his death in 1777, manumission was still prohibited, so ownership of the slaves passed to his son Jonathon. In deference to his father's wishes, Jonathon's will also freed the slaves at the age of thirty, should the laws of Virginia be altered to allow it. But he died shortly thereafter and the slaves (now numbering more than one hundred) passed to relatives. In 1782, Virginia liberalized its law to allow manumission, but for ten whole years the heirs of Jonathon (his brothers and sisters) refused to give up the slaves.

Wythe brought his staunchly independent eye to the facts: the wills were valid and the law had been changed, so the slaves born to females under thirty when the law was changed must have their freedom. This result, which gave retrospective force to a will freeing slaves, no doubt upset many Virginians.

But then the chancellor did something truly remarkable. He further ordered that the former slaves should be paid compensation for the years Jonathon's heirs had illegally held them captive ("profit since their respective rights to freedom accrued"). The idea that slaves could be paid compensation for a civil wrong was shocking to most Virginians. However, Wythe reasoned that if white people had been unlawfully enslaved they would receive compensation: why should the law be different for blacks? To carry out his decision he ordered that a special commissioner be appointed, to calculate the amount of the "profit."

The matter was carried to appeal, with Edmund Randolph representing the slaveholders and John Marshall for the slaves. The Court of Appeals quibbled over whether the slaves should be free immediately or when they reached thirty years. Judge Roane agreed with Wythe. It was not to be. The majority, Judges Pendleton and Carrington, ruled that the children born of mothers not yet thirty, had themselves to serve until that age. Their reasoning was that the children inherited whatever restriction applied to their mothers.

The award of profit was also denied. Judge Roane, whom Wythe recalled as a student some twenty years earlier, wrote in awful condescension:

There is yet one part of the Chancellor's decree, which I could have wished had not been made. I mean the reference to a commissioner to ascertain the profits of the slaves . . . In this country, I believe no instance can be produced of profits being adjudged to a person held in slavery, on recovering his liberty. Among a thousand cases of palpable violations of freedom, no jury had been found to award, and no Court has yet sanctioned a recovery of profits of labor, during the time of detention.

Judge Carrington agreed, denying compensation because it was "new and unprecedented. Besides, the account, when the reductions for the trouble and expense of taking care of the aged and infirm, and for rearing of the children, is made, would probably yield very little."

Chief Justice Pendleton concurred.

*

For weeks during the fall balm of 1800, an enslaved blacksmith, Gabriel Prosser, had been attending church meetings, singing ceremonies and fish feasts, spreading a messianic plan to massacre the white masters of Richmond. All he needed was one thousand men prepared to fight for their freedom.

Under Prosser's plan, a fire would be lit late at night in a block of timber-framed warehouses near the river. When the population rushed to control it, his slave army would storm the Capitol and seize the weapons reputedly stored in the attic. Others of his men would drag Governor Monroe from his bed in the nearby governor's mansion, and hold him hostage. Then the forces would combine, lie in wait, and shoot down whites as they walked back to the city after fighting the fire. Once Richmond was taken, Prosser's African troops would go from plantation to plantation to kill the white masters and their families. They would march under the banner of *Death or Liberty*, so everyone would understand they were demanding the same freedoms as Patrick Henry had, a quarter of century before.

On August 30, the day appointed for the revolt, about five hundred men awaited Prosser's call. They were armed with secretly made cutlasses, scythes, clubs, swords and pikes. Just as the rebels were preparing to assemble, a tremendous thunderstorm burst on Richmond, turning creeks into flooding torrents, and washing aside bridges and roads. Only a few of those hastening to meet up with Prosser arrived. Prosser decided to delay the revolt for a day. Meanwhile two slaves, Pharaoh and Tom, fearing the revolt was now doomed, crept away to alert their master. The news of the revolt was carried through pouring rain, reaching Governor Monroe early the next morning. He called out the militia to guard the Capitol and its armory, and to patrol the roads to Richmond. The revolt had collapsed even before it had begun.

Repression was swift. Responding to a frenzy of fear and revenge the militia arrested anyone remotely associated with the conspiracy. Thirty-five were hanged, and many more were marked down for hanging, when Governor Monroe received a letter from Vice-President Jefferson. His letter warned that the "other states and the world at large will forever condemn us if we indulge in a principle of revenge, or go one step beyond absolute necessity." Monroe shipped forty of the conspirators to South American plantations. A grateful white citizenry granted Pharaoh and Tom their freedom.

Virginians were chilled to the bone by the realization that Gabriel Prosser had managed to persuade hundreds of men in farms and households across the county to join his scheme of insurrection and murder. The House of Delegates responded by tightening laws controlling both freed blacks and slaves. Slaves who were freed had to leave Virginia within twelve months of their emancipation, or risk being seized and sold into slavery.

White people were not allowed to teach slaves aged eighteen or more to read or write, or do mathematics. A number of schools for black children were closed. A slave could not act as a pilot on boats or work barges. And in every county of Virginia, the militia rode the countryside at night to ensure that black people were not wandering down dark lanes or trespassing on private property.

The contrast could not be starker. Virginians rejoiced to be living in a commonwealth where white people were as free as any in the world, while black people were entombed as securely as the free could make them.

*

Ripe in years and honors, surrounded by friends and his dear wife, Martha, on a snow-struck evening in December 1799 the giant, Washington, began to falter. Two days earlier, during a ride around Mount Vernon under a dark-gathering sky, he had unexpectedly been caught by sleety winds and rain. He returned home wet and shivering. Overnight he contracted a fever that intensified into shaking chills, a gasping breath and inflammatory quinsy. After suffering much, including several bleedings by his attending doctors, he feared he would not recover.

He gave instructions regarding his will and interment. Then he sat beside the fire, to await the end. A little after 10 p.m. on December 14, Washington took up his wrist to count his pulse. Suddenly his hand fell back. Soon the doctor confirmed that his great heart had quivered to a halt.

The entire nation mourned. All classes, all walks of life, all creeds felt personally touched by Washington's death. He was the sturdy and wide-spreading oak beneath which they had huddled while the revolutionary war raged. He could have easily led his underpaid and badly provisioned army in a coup against the Congress, yet he spurned those who tempted him with a crown. He was the only man the people would have as leader during the initial years of the constitutional union, when self-interest and factionalism was poised to destroy the republic.

During his administration he was as innocent of political intrigue as he had been calculating in battle, and as mild in peace as he had been brave in war. When urged to plunge headlong into a European war during his second term he sought a way to concord. And when it came time for him to depart he made no vain attempt to anoint a successor, rather in a valedictory to the American people he urged his fellow citizens to watch over the preservation of the union with jealous anxiety.

*

The opening months of the nineteenth century saw the United States engaged in a vindictive and bruising presidential election campaign. The incumbent, John Adams, and his running mate, Charles Pinckney, were opposed by Jefferson and Aaron Burr. Washington's ideal of men of good will joining together to serve the national interest was torn to tatters as fledgling political parties and their supporters ran bitter campaigns of scurrilous abuse.

Jefferson was condemned from the pulpit for being an anti-Christ, and on the public platform and in the press for being an anarchist and an apologist for the Terror (always with a capital T) of the French Revolution. Congregationalist ministers told their parishioners they would have to hide their bibles and worship in secret if Jefferson came to power. Newspapers excoriated the "ruffian" Adams as a monstrous, hermaphroditical father of repressive laws, an elitist and monarchist to boot.

This acrimonious campaign brought forth the worst of results. Adams and Pinckney were defeated, but Jefferson and Burr tied at seventy-three votes each—doubly unexpected because Burr had campaigned as vice-president to Jefferson. Burr was a tenacious fighter who had distinguished himself in the Canadian campaign during the Revolutionary War without achieving the promotion he felt was his due. Now, he declined to give way to Jefferson, instead remaining inconspicuous in his New York home, hoping that the federalist majority in the House of Representatives might grant him the presidency.

The balloting lasted five days, and it was not until the thirty-sixth vote that the federalists realized that much as they despised Jefferson, they distrusted the wild-eyed Burr even more. Jefferson became President of the United States.

He was the first president inaugurated in Washington, a city-yet-to-be, standing in glorious isolation on the swampy banks of the Potomac, surrounded by boardinghouses, oyster taverns, whipping stocks and departmental offices. Jefferson, displaying a carelessness of solemnity, and dressed like a country gentleman, walked from his boardinghouse to the ceremony at the unfinished Capitol building, and began his address by saying that the task before him was above his talents. He further disarmed his opponents with a speech that elevated disharmony to a virtue: "We are all Republicans, we are all Federalists. If there be any among us who would wish to dissolve the Union or to change its republican form, let them stand undisturbed as monuments of the safety with which error of opinion may be tolerated."

*

In the spring of 1801 James Callender, a drunkard, wife-beater and Grub street journalist traveled to Charlottesville, a town in the valley below Monticello, on the trail of scandal. In the city's taverns and farms he gathered bits of gossip from Jefferson's neighbors. More than pleased with his outing, back in Richmond he wrote a lurid article which appeared in the *Richmond Recorder* the following year. It concerned President Jefferson:

It is well known that the man, whom it delighteth the people to honor, keeps, and for many years past has kept, as his concubine, one of his own slaves. Her name is Sally. The name of her eldest son is Tom. His features are said to bear a striking although sable resemblance to those of the president himself. The boy is ten or twelve years of age ...

By this wench Sally, our president has had several children. There is not an individual in the neighborhood of Charlottesville who does not believe the story; and not a few who know it ... Mute! Mute! Mute! Yes very Mute!

Once the story was hot in the air, James Madison and other supporters of Jefferson jumped in to say it was not to be believed. The president was morally above such behavior. One only had to know the man to be aware he regarded inter-racial sex as abhorrent. Nor would he ever sully the memory of his dear, departed wife. No, whatever sensual urges remained with Jefferson after the death of his Martha were devoted to the service of his nation.

This was from his defenders. Others were not so kind. Newsmongers across the country, not caring if the story was true or not, reprinted Callender's sensations with glee. Poets and satirists sprinkled columns with witticisms and rhymes. Editors opined that for the honor of the nation Jefferson should present evidence of his innocence as soon as possible. Others, assuming guilt, asked unctuously why the president had not married some worthy woman of his own complexion. Meantime, bawdy ballads celebrated Sally's allure:

Of all the damsels on the green,
On mountain, or in valley,
A lass so luscious ne'er was seen,
As Monticellian Sally.
Yankee doodle, who's the noodle?
What wife were half so handy?
To breed a flock of slaves for stock,

A blackamoor's the dandy.

When press'd by loads of state affairs,

I seek to sport and dally

The sweetest solace of my cares

Is in the lap of Sally.

Dreadful stuff, worse verse.

Jefferson's response to Callender was silence—seen by Virginia as a mark of character, and indicating he regarded Callender as below the notice of a gentleman. Nor did he remove Sally Hemings and her brood from Monticello—to the contrary she bore more mixed-race children.

There the story faltered, though it was never quite vanquished. Few in Virginia thought it surprising that after the death of his wife in 1782 Jefferson might have sought solace with one of his slaves. After all most plantations had their dusky stories. Parallel families abounded. Evasion and denial were unnecessary in such matters, for carnal matters between masters and servants were never mentioned in polite society. Discretion was everything. The child should never be acknowledged and public affection toward the mother should be avoided. The outrage, such as it was, was not at the accusation, but at that scoundrel Callender for airing it.[27]

From time to time Jefferson's opponents resurrected the Callender allegations. Visitors to Monticello noted that Jefferson had favored the Hemings family by making them domestics rather than field hands. The women were maids, cooks and cleaners. The men were butlers, cooks, carpenters, wagoners, weavers and gardeners. Deniers suggest that noth-

---

27   Most scholars now accept that Jefferson fathered the children of Sally Hemings. This conclusion is based in part on DNA tests, first reported in 1998, raising the strong possibility that he was the father of one of the Heming children. Also adding support were longstanding assertions of paternity from the Hemings family, enhanced by records showing that Jefferson had access to Sally Hemings approximately nine months before the birth of all her children and that she conceived no children when he was absent. Further, the only slaves Jefferson ever freed were from the Hemings family, which Sally's son said was because of a bargain she struck with him in Paris to free her children at twenty-one years. Sally had six, possibly seven children, so perhaps it was a relationship of longstanding affection.

ing should be read into this because many of the Hemings family were sired by Jefferson's father-in-law, John Wayles, a planter and slave trader. This included Sally herself. Thus Jefferson's wife, Martha, used her six half-brothers and sisters as servants, a relationship that is uncomfortable to dwell on, because it means the president accepted the enslavement of his in-laws.

Nor did the Callender allegations faze American voters: despite the best hopes of his political opponents, Jefferson was returned for a second term in 1804. As for Callender, he was found dead in a three-foot shallow of the James River on July 17, 1803. The coroner's jury concluded that Callender, "with intent to bathe, but being in a state of intoxication . . . came to his death by an accidental drowning."

*

The relationship of George Wythe with his servant Lydia Broadnax has also long been the subject of speculation, first to local gossips, later to historians. Scraps of information indicate that, by 1797, Wythe's house-keeper had accumulated considerable wealth. Tax records for that year show that she owned land on a block bounded by Fifth and Leigh Streets. The property seems to have been a tenement, because other records show Broadnax from 1799 through 1801 collecting annual rent of sixteen dollars from a man named William Francis. She must have added some rooms to the property, because the 1810 census records that the dwelling was occupied by six freed persons and two slaves. Although Virginian law until 1832 allowed free blacks to own slaves, it is more likely that they were domestic servants of nearby masters.

How Broadnax accumulated the money to purchase this property is unclear. One assumes Wythe provided her with board and lodgings, so perhaps she was able to accumulate a nest egg from her wages. There is further indication of her steady accumulation of wealth, in a letter that Wythe wrote to Jefferson in 1801. It seems that some years earlier his housekeeper had lent money to Captain Tinsley of the United States Army, the brother of Peter Tinsley, the clerk of Wythe's court. Captain Tinsley, upon being transferred to the southern frontier, presumably felt he could ignore a black woman's demands for repayment. Unfortunately for him, he failed to take into account his lender's powerful friends. Lydia told her story to Wythe, and he wrote to President Jefferson. The commander in chief made enquiries and promptly ordered that the debt should be deducted from Tinsley's pay.

Also living with Wythe in the house on Shockoe Hill was a freed slave named Ben, probably employed as a gardener and handyman. Nothing more is known about him.

The third person living under Wythe's roof was a free-born youth of mixed race, named Michael Brown. His identity and the identity of his father have been the subject of longstanding folklore in Virginia, a common claim being that he was the son of Lydia Broadnax and George Wythe. This assertion is given some historical authority by a curious manuscript known as the Dove Memorandum. A Dr. John Dove, approaching the end of his life in 1856, and then living in California, wrote in his own hand a recollection of his life in Richmond in the early 1800s. Among the tidbits it contained was the following:

Judge Wythe had a yellow woman by the name of Lydia who lived with him as wife or mistress as was quite common in this city fifty years ago with gentlemen of the olden time. By this woman he had a son named Mike who was not only fine looking but very intelligent and the Judge took great pleasure in educating him and made him an accomplished scholar.

George Wythe Munford, the son of the student who had lived with Wythe when he first came to Richmond, rather coyly wrote of the relationship between Broadnax and her employer: "Lydia Broadnax ... understood his wants and ways. She was a servant of the olden time, respected and trusted by her master, and devotedly attached to him—one of those whom he had liberated, but who lived with him from affection."

In 1803, Wythe wrote a will favoring "my freed woman Lydia Broadnax, and freed man Benjamin, and freed boy Michael Brown." He appointed "my friendlie neighbour William DuVal executor" to distribute the rent of a house and the interest from his stocks to support them. To leave the interest from the bulk of his estate to the Africans living in his house must have raised eyebrows in slave-owning Richmond.

To many it was proof that Wythe was anxious to provide Broadnax and Ben with the income to raise his son in an advantageous manner.

18

His Last Great Case

*The descendants of Butterwood Nan—Edmund
Randolph argues for a slaveowner—Washington
demands an explanation—George Taylor for
Jackey Wright and her children—the enslavement
of Native Americans—elderly citizens with long
memories—Wythe considers his ver-
dict—Massachusetts rids itself of slavery—Wythe
reaches for the Bill of Rights*

Property attracts lawyers as bees to a cider press, and in Virginia property in slaves came second only to land in total value. Just about any
transaction that involved land could be entered into with slaves—thus
cases involving the mortgage of slaves, the rental of slaves, trespass
by slaves, warranties and title to slaves arrived regularly in Wythe's
court. In fact more than half of the property cases he heard concerned
slaves.

Wythe's most famous decision on slavery, *Hudgins v. Wrights*,
centered on the question of whether the descendants of a woman known
as Butterwood Nan should be free. In 1806, a frightened mother and her
three infant children came to his court asking to be released from bondage. Wythe, the judge, picked up the mask of the law, and began to decide
the case according to statute and precedent. Yet, his opinion in this case

sent shockwaves through the state, and brought him as much scorn as any opinion he had previously delivered.

In commencement, Edmund Randolph rose from the bar table to announce that he stood suit for Mr. Houlder Hudgins, ship builder and plantation owner of the James River. Mr. Hudgins's valuable property was under seizure, Randolph informed the court. He turned and pointed to Jackey Wright and her three daughters sitting in the dock. Mr. Hudgins intended to retain the eldest child for himself, said Randolph, though he had recently sold Jackey and the other two girls to Richard Cox.

The court documents described Cox as "a negro trader, who was proceeding with them to one of the southern states."

Edmund Randolph was a regular in Wythe's court, over the years appearing in many significant cases. He had acted for the Anglican Church in the Glebe Case and for the slave owners in *Pleasants v. Pleasants*. Later, in 1807, he was senior counsel in the defense of Aaron Burr in his treason trial.

Despite his pre-eminence at the Virginia bar, Randolph still carried a burden of public humiliation and disgrace. In 1795, President Washington had forced him to resign from his cabinet. It is difficult to say what Randolph was guilty of, but recounting the episode becomes less byzantine if one accepts there is no loyalty in diplomacy. After opposing, then supporting, ratification of the United States Constitution, Randolph's doglike devotion to Washington had led to his appointment as the nation's attorney general. In that role, he became trusted counselor to a president beleaguered by the quarreling Jefferson and Hamilton. In 1794, when Jefferson retired to Monticello, Randolph became secretary of state in his place.

The story of Randolph's downfall begins with a British man-of-war intercepting a French ship on the high seas. Among the booty were gossipy notes made by a French minister about meetings with Randolph. The British mischievously handed the notes to American officials and, with Hamilton wire-pulling behind the scenes, they were presented to Washington as proof of Randolph's disloyalty.

The notes were incomplete, ambiguous, and poorly translated. Yet Washington took them at face value. A malevolent interpretation might lead one to believe Randolph had been soliciting bribes in exchange for cabinet secrets; a benign reading would lead to the conclusion he had been blathering to impress the French with his importance. In the presence of the entire cabinet, Washington confronted Randolph with the incriminating documents and demanded an explanation. Randolph, one of the greatest courtroom attorneys of the era, was struck dumb. He stumbled in confusion back to his office, where he wrote out his resignation. Then he fled with his family to Virginia.

Recovering his wits, Randolph wrote an overlong pamphlet protesting his innocence and waited for forgiveness from Washington. It never came. His misfortune was compounded when the U.S. Treasury demanded he account for a vast amount of public funds he had dispersed while secretary of state. Embittered and bewildered, he returned to embrace his loyal mistress, the law.

He soon regained his position of leader of the Virginia bar, but he was a changed man, his former calm, polite certainty replaced by an acerbic, cynical, sneering sort of advocacy.

*

In *Hudgins v. Wrights*, Randolph was opposed by George Taylor, appearing for Jackey Wright and her children. Taylor argued the case in *forma pauperis*. A law of Virginia of 1795 had instituted a system for legal representatives for pauper slaves claiming to be free. As a first step, the slave had to petition a magistrate, who could commission an attorney to report on the case. If the report convinced the magistrate the claim had merit, the court would appoint a lawyer to prosecute it further. However to protect masters from "nuisance suits," Quakers were banned from the jury and counsel for the pauper had to appear for no fee. This, Taylor was prepared to do.

Taylor began by asking Chancellor Wythe to note the color of the skin of the three little girls. They were perfectly white. Jackey also looked white, said Taylor. Wythe noted this as well. Jackey's mother Phoebe (no surname recorded in the law reports) was in court watching proceedings. Taylor informed the chancellor that she was a now a free woman, but that she had given birth to Jackey when she was a slave. Wythe was asked to cast his eyes toward her. The chancellor peered beyond the bewigged counsel, their appended clerks, Mr. Hudgins and a few curious onlookers. Phoebe stood for Wythe's inspection. He now had three generations before him: grandmother, mother and granddaughters—three generations of progressively lighter-colored slaves.

Nothing in the court papers reveals how Jackey and the two girls escaped from the slave trader, Richard Cox. One possibility was that because they looked white they attracted the sympathy of strangers, who issued writs bringing them back to Richmond and so to Wythe's court.

Taylor only had two points to argue. The first, of great emotional force though of scant legal merit, was that Jackey and her daughters could pass as white. His second and strongest, indeed his only viable argument, was that Jackey Wright and her daughters were descendants of an American Indian, and not an African. Taylor told the court that he had witnesses ready to trace Jackey Wright's lineage back through four generations to a woman called Butterwood Nan, an Indian. The family tree, said Taylor, through the maternal line, descended from Butterwood Nan, to her daughter Hannah, then to her daughter Phoebe, and so to her daughter, Jackey Wright and her children.

Taylor then referred to several Virginian cases that said that it was only lawful to enslave Indians until 1705. Thereafter, taking Indians into slavery was prohibited. Thus, only those descendants of an Indian woman who had been a slave prior to 1705 could be enslaved.

Rising to the challenge, Randolph said he would call witnesses to say that Butterwood Nan was a slave before 1705. If Butterwood Nan was legally acquired before 1705, this would ensure the continued bondage of her children all the way down to Jackey Wright, and her daughters, he argued.

*

The first slaves in Virginia were Amerindians, not Africans. Soon after arriving in 1607, the Jamestown colonists purchased from Indians the captives they had taken in tribal wars. After the surprise attack on white settlements in 1622, Indians were also captured in war. By 1650,

Indian slaves were appearing in wills, inventories of estates and in deeds of sale.

There was no law justifying Indian slavery—permission being assumed by the lack of contrary instruction from England, backed by the ancient lore of conquest that it was more compassionate to enslave than to slaughter. The House of Burgesses, in adopting this reasoning, declared in 1679 that for the better encouragement of the militia, Indian prisoners taken in war became the property of serving soldiers.

Once captured, some masters brought the godless into Christianity. This gave rise to the question of whether Christians could be slaves. The Burgesses provided the answer with a statute in 1667 ruling that baptism did "not alter the condition of the person as to his bondage or freedome; that diverse masters freed from this doubt, may more carefully endeavour the propagation of Christianity."

However, as the colonists soon learned, dispossessed people rarely make obedient vassals on land they regard as their birthright. The distant mountains were the Indians' sanctuary, and too often the moment they could slip their chains, they ran. They were sullen and proud. They were hunters and warriors, they ranged free, they were not born to feed animals and tend crops. They were also defenseless against European diseases, and withered from a sickness of the spirit. Surely, thought the colonists, there must be an easier race to enslave than the American Indian. Thus it became a common practice when Indians were captured in war to sell them to plantations in the West Indies.

The first Africans came to Virginia in 1619 aboard a Dutch trader. Only twenty in number, they were purchased not as slaves, but as forced servants who might hope to be eventually free. Unlike the Amerindians, they were a long way from home and had nowhere to flee. They resisted disease, and could be made to work the fields. A vulnerable and productive source of wealth was thrust before the colonists, and it was beyond their moral strength to resist. So when the next slave ship arrived, Virginians gathered on the docks to trade tobacco, furs, tar and turpentine for dark-skinned humans. In a mere thirty years, the African in Virginia had descended in status from servant to slave.

By the 1700s, Indians were no longer taken into slavery. What the white man wanted from Indians was not their labor but their lands. Sullen and resentful, these Native Americans were rolled back beyond the Tidewater; back to the foothills, and then into the mountains and beyond, nation upon nation, leaving behind beggars and vagrants in lands bequeathed to them by their ancestors.

*

Elderly citizens with long memories came to the High Court of Chancery in Richmond to give evidence about Jackey Wright's forebears. Robert Temple said he knew Butterwood Nan. That was some fifty years ago, and she was not less than sixty then. Temple also said he knew Butterwood Nan's father, and he was an Indian. Temple's daughter, Mary Wilkinson, said she had "seen an old Indian called Butterwood Nan, the reputed mother of Hannah. She supposed she was about sixty years old." Mary Wilkinson said she was about ten or twelve at the time. About Hannah, she said: "she had long black hair, was of a copper colored complexion, much darker than Phoebe—and in the family was always called Indian Hannah."

Francis Temple, the brother of Robert, could not remember Butterwood Nan, but he knew Hannah, and she was generally called an Indian in the neighborhood. Francis Temple recalled people saying over the years that if Hannah tried for freedom she would get it. In fact Hannah never stopped claiming she was free and her master threatened to whip her for saying so. "She was of a copper color, with long black hair, of the right Indian color. ... She was called by all who knew her as Indian Hannah."

Edmund Randolph began his final address with all the confidence of an attorney satisfied that the facts and the law were on his side. He pointed out that the testimony of witnesses, all reliable, upright Virginians, was consistent. Jackey Wright and her daughters were descendants of Butter-

Our constitution . . . is totally repugnant to the idea of being born a slave. This being the case, I think the idea of slavery is inconsistent with our own conduct and Constitution; and there can be no such thing as perpetual servitude of a rational creature.

wood Nan. And she was of Indian descent. And she was born earlier than 1705. Witness Robert Temple had said he had known her fifty years ago and she was upwards of sixty then. Mary Wilkinson had said much the same thing.

The fact that Jackey and her children looked white was of no matter. What counted was the evidence that Butterwood Nan was a slave prior to 1705. At that time Indians could be slaves and, under Virginia law, if she was a slave so were all her descendants.

The legal arguments ended and Wythe retired to write what would be the most important decision of his life.

He feared that Randolph was correct. From his observation it would seem that Jackey Wright's three daughters, being paler than their mother, were fathered by white men, though no mention was made of this in the court proceedings. Legally, the identity of the father was irrelevant. Must he then rule that Jackey's family could be split up and sold because the Wrights were descendant from Butterwood Nan? So that a slave trader could take them to a southern state where prices were higher? Probably to a cotton plantation in Georgia or to the rice fields of Carolina. Jackey's two daughters were white enough to grace a New Orleans bordello. Was this the depths to which the law in Virginia had sunk?

*

Massachusetts had rid itself of slavery in 1783. There, change came not as the result of some great legislative reform, huge abolitionist campaign or public protests. A judge was responsible.

A runaway African, Quock Walker, was recaptured by his master, Nathaniel Jennison, with the aid of his neighbors. Walker was badly beaten and imprisoned on Jennison's farm. Such was the community's opposition to slavery that three court cases were instituted to free Walker. The final and most decisive was that of the *Commonwealth v. Jennison*, brought by the attorney general of Massachusetts, charging Jennison with assault and battery. In his defense Jennison argued that "the black was his slave, and that the beating and etc was the necessary restrain and correction of the master."

Counsel for Walker argued that the law of nature and the law of God had found expression in the Massachusetts Bill of Rights. Picking up on this, Chief Justice William Cushing of the Supreme Court read to the jury the first article of the Massachusetts Bill of Rights, written by the esteemed John Adams. It proclaimed all men were born free and equal, and had "certain natural, essential, and unalienable rights; among which may be reckoned the right of enjoying their lives and liberties." In an historic address to the jury the chief justice proclaimed:

> Our constitution . . . is totally repugnant to the idea of being born a slave. This being the case, I think the idea of slavery is inconsistent with our own conduct and Constitution; and there can be no such thing as perpetual servitude of a rational creature.

The jury accepted his direction and Quock Walker was freed. Thus was slavery ended in Massachusetts.

In Richmond, five hundred miles south and twenty years later, Wythe began to wonder if a frail judge of eighty years—the most overturned judge in Virginia—could stand up for what was right.

*

As Wythe prepared to write his decision in the case of the descendants of Butterwood Nan, he must have pondered the pattern of public life in Virginia as he had experienced it—the way that themes of independence and liberty were so often intertwined. Perhaps he thought back to that time in 1776, when Thomas Jefferson and Wythe were at the Continental Congress in Philadelphia doing their part in pushing the weakest spines toward a declaration of independence. Meanwhile the Virginia Convention in Williamsburg was rushing pell-mell toward state independence. Unable to be in two places at once, Jefferson had asked Wythe to ride to Williamsburg with his newly drafted constitution.

By the time Wythe arrived the Virginian Convention had already adopted the Bill of Rights. Its opening article was a ringing declaration: *That all men are by nature equally free and independent, and have certain in-*

herent rights, of which, when they enter into a state of society, they cannot by any compact, deprive or divest their posterity; namely, the enjoyment of life and liberty, with the means of acquiring and possessing property, and pursuing and obtaining happiness and safety.

All men are by nature equally free and independent. These wonderfully precise, simple and unambiguous words powered the revolution. These words, in their ordinary meaning, did not exclude any person.

The judgment Wythe wrote in the Butterwood Nan case has been lost, although the court papers of the subsequent appeal summarize his opinion:

> On the hearing, the late Chancellor, perceiving from his own view, that the youngest of the appellees was perfectly white, and that there were gradual shades of difference in color between the grandmother, mother, and granddaughter, (all of whom were before the Court,) and considering the evidence in the cause, determined that the appellees were entitled to their freedom; and, moreover, on the ground that freedom is the birth-right of every human being, which sentiment is strongly inculcated by the first article of our "political catechism," the Bill of Rights—he laid it down as a general position, that whenever one person claims to hold another in slavery, the *onus probandi*[28] lies on the claimant.

Wythe did not go so far to say that the Bill of Rights acted to free slaves. He only ventured that a person held in bondage did not have to prove a right to freedom. On the contrary, it was up to the master to establish right of possession. But what a precedent Wythe set! The suggestion that the Bill of Rights applied to all, regardless of color, was startling. It would allow a cornucopia of legal challenges to the machinery and minutiae of slave law and the entrenched discrimination applying to free black people.

Wythe would have known that the words "when they enter into a state of society" had been inserted into the Bill or Rights at the suggestion of

---

28   Onus of proof.

Edmund Pendleton for the purpose of excluding those of African descent. Because Wythe's judgment has been lost it is impossible to say how he addressed this issue.

However, from his other decisions it is clear that he believed that the words in a statute should be given their plain and literal meaning. His role as a judge was to apply the law as it read, not as some would like it to read. The issue before him was whether persons claiming to be free should have the protection of the Bill of Rights. He decided they should, because they had entered the society of Virginia. It was too late to claim that Africans were not part of Virginia's society. They had been in Virginia for well over a century and a half. They worked in most households, in every village and in every city. They were essential to the economy. Virginia's reputation for gentlemanly behavior, honor and elegance was dependent on the labor of its servants. And the proof was there. It was Virginians at ease, attended by slaves, who guided the nation to freedom. The Declaration of Independence was penned by a Virginian. A Virginian commanded the army to victory. Virginians wrote much of the United States Constitution and its first ten amendments introducing the Bill of Rights. The first and third presidents of the United States were Virginians. All great men, all slave owners. That Africans were part of Virginia society could not be doubted. Virginia, its society and its economy depended on them.

Much as Wythe expected, as soon as he announced his decision freeing Jackey Wright and her daughters, Randolph climbed the stairs to the Court of Appeals and lodged an appeal with the clerk of court. It was scheduled for hearing in November 1806.

19

Murder!

George Wythe Sweney—Lydia Broadnax cooks breakfast—Sweney reads a will—George Wythe Munford's account—Wythe redistributes his wealth—it's monstrous strange, thinks Broadnax—DuVal finds an ill man—Tinsley and the forged checks—Sweney considers suicide—the death of Michael Brown—Randolph varies a will—DuVal writes to Jefferson—the death of a chancellor

Sometime around 1805, into Wythe's house of settled routine came a youth of about sixteen. His name was George Wythe Sweney,[29] and he was the grandson of Wythe's sister, Anne. His Christian names were intended by his parents to honor his famous great-uncle.

Why the chancellor took Sweney into his care is unclear: he had not accepted students in his house for over a decade. Perhaps the old man was lonely, and welcomed the company of a young man whom he could instruct in classical languages. More likely, Wythe was doing a favor for relatives. Sweney was a troubled boy, and had been in dif-

---

29 Sources vary in the spelling: Sweeny, Swinney and Sweney. The last mentioned is used in this book because that is how Wythe spelt the name in his will.

ficulties with the law, so perhaps the youth was sent to Richmond to escape bad influences.

The only information about his first months with Wythe comes via a piece of chitchat preserved in a letter Elizabeth Cabell sent to her sister: "To test the theory that there was no natural inferiority of intellect in the negro, compared with the white man, he [Wythe] had one of his own servant boys and one of his nephews both educated exactly alike. I believe, however, that neither of them did much credit to their teacher."

As well as being an indifferent student, Sweney proved to be a sneak thief, and of the most incompetent kind. These were crimes certain to be detected. Who would not be suspicious of a boy selling trunks of books with the words *exlibris George Wythe* on the flyleaf, when everyone in Richmond knew that although the old man often purchased, he rarely sold. Soon after that, a terrestrial globe disappeared from Wythe's study. With a convincing show of innocence, Sweney denied all knowledge.

Whatever punishment the old man inflicted on his grandnephew for the theft of his books remained private to the household, but Wythe did alter his will. In a codicil dated January 19, 1806, the chancellor noted that Ben had died. (Nothing is known of the circumstances.) His death meant increased shares of Wythe's estate for Broadnax and Brown, but no extra benefits to Sweney. Instead Wythe directed that "the residuary estate devised to him is hereby charged with debts and demands." This strongly implied that Sweney had run up debts, probably through gambling, and Wythe wanted them repaid before the young man got his hands on the estate.

In an additional variation to the will, Wythe bequeathed his "books and small philosophical apparatus to Thomas Jefferson, president of the United States of America."

Then: "To the said Thomas Jefferson's patronage i recommend the freed boy Michael Brown, . . . for whose maintenance, education or other benefit, as the said Thomas Jefferson shall direct."

When Wythe's will became public knowledge this was seen as an extraordinary provision. To expect the President of the United States to accept guardianship of Brown appeared to be a clear confession of Wythe's paternity of the boy. It must be that Wythe had discussed this provision with Jefferson beforehand, or he would not have written it.

At the end of the will appears a verse that may be read as a confession of undisclosed guilt:

Good Lord, most merciful, let penitence
Sincere to me restore lost innocence;
In wrath my grievous sins remember not;
That, after death's sleep, when i shall awake,
Of pure beatitude i may partake.

*

On Sunday morning May 24, 1806, Lydia Broadnax was in the kitchen, toasting bread before the stove. Michael Brown was with her, waiting for his breakfast. Wythe was upstairs in bed. George Sweney came into the kitchen: "Aunt Lydy, I want you to give me a cup of coffee and some bread, because I haven't time to stay to breakfast."

"Mars George," she replied, "breakfast is nearly ready; I have only got to poach a few eggs, and make some toast for old master; so you had better stay and eat with him."

"No," he said, "I'll just take a cup of hot coffee now, and you can toast me a slice of bread."

Broadnax continued:

He went to the fire, and took the coffeepot to the table, while I was toasting the bread. He poured out a cupful for himself and then set the pot down. I saw him throw a little white paper in the fire. He then drank the coffee he had poured out for himself, and ate the toast with some fresh butter. He told me good-bye and went about his business. I didn't think there was anything wrong then.

In a little while I heard old master's bell. He always rings it when he is ready for his breakfast; so I carried it up to him. He poured out a cup of coffee for himself, took his toast and eggs, and ate and drank while he was reading the newspaper.

The above narrative appears in the pages of a book by George Wythe Munford published in 1884, which contained a detailed account of Wythe's death. Munford was given his Christian names by his father, William Munford, who was the impoverished student Wythe took into his house from 1791 to 1793. Munford junior was three when Wythe died, so his description of these events must come from hand-me-down sources, perhaps his father or Broadnax herself. Another possibility is that Munford senior, who was a lawyer, took a statement from Broadnax that his son used in his account.

Munford's book relates that Broadnax had something important to report to her master on that Sunday morning. While Wythe was consuming his breakfast of eggs, toast and coffee, she told him that the day before she had seen Sweney enter his study. She had crept up behind the young man, and saw him go to her master's private desk and pull out a bundle of papers. He unfolded a document and began to read. Broadnax knew that Sweney had Wythe's will in his hand. She stepped forward. Her appearance brought forth an immediate explanation: "The Chancellor sent me to read it, and to tell him what he thought of it."

After relating her story to Wythe, Broadnax waited for a response. If she expected her master to break the code of the South and criticize a white person in front of a black, she was to be disappointed. "I fear I am getting old, Lyddy," he muttered, "for I am becoming more and more forgetful every day." Then as an indication that the matter was closed, he said: "Take these things away, and give Michael his breakfast, and get your own, Lyddy."

It is understandable that Sweney was anxious to read Wythe's will, because as recently as February 24, Wythe had further altered it. The will now provided that on Wythe's death Brown would receive half the bank stock, with the other half going to Sweney immediately. There was also a proviso: "If Michael die before his full age, I give what is devised to him to George Wythe Sweney."

Broadnax then returned to her kitchen. She and Brown drank coffee from the pot. By her account:

After that, with the hot water in the kettle I washed the plates, emptied the coffee grounds out and scrubbed the coffeepot bright, and by that time I became so sick I could hardly see, and had a violent cramp. Michael was sick, too; and old master was as sick as he could be. He told me to send for the doctor. All these things makes me think Mars George must have put something in the coffeepot. I didn't see him, but it looks monstrous strange.

*

The next person to arrive on that Sunday morning was not a doctor fetched by Broadnax but the next-door neighbor, Major William DuVal. He was a local eminence, a magistrate and former mayor of Richmond, who had served under Patrick Henry during the Revolutionary War. He found Wythe's house in silence. He climbed the stairs and entered Wythe's bedroom, where, as he told the court later, he discovered the old man "very ill extended on his back":

Mr Wythe said he had not caught cold, that he was as well as usual in the morning, & ate his breakfast as usual; but was immediately taken extremely ill, confined on his back except when forced up, which was upwards of forty times, and had fifteen evacuations.

Soon after, a doctor, William Foushee arrived. An elderly, balding gentleman with only one eye—the other had been gouged out in a youthful billiard-room brawl—this Edinburgh-trained physician was one of Richmond's leading medical practitioners. He examined the old man, heaving in perspiration on his bed. The chancellor, according to the doctor, complained of a "great thirst, dryness of the throat and mouth, restlessness and anxiety." Foushee also examined the other patients. Broadnax could "hardly see, and had a violent cramp." He concluded she was "not so ill, but seriously sick." Michael Brown was "worse than either—cold in his extremities and having convulsions."

It is not known what treatment Dr. Foushee prescribed, however when DuVal called on Sunday night, Wythe whispered to him that he had "never suffered more in his life."

On Monday morning, one of the most distinguished medical men in Richmond responded to DuVal's call. Dr. James McCaw, who had also trained in Edinburgh, was a founding member of the Medical Society of Virginia. He was fondly remembered in Richmond for tirelessly inoculating the poor during the smallpox epidemics of 1794 and 1802. McCaw noted that Wythe "had been up with a violent puking and purging," and prescribed an opiate which gave him immediate relief.

As Wythe and Brown showed no improvement DuVal called in Doctors McClurg and Currie to add to the opinions of McCaw and Foushee. During the Revolutionary War, Samuel McClurg had been surgeon to the embryonic American navy and director of hospitals for Virginia. He had known Wythe for many years. They had been colleagues on the faculty of William and Mary, and he had served with Wythe in Virginia's delegation to the constitutional convention of 1787.

*

On Tuesday afternoon, Wythe's clerk at the Chancery Court, Peter Tinsley, came to visit. He sat beside Wythe's bed holding a vellum-covered folder. He told Wythe that earlier in the day William Dandridge of the Bank of Virginia had called at the courthouse. Dandridge had shown Tinsley a check for one hundred dollars. Tinsley held up the check for Wythe's examination. It was signed G. Wythe. Dandridge had explained to Tinsley that earlier in the day young Sweney had presented the check at the bank. After cashing the check, Dandridge had felt uneasy about the signature. He had run out of the bank, caught up with Sweney and suggested "there was a mistake in the check." The boy immediately handed back the money. Returning to the bank, Dandridge had gone through all the checks recently drawn against Wythe's account. He had found a number where the signature looked doubtful.

Tinsley placed seven checks across the ill man's bedspread.

Wythe proceeded slowly. He picked up one of the checks. "I signed this one," he said. Tinsley put it aside.

"And the others?"

Wythe looked at them one by one. Sadly he placed them in a pile. "None of them bear my signature," he replied.

*

While this was happening Sweney, in a distraught state of mind, was lying low at the house of a youthful friend, Tarlton Webb. Webb was to later testify that Sweney had showed him a substance wrapped in paper "which he said was Ratsbane." Sweney then blurted out that he intended to kill himself. Webb asked Sweney what was the matter. Sweney replied "that he was very unhappy and something pressed upon his mind." Sweney then offered some of the poison to Webb should he wish to die as well.

There was no double teenage suicide that day, and by nightfall Sweney was in the Richmond jail. The next morning the city awoke to the sensational news that the grandnephew of one of the city's most distinguished citizens had been arrested for forging his uncle's checks, even while the old man, laid low by a mysterious illness, struggled for his survival.

Enter a neighbor, William Claiborne, who was prepared to think the unthinkable, even if others were not. He visited Wythe on Wednesday, May 28. The chancellor told him "he was taken with *cholera morbus*"—meaning diarrhoea, cramps and vomiting, probably caused by eating contaminated food. Wythe thought the strawberries and milk he ate on Saturday night might be the culprit.

Claiborne found Brown and Broadax in the kitchen. Both of them were ill. Broadnax told him of her suspicion that Sweney had placed something in the breakfast coffee on Saturday morning and that he had been caught reading the master's will. This was enough for Claiborne. He hastened to tell DuVal of his belief that the family had been poisoned by Sweney. As for the motivation, he had a theory for that as well. If Wythe, Broadnax and Brown were no more, the chancellor's entire wealth would fall to Sweney.

On the same day, Dr. McCaw called on his patient. He noted that Wythe "was better until the discovery of the prisoner's forgery, when he became worse and continued to grow worse." In the following days more evidence of Sweney's murderous purpose emerged. Pleasant, the slave of William Rose, the Richmond public jailer, found a tight ball of paper in the yard adjacent to Sweney's cell. Inside she found a powdery substance. Rose just knew it was arsenic. He told Dr. Samuel McCraw, an eminent physician of the city, of his find. McCraw walked around the yard of the jail with Pleasant. He found more paper and powder sprinkled among the fennel.

Then a Mr. Nelson Abbott came forward to say that he found a hammer in Wythe's yard, "much stained with yellow." Abbott was told by some "negroes" they had seen Sweney "beat something they did not know what on the side of the ax with the hammer."

Dr. McClurg visited Wythe again on Saturday. He "found him with a fever, his tongue very foul." Wythe told him he hadn't had a passage for twelve hours and he was in no pain—probably due to the opiate prescribed by McCaw.

*

Early Sunday morning, a week after Wythe and his small family were struck down, Parsons Buchanan and Blair paid a call. They found Wythe accepting of his fate as this account from Mumford depicts:

> The old gentleman was suffering intense agony, complaining of excessive heat, accompanied by occasional spasms. In the intervals of pain he was calm and composed, but said he felt his end was approaching.
>
> He extended his hands to the good Parsons, and gave to each a kind of pressure of recognition; and when asked how he felt, said that a man of his age could not endure such intense suffering and live long; that the remedies his physicians had administered had as yet afforded him no permanent relief. He said he had no fear of death, but regretted the manner in which it had been brought about.

He then asked that Edmund Randolph be summoned so he could prepare a codicil to his will. Before the two parsons departed, they knelt beside his bed. "And with your permission, my old friend, we will unite with you in prayer," said Parson Buchanan. After he had finished, the chancellor took his hand. He then extended it to Parson Blair, and said, "We will meet hereafter, around the throne of grace, where pain and sorrow shall be felt no more."

Munford's account of the visit of the two parsonscontinues:

> Dr. Foushee came to the door. The Chancellor beckoned to him, and said, almost in a whisper, "How are Lyddy and Michael?"
>
> "Lyddy," said the doctor, "feels more comfortable. But Michael is dead. The effect of the poison has been rapid indeed."
>
> "I shall not be far behind," the Chancellor said. He uttered a groan, and tossed to and fro in visible agony.
>
> As our Parsons prepared to leave him, seeing he was too ill for them to be of any service, they said, "We hope to see you again. God be with you."
>
> "Not in this world," said he, and they passed out sorrowing.

DuVal's recollection of Wythe's response to the news of Brown's death was more heartfelt. The old man "drew a long death   and pathetically said—Poor boy ... The boy was humble and good."

*

Within hours, Edmund Randolph was standing at the end of Wythe's bed with pen and paper in hand. He took Wythe's instructions to disinherit Sweney and give his share to the boy's brothers and sisters.

After Randolph had departed, four gentlemen presented themselves at Wythe's house, not to visit the sick old man, but to conduct a search of Sweney's room. They were DuVal, Dr. McCraw and two men of business in the city, William Price and Samuel Greenhow.

After a short absence they returned from Sweney's room with a clutch of objects to show the chancellor—all indicative of the young man's guilt. On Sweney's writing table were six wilted strawberries with a yellow substance attached, which the men agreed looked like arsenic. Upon opening a chest they had found a quire of blotting paper that McCraw affirmed was the same as that found in the prison garden. Next, McCraw had discovered a phial of liquid with a suspicious-looking material adhering to the glass; and two pieces of coarse brown paper with "something adhering to them which was also declared to be arsenic and sulphur."

That afternoon Randolph returned with the codicil cutting Sweney out of Wythe's will. Price, Greenhow and McCraw were called in to witness the old man's signature. After sealing the document, Wythe wrote on the envelope, "To William DuVal, to be opened when G. Wythe shall cease to breathe, unless by him required before that event."

*

On Monday morning, George Sweney was brought before Mayor Edward Carrington and five of Richmond's aldermen at the Court of Hustings, a court of local jurisdiction, which had the power to commit accused people to trial. The charge was forgery. Only two witnesses were called. William Dandridge from the Bank of Virginia told of Sweney presenting a check in Wythe's name for one hundred dollars, then returning the money when confronted. Peter Tinsley then swore that he had showed Chancellor Wythe seven checks drawn on his account. Wythe had denied signing six of them. In a quick, unanimous decision, Sweney was committed for trial at the next sitting of the District Court. Bail was set extraordinarily high, at one thousand dollars.

DuVal, being a magistrate, had the right to go into the city jail and stare at Sweney through the bars. DuVal may have hoped for a confession, or at least an explanation, but the boy gave neither. He sat on the edge of a wooden bed, with his head in his hands, and barely glanced at DuVal. The magistrate's questions brought no response. Then just as DuVal was departing, Sweney handed him a letter which asked that he be bailed from prison. DuVal took it to Wythe.

In some ways it was a skillful letter. Most criminals are convicted not by conscientious detective work, but by confession: but no confession appeared. Instead, Sweney described his awful predicament. The boy, of course, did not have one thousand dollars for bail: would his uncle help?

Sweney faced at least three months imprisonment in Mr. Rose's jail before his trial came on. The cells were notoriously dank, stank of urine, and were crowded with thieves, runaway slaves and debtors. However the chancellor was not moved. "Mr. Wythe would have nothing to do with bailing," DuVal later told the court.

DuVal decided it was time to inform President Jefferson of the tragedy that had befallen his old teacher and friend. He wrote on June 4:

Geo. W. Sweeny, who lived with Mr. Wythe was committed to goal on the 27th of May last for forging six checks on the Bank of Virginia. On the 25th of May Mr. Wythe was taken with a Cholera Mortus. On the 25th and 27 all the rest of his family were seized with the same violent disorder. On the 27 we had no idea that Sweeny had poisoned the whole family. On Sunday morning June the first last, Michael the mulatto boy died. Yellow arsenic was found in Sweeny's room and many other strong circumstances concurred to induce a belief that he had poisoned the whole family. As a magistrate I requested four eminent physicians to open the body of the boy. They did so, from the inflammation on the stomach and bowels they said it was the kind of inflammation produced by poison.

His letter to Jefferson continued:

Our worthy friend is still alive. He has suffered greatly … I had Doctors McClurg, Currie and McCaw to attend him. They pronounce his Death to be certain in a day or two. They say his constitution was remarkably strong for a person of his age. Thus by the hand of a youth to whom he was kinder than a father, is about to be taken from us, the most virtuous and illustrious of our citizens. One among the best of men—whom even Death can't terrify or alarm.

*

The next day, Major DuVal sat vigil besides his neighbor's bed, listening to his labored, irregular breath. It seemed to DuVal unlikely that Wythe

261

would regain consciousness yet, after several hours of silence, Wythe suddenly called out, low and clear, "I am murdered."

DuVal could obtain nothing more from him. Later, when Parsons Buchanan and Blair visited he was "too far gone to recognize them."

George Wythe died on Saturday morning, June 8, 1806, almost two weeks to the day of first falling ill. DuVal was by his bedside at the end. Was Lydia Broadnax, the woman who had shared his life for fifty years, allowed to sit by his bed in the final hours? If she was, none of the white men noted her presence.

That evening DuVal wrote a second letter to Jefferson:

Our venerable, great, and pious Friend, departed this Life about a half-hour after Nine of the Clock. Doctors Foushee, Currie, Greenhow, McClurg, and McCaw opened his chest and bowels. There was considerable inflammation in his Stomach. It is strongly suspected that he and Michael Brown were poisoned with Yellow Arsenic by Geo. W. Sweeny. On Thursday he said I am murdered but mentioned no name. The day before yesterday, he said Let me die righteous. He during his severe complaint displayed uncommon patience and fortitude. He called on the Lord Jesus Christ to have mercy on him.

The Governor and Council have desired that his body shall be conveyed to the Capitol. Tomorrow at four o'clock in the afternoon his Funeral Oration will be pronounced by Mr. Wm. Munford who lived with Mr. Wythe formerly, and is a member of our Council of State.

*

In an emotional funeral oration delivered the next day Munford spoke of visiting the ailing chancellor during the last weeks of his life: "When on his death-bed racked with agonizing pain, I saw him with a large bundle of papers, relative to an injunction in the chancery, lying by his bedside. He told me that he had been studying them and hoped to be better the next day, that he might be enabled to hold court again."

Recognizing the more than forty years in which Thomas Jefferson and Wythe had been companions and regular correspondents, Munford said:

Between those two extraordinary men the warmest friendship has ever existed and the President of the United States has always been prepared to acknowledge himself the pupil of the wise and modest Wythe.

Most of the heroes and patriots of the revolution are gone to their graves with glory and George Wythe, one of the oldest and best of those venerated fathers of the country, has now followed Washington, Franklin, Samuel Adams and many others who are removed from this troublesome world.

At the conclusion of Munford's oration, the mourners walked in solemn procession from the Capitol to Saint John's on Church Hill, for a service witnessed by a great crowd of Richmond's citizens. Saint John's was the church in which Patrick Henry had in 1775 made his famous speech "Give me Liberty or Give me Death," a speech Wythe had heard delivered.

As befitted a revolutionary patriot and signer of the Declaration of Independence, Wythe was buried in the church grounds outside the western porch. In keeping with his self-effacing nature, no plinth, column or stone marked his grave.

The next day, the *Richmond Enquirer* dressed its pages in mourning borders. Under the heading "Full of Years; and Full of Honour," the editor wrote:

On Sunday morning of the 8th inst., departed this life, the venerable chancellor of the Richmond district, GEORGE WYTHE. Over the suspected causes of his death, let us for a moment draw the veil. Every situation in life has its rights and its duties. Let us therefore respect the rights of the accused.

But of the deep, the solemn, the almost unparalleled impression produced by his death we may be permitted to speak. ... Kings may require mausoleums to consecrate their memory; saints may claim the privilege of canonization; but the venerable George Wythe needs no other monument than the services rendered to his country, and the universal sorrow which that country sheds over his grave.

Within days, from Washington, President Jefferson replied to Duval's earlier letters:

[A] purer character has never lived. His advanced years had left us little hope of retaining him much longer, and had his end been brought on by ordinary decays of time and nature, altho' a subject of regret, it would not have been aggravated by the horror of his falling by the hand of a parricide.

In a following letter, Jefferson expressed regret at Michael Brown's death "not only for the affliction it must have cost Mr. Wythe in his last moments, but also as it has deprived me of an object of attentions which would have gratified me unceasingly with the constant recollection and execution of the wishes of my friend."

At the next sitting of the Virginia Assembly, the members of both houses resolved to wear black armbands in Wythe's memory.

Thus, amid ceremony and sad remembrance, one of America's revolutionary heroes was laid to rest.

Nothing is known of the last rites for Michael Brown.

20

A Trial and an Appeal

Sweney at the Court of Hustings—doctors with doubts—Sweney sent to trial—Randolph for the defense—William Wirt calms his conscience—a puzzling trial—theories and conspiracies—Sweney convicted of forgery—Sweney's fate—what happened to Broadnax—Judges in appeal—the descendants of Butterwood Nan—Judge Tucker tries to be helpful

George Wythe Sweney now faced indictments in three separate proceedings: one for forgery, another for the murder of George Wythe, and a third for the murder of Michael Brown.

The two charges of murder were the subject of a preliminary hearing by the Court of Hustings in Richmond to establish if there was sufficient evidence to send Sweney to trial. This took place two weeks after Wythe's death, on July 23, before a court composed of Mayor Carrington and five aldermen.

Tarlton Webb, a young friend of Sweney, was the first to give evidence. The prisoner Sweney had come to his house and said he wanted to kill himself as he was very unhappy. He said there was something pressing on his mind. Later he showed Webb some ratsbane wrapped in paper and offered to give him some if he wanted to die as well.

Another youngster, Taylor Williams, said that Sweney had been talking about poison for weeks prior to his arrest. He remembered they spoke about ferrous sulphate and ratsbane being good for killing rats.

William Rose, the Richmond public jailer, related how his servant girl, Pleasant, on the day after Sweney's imprisonment for forgery, had brought him a ball of paper which she had found in the garden. Inside, he found a substance he knew was arsenic. Rose admitted he had failed to search Sweney when the youth was taken into custody.

Major William DuVal told the court Wythe's illness began after he took breakfast on 25 May; after that he went into a gradual perceptible decline. DuVal had searched Sweney's room and found paper with a substance adhering to it that Greenhow had declared to be arsenic. Further, amounts of arsenic had been found in an old smokehouse on Wythe's land. Ominously for Sweney, he concluded his evidence: "It was generally believed that Mr. Wythe had left the prisoner a great portion of his estate, and known that he had made some provisions for the mulatto boy, Brown."

Dr. Samuel McCraw said Rose had shown him the paper containing the arsenic. McCraw also said he found two other pieces of paper in the garden of the jail and some arsenic on the ground. He also took part in the search of Sweney's room. He had never heard Mr. Wythe express any suspicion that he had been poisoned, although one time he heard Wythe call out "cut me," which the doctor understood as a request to perform a postmortem.

Samuel Greenhow and William Price gave evidence similar to McCaw's and DuVal's relating to the search of Sweney's room. Price also heard Wythe say to Dr. McCraw he wanted to be cut open. Another witness, Nelson Abbott, had seen a hammer and an ax stained with yellow in a workshop in Wythe's yard. William Claiborne swore that after finding a substance on a wheelbarrow in Wythe's old smokehouse he "applied fire to it and found from the smell that it was arsenic."

Next, Edmund Randolph took the stand. He told how after the death of Brown, Wythe "wished his will to be altered so as to give to the prisoner's brothers and sisters what he had given him." On the following Wednesday, Lydia Broadnax told him more poison had been found in Abbott's shop.

He went there and spoke to a slave who told him that Sweney had been pounding something on an ax head. He believed it was ratsbane. He saw the prisoner scraping it into a piece of paper.

Both Doctors McClurg and Foushee told of performing autopsies on both Wythe and Brown. Their evidence abruptly turned the case on its head. Quite unexpectedly, both physicians cast doubt on cause of death. Dr. McClurg testified (as transcribed by the court recorder):

That he was present at the opening of the body of Michael Brown. The lower part of the stomach was very much inflamed and had the appearance of the black vomit. [He] went to visit Mr. Wythe on the day before the boy died and found him with a fever, his tongue very foul, had had no passage for twelve hours, and was free from pain. The appearance of the boy was such as arsenic might have produced; but such as might also have been produced by a great collection of bile. [He] was also present at the opening of the body of Mr. Wythe. The whole of his stomach and intestines had an uncommonly bloody appearance, that if produced by arsenic, in his opinion, death would have ensued much sooner. Mr. Wythe had been frequently attacked with disordered bowels within three years last past.

Evidence to support the latter statement is in the correspondence of William Browne of Williamsburg, who in September 1804 wrote a chatty letter to judge Joseph Prentis, exclaiming at the remarkable behavior of the eccentrics of Richmond:

The venerable Wythe is one who has fallen more immediately under my eye … He appears to me to be little removed from insanity [when] he passed thro' a hard rain down to the Capitol on Sunday last … When he goes out to answer the call of nature he with little ceremony sits down immediately in the street.

Dr. Foushee also hesitated to give a firm opinion on the cause of Wythe's death. "The stomach was very much inflamed, and appeared as if a new inflammation was coming on. There was very little bile in the liver.

The same appearance that his stomach and intestines exhibited might have been produced by arsenic, or any other acrid matter."

Although Dr. McCaw was present at the opening of Wythe, curiously he gave no opinion on the cause of death. Of Brown, he recalled that he "saw the boy on the day before his death, when he had a fever and complained of great pain. The deponent saw him opened after his death, and thinks that his death might have been occasioned by a great accumulation of bile."

Richmond's mayor and aldermen were not held back by the physicians' doubts. After a hearing lasting near five hours, the mayor announced that the court was of the "opinion that the prisoner is guilty of the offence aforesaid, and doth order that he undergo a trial before the next District Court directed by law to be holden at the Capitol in this City."

*

During the summer, grand juries endorsed bills of indictment against George Wythe Sweney for the murder of George Wythe and Michael Brown, for a hearing to commence on September 2, 1806.

The trial for the murder of Chancellor Wythe was heard first, by a jury before two judges of the District Court, Joseph Prentis and John Tyler. The state Attorney General, Philip Norborne Nicholas, prosecuted. Sweney was defended by the very best at the Virginian bar, Edmund Randolph and William Wirt.

Even taking into account that early in the nineteenth century the rules relating to conflict of interest were at a rudimentary stage, Randolph's appearance for the accused seems extraordinary. He had several reasons to disqualify himself: he was well acquainted with the deceased, had testified for the state at the preliminary hearing and, because he had discovered some of the evidence, was a potential witness. His involvement only adds to the mysteries associated with this trial.

The second attorney in defense, William Wirt, was a member of the interconnected aristocracy of Virginia. He was the brother-in-law of Governor Cabell and the grandson of Patrick Henry. Later, he became attorney general of the United States during the presidencies of James

Monroe and John Quincy Adams. Wirt also knew Wythe extremely well because from 1802 he had been of equal judicial status as chancellor for the eastern part of the state. He resigned in 1803 because the pay was too low. He had no wish, he wrote to a friend, to be "like Mr. Wythe, grow old in judicial honors and Roman poverty. I may die beloved, reverenced almost to canonization by my country, and my wife and children, as they beg for bread, may have to boast they were mine."

When first Wirt heard of Wythe's death, he had no doubt of Sweney's guilt. He wrote of his hope that "no one would undertake the defense of Sweney, but that he would be left to the fate which he seemed so justly to merit." To James Monroe he said: "The young villain (only about 16 or 17) had been in the habit of robbing his uncle with a false-key, had sold three trunks of his most valuable law-books, had forged his checks on the bank to a considerable amount, & wound up his villainies by this act."

Within weeks Wirt had changed his mind. He had recently married for a second time, and the newlyweds had expensive tastes. He confided in a letter to his wife that the trial might "give me a splendid debut in the metropolis." To calm his troubled conscience, Wirt consulted the elderly Judge William Nelson. The judge offered reassurance, which Wirt conveyed to his wife:

> Judge Nelson says I ought not to hesitate a moment to do it; that no one can justly censure me for it; and, for his own part, he thinks it highly proper that the young man should be defended. Being himself a relation of Judge Wythe's,[30] and having a most delicate sense of propriety, I am disposed to confide very much in his opinion.

*

What happened at Sweney's trials for double murder is a puzzle. Not even the sketchiest outline of the course of the trial remains as the court documents were destroyed in 1865, during the burning of Richmond in the

---

30 Judge Nelson was related to Wythe's second wife, Elizabeth Taliaferro.

Civil War. All that has survived is a brief report in the *Richmond Enquirer* of September 9, 1806:

> On Tuesday, came on the celebrated trial of George W. Sweeny, on the charge of administering arsenic to his great uncle, the venerable George Wythe; P. N. Nicholas (attorney general for the prosecution) William Wirt and Edmond Randolph, Esqrs. counsel for the defendant. After an able and eloquent discussion, the jury retired, and in a few minutes, brought in a verdict of not guilty …

> The pen yet lingers to add, that some of the strongest testimony exhibited before the called court and before the grand jury, was kept back from the petit jury. The reason is, that it was gleaned from the evidence of negroes, which is not permitted by our laws to go against a white man.

The charge against Sweeny of murdering Michael Brown was quashed without even proceeding to trial.

What in the world had transpired?

The law forbidding the reception of evidence from black witnesses against white people had graced Virginia's statute books at least since 1705. Jefferson had an opportunity of repealing the provision during his great reforms of 1777–79 but failed to do so. There is enough in Jefferson's *Notes on the State of Virginia* to conclude that he thought that Africans, slave and free, were inferior in reasoning and imperfectly understood the Christian concept of swearing on the Bible.

Had she been allowed, Lydia Broadnax could have told of Sweeny reading Wythe's will, having access to the kitchen while the coffee was being brewed, and throwing a small white paper into the fire. Abbott's slaves could have told of Sweeny pounding ratsbane on an ax. And Pleasant could have told of finding a substance wrapped in paper in the garden of the jail. It was all circumstantial, though in combination a jury might have believed it established guilt beyond reasonable doubt.

With the evidence of the Africans excluded, the prosecution foundered. It also faced the difficulty, present in most cases of poisoning, that no one had actually seen Sweeny secreting arsenic in the food.

Then there was the question of Sweney's motivation. If he was bound to inherit a substantial portion of Wythe's wealth on his death (which could not be far off for a man in his eightieth year), why poison him? Because Sweney was a boy who could not wait? Or because he had run up gambling debts and was under pressure to pay?

Or were the intended victims Brown and Broadnax, and the murder of Wythe a mistake? Perhaps Sweney never intended the coffee to be taken upstairs to the chancellor that Sunday morning. Did he assume if the victims were two free Africans, then there would not be a proper investigation, and he would eventually inherit all?

What of the extraordinary amount of yellow powder found in so many places? It was smeared on an ax and on a hammer in the workshop. DuVal had found powder in Wythe's old smokehouse. Claiborne had found arsenic on wheelbarrow. The search party discovered more yellow powder in Sweney's bedroom. Rose's slave Pleasant came across poison wrapped in paper in the garden of the jail. McCraw had found it sprinkled among plants.

So much poison beggars belief. Did Sweney make no attempt to hide the means of his crimes? Was the jury supposed to believe that Sweney, after poisoning everyone in his house on Sunday morning, still had the poison wrapped in his pocket when imprisoned for forgery on Wednesday? There is little doubt that Sweney was a deeply disturbed young man. His friends told of a youth obsessed with poisons and a desire to kill himself. Could it be that, in a distraught mental state, he had been collecting poison for his own suicide? Perhaps this explains why the poison was in his pocket when locked in jail.

It appears that no chemical analysis of the yellow powders was undertaken by the authorities. Understandable perhaps, as at that time the recognized method for detecting arsenic relied on unstable ammonia solvents, which often produced inconsistent or inconclusive results. It was not until 1836 that a British chemist, James Marsh, devised a test to produce certain identification of arsenic. Several years earlier Marsh had been called to give expert testimony at the trial of a man accused of murder by administering arsenic-laced coffee. While he was able to identify the poison as arsenic, by the time the trial commenced his samples had deteriorated, the prosecution case collapsed and the accused escaped conviction. Irritated by this, Marsh returned to his laboratory and four years later emerged to announce a test that involved identifying arsine gas within hydrogen emanating from the poison. His test was so sensitive it could detect arsenic in a sample as small as one-fiftieth of a milligram. But this was too late to solve the mystery of the deaths in Wythe's household.

*

Had Wythe and Brown died of natural causes? This strong possibility emerges from the evidence of the doctors, McClurg, McCaw and Foushee. McCaw went so far as to say that Brown's death "might have been occasioned by a great accumulation of bile." McClurg noted that Wythe had a history of "disordered bowels."

Historian Fawn Brodie in her celebrated study, *Thomas Jefferson, an Intimate History,* put forward an alternative explanation. She asserted that many of the citizens of Richmond were "aghast" at the implications flowing from Wythe's will, which benefited "his housekeeper" and "her yellow son" and asked the President of the United States to take care of the boy's education:

> Thus the whole legal paraphernalia of Virginia law was perverted to absolve the forger and murderer and to dramatize the legal sanction of the murder of a man who would so advertise his miscegenation. The fact that Wythe was one of Virginia's most distinguished sons, and a signer of the Declaration of Independence, only served to make it more imperative that his gesture be repudiated and buried in the most expeditious fashion possible.

As many have pointed out, Brodie's argument falters at a number of points. The citizens of Richmond were, in fact, unlikely to be aghast at Wythe's "obvious advertisement of the boy's paternity." The mild reaction of Virginians to Callender's allegations that Jefferson regularly bedded one of his slaves seems to indicate that this sort of behavior left no one aghast, so long as it was handled discreetly.

Nor did Brodie's assertion that Wythe was "buried in the most expeditious fashion possible" accord with the reality that Richmond was deeply saddened by Wythe's death, and that his passing was marked with substantial ceremony. Perhaps most telling, for the "whole legal paraphernalia of Virginia law" to be "perverted," as Brodie suggested, would have required the judiciary, the bar, the jury and the press to be enlisted in an elaborate conspiracy of injustice. There is simply nothing to suggest that that occurred.

In his book, Munford presented another theory of how Sweney escaped conviction. He wrote of Edmund Randolph sitting beside the dying Wythe to receive instructions on a codicil to disentitle Sweney of the benefits of the will. After the formalities were complete, Wythe told Randolph:

It is not my desire that this unfortunate nephew of mine shall be prosecuted or punished, further than this codicil will punish him, for the offences with which he stands charged. I dread such a stigma being cast upon my name or my sister's. I do not believe he can be convicted in the teeth of our statute law, which prohibits negro testimony from being received against a white man under trial. And without such testimony he will be acquitted. For myself, I shall die leaving him my forgiveness.

In the next sentence, Munford commented: "This will explain the reasons why Edmund Randolph appeared as counsel for the defense."

Both Munford senior and Edmund Randolph visited Wythe shortly before he died, so this version of events must be given respect. If it is accurate, it also raises the possibility that Randolph, or perhaps Wythe himself, requested the attending doctors to assist Sweney by reporting that they were unable to establish the cause of death or to identify the yellow powder as arsenic.

An even more striking theory comes from an article published in 1999 in the journal of Colonial Williamsburg, and entitled: *Jefferson's "Alleged Child"—Could He Have Been Michael Brown, Murdered with George Wythe?* The author, Polly Longsworth, again placed Edmund Randolph in the midst of a conspiracy—this one designed to protect Thomas Jefferson "from political enemies far too interested in the president's purported mulatto son." She argued that Jefferson feared that during Sweney's trials for the murder of Wythe and Brown, his enemies might have learned too much about the murdered boy. But what was there to learn?

The answer provided by Longsworth concerns the identity of a boy named Tom. James Callender, in his muckraking articles of 1802, wrote that a twelve-year-old boy whom he scandalously called "our little mulatto president" was the child of Jefferson. After investigating Callender's story, the editor of the *Frederick-Town Herald* wrote that this boy "we are assured, bears a strong likeness to Mr. Jefferson." Soon after these reports, Tom disappeared from Monticello. Longsworth suggested (with scant evidence) that Randolph may have helped convey the boy to Richmond, to live with Wythe under the assumed name of Michael Brown.

*

The day after his acquittal for murder, Sweney faced court on charges of forgery. He was convicted. William Wirt then obtained an arrest of sentence to allow an appeal to the General Court.

On November 17, six judges assembled to hear Wirt. He pointed out that the statute making forgery a crime referred to "any false tokens or counterfeit letter, made in *any other man's name.*" (author's italics) The present charge related to forgery perpetrated on a bank, but a *bank* was a corporation and not a man. According to Wirt, this made sense because when the Assembly passed the law against forgery in 1789 no banks existed in Virginia. It also made sense to the six judges. However Wirt's arguments only went to the times Sweney received notes issued by the bank. On one occasion, he had been handed fifty dollars in "money current" (cash). The judges ruled this was Wythe's property.

The court returned this single count to the District Court for sentencing. Sweney received six months' imprisonment plus an hour locked in the pillory outside the Richmond market—a location where rotten fruit and rancid meat were in ready supply. However, for reasons unknown, this sentence was not carried out, and the attorney prosecuting for the Commonwealth of Virginia declined to proceed further. Sweney was released.

By year's end the Virginian legislature had closed the loophole that allowed forgery against a bank to go unpunished. The law prohibiting black evidence against whites remained on the books until 1867.

Sweney then dropped out of view. Dr. Dove in his Memorandum said that "the young man went to Tennessee, stole a horse and was sent to the penitentiary." B. B. Minor said something similar: "The unfortunate man then sought refuge in the West; where his career was brought to a premature and miserable close."

*

With the death of Wythe, Lydia Broadnax gained the rent of his house and the interest on his stocks for so long as she lived. Yet, in 1807, she wrote to Thomas Jefferson asking for money:

> I have already labored under many tedious difficulties, and what is more unfortunate my eyesight has almost failed me. I believe it is owing to the dreadful complaint the whole family was afflicted with at the decease of my poor Master—supposed to be the effect of poison. It is true I have a tolerable and comfortable house to live in, but being almost intirely deprived of my eyesight, together with old age and infirmness of health I find it extremely difficult in procuring the daily necessities of life—and without some assistance I feel I shall sink under the burden.

The president sent her fifty dollars. Broadnax may have regarded Jefferson as a soft touch, for she was not at all impoverished. As mentioned earlier, the census of 1810 showed that six freed blacks and two slaves were residing in the building she owned, suggesting she was running a boardinghouse. In 1820 she wrote a will that included among her assets a house and a vacant lot in Richmond that she left "to Philip Wythe and Benjamin Wythe, free boys of color, grandsons of my sister Letty Robinson, deceased." The choice of the two boys' surname shows the high regard felt by many in the black community for Chancellor Wythe.

She died soon after, probably in 1821.

*

The appeal in the descendants of Butterwood Nan (*Hudgins v. Wrights*) commenced in November 1806, five months after Wythe's death and seven weeks after the trial of George Sweney for murder. Being a matter of great consternation and controversy, the appeal was heard by a panel of five judges.

Every member of the bench had known Wythe personally. At William and Mary, Wythe had taught three of them, namely Spencer Roane, William Fleming and the presiding judge, St. George Tucker. In fact, some thirty years earlier, Tucker had sat in a corner of Wythe's chambers as a law clerk and carried his books and papers to courts. Wythe had also signed his admission papers. Tucker was a man troubled by slavery (while holding more than one hundred slaves himself), and had published a pamphlet urging its gradual elimination coupled with harsh laws encouraging former slaves to "voluntarily" migrate to the West. Wythe had also served with the other two judges, Paul Carrington and William Fleming, at the Virginia Ratifying Convention of 1788.

Thus, it appeared that the fate of Jackey Wright and her daughters depended on whether Wythe's distinguished former students and colleagues would decide that the first article of Virginia's Bill of Rights applied to all, or that it excluded people with dark skins.

Edmund Randolph, in opening his onslaught on Wythe's decision, complained that the late chancellor had mentioned the white color of Jackey White and her daughter "more to excite the feelings of the Court as men, than to address them as Judges." He should never have allowed the circumstances of their being white "to operate on his mind." Randolph then turned to what he saw as the decisive issue: that Butterwood Nan was taken into slavery before 1705, and until that date it was legal to enslave Indians. Thus, all her descendants were slaves.

In the midst of this address, Judge Tucker dropped a bombshell. "Is not that a mistake?" he said. Randolph looked at him in surprise. Tucker explained he had been doing some research of his own. He had unearthed some old Virginian statutes and found that the law that meant Indians could not be enslaved after 1705 was a mere repetition of a law made in 1691. On the evidence it was likely Butterwood Nan was enslaved between those dates; therefore, her descendants over three generations should never have been slaves.

The opposing attorney, George Taylor, jumped on this offering from the bench as the salvation of his case. He promptly altered his final address: "From the beginning of the world till the year 1679, all Indians were, in fact as well as right, free persons," he declared. "In that year an act passed declaring Indian prisoners taken in war to be slaves: and in 1682, another, that Indians sold by us by neighboring Indians and others trading with us should be slaves. These acts remained in force till 1691 (as supposed by one of the judges) ..."

In the end, Taylor did not mention Wythe's reliance on the Virginian Bill of Rights—presumably he thought that point a lost cause.

*

Judgment was delivered on November 11, 1806. Every one of the five judges specifically disowned Wythe's assertion that freedom was the birthright of all regardless of color, or that the Bill of Rights applied to slaves. The leading opinion was written by St. George Tucker:

I do not concur with the Chancellor in his reasoning on the operation of the first clause of the Bill of Rights, which was notoriously framed with a cautious eye to this subject, and was meant to embrace the case of free citizens, or aliens only; and not by a side wind to overturn the rights of property, and give freedom to those very people whom we have been compelled from imperious circumstances to retain, generally, in the same state of bondage that they were in at the revolution, in which they had no *concern, agency or interest.*

The other judges concurred, "not approving of the Chancellor's principles and reasoning ... except so far as the same relates to white persons and native American Indians, but entirely disapproving thereof, so far as the same related to native Africans and their descendants, who have been and are now held as slaves."

However, on the crucial issue, all judges accepted, on the evidence, that Butterwood Nan had been made a slave after 1691, so her descendants must be free. Thus Jackey Wright and her three "perfectly white" daughters walked out of the courtroom, slaves no more.

Into this moment of liberty Judge Tucker added a discordant note. In his written opinion, he took the opportunity of setting guidelines for judges in Virginian courts where those applying for freedom were of doubtful heritage:

> Nature has stampt upon the *African* and his descendants two characteristic marks, besides the differences of complexion, which often remain visible long after the characteristic distinction of colour either disappears or becomes doubtful; a flat nose and wooly head of hair ... So pointed is this distinction between the natives of *Africa* and the aborigines of *America*, that a man might as easily mistake the glossy, jetty clothing of an *American* bear for the wool of a black sheep ...
>
> Suppose three persons, a black or mulatto man or woman with a flat nose and wooly head; a copper-coloured person with long jetty black, straight hair; and one with a fair complexion, brown hair, not woolly nor inclining thereto, with a prominent *Roman* nose, were brought together before a judge ... How must a judge act in such a case? I answer that he must judge from his own view. He must discharge the white person and the *Indian* out of custody, taking surety... that the holder may have an opportunity of asserting and proving them to be lineally descended in the maternal line from a female *African* slave; and he must redeliver the black or mulatto person, with the flat nose and wooly hair to the person claiming to hold him or her as a slave, unless the black person or mulatto could procure some person to be bound to him, to produce proof of his descent, in the maternal line, from a *free female ancestor.*

Thus did the highest court in Virginia affirm that slavery was racially based, and set the course for decades of degrading trials in which people seeking freedom were exhibited before judge or juries while the lawyers pointed out their skin color, hair texture and the shape of their noses.

Epilogue

After George Wythe's death, President Jefferson did not forget his friend. He wrote to Major DuVal asking if a portrait of Wythe existed, that he could have as a keepsake of his old teacher and friend. The only painting DuVal could find belonged to Lydia Broadnax. He wrote back to the president:

If you preferred the original, Lydia would be contented with a profile copy—I know from what Mr. Wythe often said, that you were dearer than any relation he had—that his attachment arose from that impulse that unites great minds, the sincere Love of Virtue.

*

In 1922, a plaque was placed in the grounds of Saint John's Church, Richmond, close to where George Wythe was thought to be buried. Its inscription reads:

THIS TABLET IS DEDICATED
TO MARK THE SITE WHERE LIE
THE MORTAL REMAINS OF
GEORGE WYTHE
BORN 1726—DIED 1806
JURIST AND STATESMAN
TEACHER OF RANDOLPH
JEFFERSON AND MARSHALL
FIRST PROFESSOR OF LAW IN THE UNITED STATES
FIRST VIRGINIA SIGNER OF THE
DECLARATION OF INDEPENDENCE

Postscript

At this point, amid the book's final pages, the author steps out reluctantly from under the cover of the narrator's role, to speculate on the mysterious outcome of Sweney's trials for murder. After living in close quarter with Wythe and his family for more than half a decade, I trust my readers may concede that I have an opinion worth expressing.

The household of George Wythe in Richmond comprised Wythe, his fellow victim Michael Brown, the accused George Sweney, and Lydia Broadnax—yet suspicion immediately fell only on Sweney. Perhaps this was not surprising, given his record of dishonesty and the discovery of a substance that looked like poison in various incriminating locations, including his room and the garden of the prison where he was held on a charge of forgery. Broadnax added to the mounting evidence by suggesting that the young man had put something in a coffee pot before the coffee was drunk by the rest of the family. 'I didn't see him, but it looks monstrous strange,' said Broadnax.

But in the rush to condemn Sweney, was another member of the household completely overlooked? In the catalogue of heinous crimes that the slaveholding South feared, poisoning by a black domestic servant eclipsed most others—perhaps even arson or the rape of a white woman. It was the crime of a person embedded in the home; hard to detect and devastating in its effect. A member of the master's family suddenly died, and when the doctor was called he was unable to say what the cause was.

Amid the grief of the moment, the master's family remembered that a particular servant had been resentful for months past because of some fancied ill treatment. As suspicion turned to certainty, the white members of the household wondered who could be trusted. How could one know what was going on behind that dark face? Fear and uncertainty stalked the house.

Eugene D. Genovese, in his classic study of American slavery, *Roll, Jordan Roll, the World the Slaves Made,* observed that poison "held a special place in the arsenal of slave weapons throughout the Americas":

> Long before Africans fell prey to the slave trade they had mastered the art of poisoning as a means of dealing with enemies. From the moment they embarked for the New World, they resorted to poison against the whites ...

When Thomas Jefferson rewrote the criminal law of Virginia in 1788 he gave voice to the general horror of this crime by proposing a special punishment for poisoners, namely that they suffer death by poisoning themselves. For similar reasons the state of Virginia passed a law making it a felony for any black person to prepare or administer medicine. The opening words of this statute justified the prohibition: "Whereas under pretence of practicing physic, Negroes have prepared medicine by which many persons have been murdered or have languished." In 1761, this law was applied with ferocious severity by Judge Edmund Pendleton to a slave named Cupid who had given medicine to a fellow slave. Keen to set an example, Pendleton and his co-justices sentenced Cupid to death by hanging.

Despite the acquittal of Sweney for murder, at no time did anyone consider the possibility that the real perpetrator might be Broadnax. Yet she had both the opportunity and, potentially, the motive. As the person preparing breakfast on that fateful day, she certainly had the opportunity to secrete poison in the coffee pot. She also could have easily sprinkled poison in the various locations where it would best implicate Sweney. With Brown, Wythe and Sweney out of the way, she stood to gain the entirety of Wythe's estate.

I hasten to add that this theory is no more than wild speculation on my part, and quite devoid of supporting evidence. So if Broadnax is excluded, as indeed she rightly must be, then one is left with the strong possibility that the reason no one was found guilty of murder was because there were no murders committed.

None of the doctors who treated Brown and Wythe during their illness, or conducted their autopsies, was prepared to state positively that the pair had been poisoned. The key words in Dr. McClurg's evidence read:

> The appearance of the boy was such as arsenic might have produced; but such as might also have been produced by a great collection of bile. Was also present at the opening of the body of Mr. Wythe. The whole of his stomach and intestines had an uncommonly bloody appearance, that if produced by arsenic, in his opinion, death would have ensued much sooner. Mr. Wythe had been frequently attacked with disordered bowels within three years last past.

Dr. McCaw who was present at the opening of Brown thought "his death might have been occasioned by a great accumulation of bile." The most that Dr. Foushee would say of Wythe was that the appearance of his stomach and intestines "might have been produced by arsenic, or any other acrid matter."

At Sweney's trial, any competent lawyer (and Sweney had two of the smartest lawyers in Virginia) would have pointed out that Brown and Wythe may have died of unexplained natural causes. Perhaps the evidence of Broadnax, Abbott's slaves and Pleasant may have tipped the balance towards a conviction, however, as the *Richmond Enquirer* pointed out, "some of the strongest testimony exhibited before the called court and before the grand jury, was kept back from the petit jury. The reason is, that it was gleaned from the evidence of negroes, which is not permitted by our laws to go against a white man."

Thus in the absence of cogent evidence to support a conviction, it becomes perfectly understandable that the jury brought in verdicts of not guilty.

No conspiracy theory is required.

Acknowledgments

Thanks to my patient wife, Annie.

Thanks to the staff at the Colonial Williamsburg Foundation (www. colonialwilliamsburg.com), a not-for-profit educational and cultural organization dedicated to the preservation, interpretation and presentation of the restored eighteenth-century Revolutionary capital of Virginia.

Thanks to my editor, Sybil Nolan, who tactfully guided me and this book away from many shoals.

John Bailey
Mullumbimby, 2013

Notes on Sources

The history of the American Revolution and its aftermath is so well documented that readers can find references to the major events in the standard texts, or by trawling the internet. There is little value, therefore, in providing citations for such well-known events as George Washington's famous crossing of the Delaware, or for quotations from *Common Sense*, by Thomas Paine.

Mindful that *Jefferson's Second Father* is primarily a book about the lifelong relationship between George Wythe and Thomas Jefferson, I have identified the more obscure references relating to those two figures, along with some others I felt were of such significance to the lives that they deserved a note of their own.

Where a short version of a reference appears, the full citation is given in the select references.

PROLOGUE

Exchange of letters DuVal & Jefferson: Special Collection of the International Center for Jefferson Studies, Monticello, Va. The originals are in the Jefferson Papers of the Library of Congress: 28475, 27874, 27882, 27898, 27915, 27941, 28044, 28523, 28533.

For the description of Wythe and Brown's illness: W. Edwin Hemphill's 'Examination of George Wythe Swinney for Forgery and Murder', Julian P. Boyd's 'The Murder of George Wythe' and George William Munford's, *The Two Parsons*.

1. The Young Wythe

'Jefferson noted that his friend was born': Andrew A. Lipscomb and Albert Berg, eds, The Writings of Thomas Jefferson, appendix, p. 167.

For W's childhood, forebears and parents see Imogene E. Brown, *American Aristides, A Biography of George Wythe*, p. 15ff.; Joyce Blackburn, *George Wythe of Williamsburg*, p. xiv; William Clarkin, *Serene Patriot: A Life of George Wythe*, p 19ff.

'the celebrated preacher George Keith': James Bowden, *The History of the Society of Friends in America*, pp.77-100; Blackburn, p. 6; Robert B. Kirtland, *George Wythe: Lawyer, Revolutionary, Judge*, pp. 24-6.

'is fully come off from the Quakers': 'Old Kecoughtan', *William and Mary Quarterly*, vol. 9, no. 2 (1900), p. 127; William E. Hemphill, *George Wythe, the Colonial Briton*, p. 21.

'English clergyman and writer, Andrew Burnaby': Alonzo Thomas Dill, *George Wythe Teacher of Liberty*, p. 7.

'He had not the benefit of a regular education': Andrew A. Lipscomb and Albert Berg, eds, *The Writings of Thomas Jefferson*, vol. 1, Appendix, pp. 166-7.

'two indentured servants and nine slaves': Brown, p. 16.

'in 1767 Chesterville was home to thirty-two slaves': Brown, p. 94.

'claim that he was treated badly by his uncle': B. B. Minor, 'Memoir of the Author', *Decision of Cases in Virginia by the High Court of Chancery*, p. xii; Dill, p. 8.

'Many troublesome suits are multiplied': Robert B. Kirtland, 'Keep Your Eye on the Bastards', *Toledo Law Review*, vol. 14, No. 3, p. 689.

'in the legal practice of Zachary Lewis': Kirtland, pp. 33-4.

'In backwoods Virginia they rode along rutted roads': An excellent description of colonial Virginia appears in Rhys Isaac, *The Transformation of Virginia 1740-1790*.

'Anne Lewis and George Wythe became man and wife': 'Old Kecoughtan', *William and Mary Quarterly*, 1st series, vol. 9, no. 2, p. 128; entry for George Wythe, *American National Biography*.

'court records which have survived': Hemphill, pp. 47-8.

2. Williamsburg

'compared its development unfavorably with Pennsylvania's': Andrew Burnaby, *Travels through the Middle Settlements in North-America*, p. 19, facsimile copy.

'Exceedingly beautiful cocks were produced': Isaac, Rhys, *The Transformation of Virginia 1740-1790*, p. 102. Elkanah Watson's cockfight was in Southampton County, though given that breeders traveled with their birds to event in different counties, his description would equally apply to the Williamsburg pit.

'noted that its elite were': Burnaby, p. 19.

'Benjamin Waller. A member of Virginia's elite': Colonial Williamsburg Interpreter, Colonial Williamsburg Foundation, vol. 23, p. 16; C. W. Tazewell, ed., Tazewell and Allied Families: Scrapbooks; Norma Lois Peterson, *Littleton Waller Tazewell*, p. 2.

'The Warwick Court records show': William E. Hemphill, *George Wythe, the Colonial Briton*, p. 55.

'in 1752 he appeared for his uncle Stephen Dewey': William Clarkin, *Serene Patriot: A Life of George Wythe*, pp. 12-3.

'His head was very round': George William Munford, *The Two Parsons*, pp. 416-7.

'Robert Dinwiddie, a deputy for a stay-at-home governor': Hemphill, p. 63.

'the master of a little vessel': Clarkin, p. 14.

'Dinwiddie was 'wounded to the soul': Imogene E. Brown, *American Aristides, A Biography of George Wythe*, p. 38.

3. Colonel Washington

'the Taliaferros had been established': 'The Taliaferro Family', *William and Mary Quarterly*, vol. 20, no. 3, (1912).

'notoriously known to be the property of the Crown': John R. Alden, *George Washington, a Biography*, p. 17.

Quotes from Washington: Alden p. 27; James T. Flexner, *George Washington: The Forge of Experience*, p. 89; Henry Wiencek, *An Imperfect God*, p. 62.

'(he's a 'raw laddie')': Marcus Cunliffe, *George Washington, Man and Monument*, p. 45.

'His last words were': Ronald W. Clark, *Benjamin Franklin, a Biography*, p. 115.

'Wythe promised that, if elected, he would serve without payment': H. R. McIlwaine, *Journals of the House of Burgesses*, p. 360-1.

'He had received only one vote!': Hemphill, William E., *George Wythe, the Colonial Briton*, p. 166.

'As a judge,' wrote B. B. Minor': B. B. Minor, 'Memoir of the Author', *Decision of Cases in Virginia by the High Court of Chancery*, p. xxv.

'compassion ought not influence a judge': Minor, p. xxv.

'When he stood in 1758 for the same seat': James Thomas Flexner, *George Washington, the Forge of Experience.* p 211; Henry Wiencek, An Imperfect God, p. 151.

'He received eight votes out of 242': Robert B. Kirtland, *George Wythe: Lawyer, Revolutionary, Judge*, p. 77.

'Sit down, Mr Washington, your modesty': William Wirt, *Sketches of the Life and Character of Patrick Henry*, p. 45.

'Roger Atkinson one of Washington's contemporaries, wrote': Wiencek, p. 150.

'I served with General Washington in the legislature': Flexner, p. 251.

'He was the successful bidder': W. W. Abbot, ed., *The Papers of George Washington*, vol. 6, pp. 409-10n.

'The commander in chief took time out': William Clarkin, *Serene Patriot: A Life of George Wythe*, p. 76.

4. The Young Jefferson

'Francis Fauquier, was another substitute governor': George Reese, ed., *The Official Papers of Francis Fauquier*, p. xxxv; 'A Portrait of Governor Fauquier', *Fauquier Historical Society Bulletin*, July 1924, p. 346.

'Pleading for better treatment of American Indians': Reese, p. xlviii n24.

'Said Burk's his *History of Virginia*': John Daly Burk, *History of Virginia*, vol. iii, pp. 333-4.

'Sparks flew at a faculty meeting in 1762': Martin Richard Clagett, *William Small, 1734-75, Teacher, Mentor, Scientist*, p. 160.

'Historian Martin Clagett writes': Clagett, p. 157.

'he found slavery 'in its nature disagreeable' and 'The Governor's answer appeared in his will': 'Francis Fauquier's Will', *The William and Mary Quarterly*, Vol. 8, No. 3 (1900), pp. 175-6.

'Jefferson wrote to a friend about this tragedy': William E. Hemphill, George Wythe, the Colonial Briton, p. 116.

'When I recollect at 14 years of age': Brodie, p. 39.

5. Revolution in the Air

About the Parson's Cause and the Two Penny Act: Norman K. Risjord, *Forging the American Republic 1760-1815*, pp. 78-80, George E. Howard, *Preliminaries of the Revolution 1763-75* p. 90ff; Richard R. Beeman, *Patrick Henry*, pp. 13-5;.

'Fauquier felt obliged to write to his London masters': Beeman, p. 14.

'He came out and called with great violence': Henry Wiencek, *An Imperfect God*, pp.142-3; Richard L. Morton, *Colonial Virginia, 1710-63*, vol. II, p. 802.

'The case was heard in 1763': 'The Parson's Cause', *William and Mary Quarterly*, series 1, vol. 20 p. 172; Arthur P. Scott, 'The Constitutional Aspects of the Parson's Cause', *Political Science Quarterly*, Vol. 31, No. 4, 1916, p. 566.

'His manners had something of the coarseness [ANNOTATION: ON '2013-04-11T07:38:46' NOTE: 'missing word?' NOTE: 'The spelling in both words is correct' NOTE: 'I have restored about the seal, but not about the oath. I think it is a nice chapter introduction and shows the relationship between W & J.' NOTE: ']': William Wirt, *Sketches of the Life and Character of Patrick Henry*, p. 14.

'Wythe, after some hesitation, signed': William Clarkin, *Serene Patriot: A Life of George Wythe*, p 30; Hemphill, p. 106.

'Defiantly Henry stood and praised the Two Penny Act': Morton, pp. 811-2.

'Jefferson once haughtily observed that Henry': Paul L. Ford, ed., *The Writings of Thomas Jefferson*, vol. xi, p. 233.

'William Wirt, conceded that Henry': Wirt, p. 18.

'Wrote Wirt: he understood the human': Wirt, p. 76.

'the case of the stunned turkey and the well-fed waggoner': Wirt, p. 372.

'a man accused of seizing two steers from a Mr Hook': Wirt, pp. 373-5.

'According to Jefferson, Wythe wrote': Wirt, Appendix.

'It defiantly insisted that': Wirt, Appendix.

'Student-at-law, Thomas Jefferson, was observing proceedings': Wirt, p. 53, Andrew A. Lipscomb and Albert Berg, eds, *The Writings of Thomas Jefferson*, vol.14, pp. 163-4.

'From this moment he [Henry] had no friends': William Wirt, *Sketches of the Life and Character of Patrick Henry*, p. 55.

'Jefferson stood in the doorway, listing in awe': Wirt, pp. 60-2; Alan Pell Crawford, 'The Upstart, the Speaker, the Scandals, and Scotchtown,' *Colonial Williamsburg Journal*, Winter 2001-2, p. 3.

'The fifth, much stronger, passed by one vote': Henry. S. Commager, *Documents of American History*, online, p. 56.

'By god I would have given 500 guineas': Wirt, p. 61.

'The version of this unknown Frenchman': 'Journal of a French Traveler in the Colonies, 1765', *The American Historical Review*, p. 745.

'The mythical sixth read': Commager, p. 56.

'The *Maryland Gazette* even published': Commager, p. 56; Edmund S. Morgan and Helen M. Morgan, *The Stamp Act Crisis*, p. 95.

6. Death and Taxes

'After outlining what had happened in the house, he commented': George Reese, ed., *The Official Papers of Francis Fauquier*, p. 1250.

'his attention was seized by the sight of a mob': Reece, pp.1291-3.

'In the words of Fauquier': Reece, pp. 1292-3.

'I even have not the common notice of there being such an Act': Reece, pp. 1295.

'Britain passed the Declaratory Act of 1766': Commager, pp. 60-1.

For Robinson and Chiswell affair: Alan Pell Crawford, 'The Upstart, the Speaker, the Scandals, and Scotchtown,' *Colonial Williamsburg Journal*, Winter 2001-2, online.

'Everything is become a matter of heat and party faction': Carl Bridenbaugh, 'Violence and Virtue in Virginia, 1766', *Proceedings of Massachusetts Historical Society*, vol. lxxvi, p. 22.

'Sir: the suit wherein you were pleased': 'M. L. Weems, 'The Honest Lawyer', The Times, Charleston, July 1, 1806, reprinted in *William and Mary Quarterly*, 1st series, vol. 25, no. 1 (1916), p. 19. Parson Weems is not regarded by historians as the most reliable of sources. His anachronistic reference to a 'fifty dollar note' also raises doubts.

'he penned a gushing letter of support': William E. Hemphill, *George Wythe, the Colonial Briton*, pp. 222.

'would be in any degree pleasing to Doctor Franklin': Leonard W. Labaree ed. *The Papers of Benjamin Franklin*. New Haven: Yale University Press, 1969.

'From a London merchant he ordered a 'robe': Imogene E. Brown, *American Aristides*, p. 86.

'he wrote to John Norton and Sons of London': William E. Hemphill, *George Wythe, the Colonial Briton*, pp. 236.

'apart from a reference in the *Virginia Gazette* of William Rind': *Virginia Gazette* (Rind) March 10, 1768.

'the ablest man who ever filled that office': Thomas Jefferson, *Autobiography*, p.2.

'Fauquier's last will and testament': 'Francis Fauquier's Will', *The William and Mary Quarterly*, Vol. 8, No. 3 (1900), pp. 174.

'An audit of Fauquier's estate': George Reese, ed., *The Official Papers of Francis Fauquier*, p. xlviiin.

7. Uncertain Times

'I have nothing to ask, but that you consider well': Douglas Southall Freeman, *George Washington, a Biography*, vol. 3, p. 217.

'Jefferson appeared for Samuel Howell': *Howell v. Netherland*, Jefferson's Reports 90.

'Jefferson backed a measure of the most adventurous kind': Paul L. Ford, ed., *The Writings of Thomas Jefferson*, vol. xi, p. 477.

'Mr Speaker and Gentlemen of the House of Burgesses, I have heard': William Wirt, *Sketches of the Life and Character of Patrick Henry*, pp. 86-7.

'He [Wythe] carried his love of antiquity': Wirt, p. 48.

'He had not indeed the poetical fancy': Jefferson, *Autobiography*, p. 26.

'With your Lordship's assistance': B. B. Minor, 'Memoir of the Author', *Decision of Cases in Virginia by the High Court of Chancery*, pp. xvi-ii.

'You had better not do that': Minor, p. xxxiv.

'in a scheme to raffle slaves': Henry Wiencek, *An Imperfect God*, p. 178; *Virginia Gazette* (Rind) April 14, 1768, Oct 19, 1769, November 23, 1769; *Colonial Williamsburg Journal*, Colonial Williamsburg Foundation, 2004, p. 56.

'the grand name of Hamilton Usher St. George': Public Records Office, Great Britain A.O. 13/8-10, PRO. 247; Brown, pp. 93-4.

8. Fasting, Humiliation and Prayer

'I have in my hand a paper published': Julian Boyd, ed., *The Papers of Thomas Jefferson*, vol. 1, p. 106n.

'Jefferson declared it a great success': Thomas Jefferson, *Autobiography*, p. 5.

'Jefferson had written in rage': Boyd, vol. 1, pp. 121, 134, 135.

'Dunmore, perceiving a 'danger': John E. Selby, *The Revolution in Virginia* 1775-83, p. 17.

'Chief Logan, now a prisoner of the militia, wrote': Thomas Jefferson, *Notes on Virginia*, pp. 188-9.

'Considering the article of tea': Henry. S. Commager, *Documents of American History*, p. 80.

'There's not a Justice of Peace in Virginia that acts': John Dos Passos, *The Head and Heart of Thomas Jefferson*, p. 169.

'Henry demanded to be heard': William Wirt, *Sketches of the Life and Character of Patrick Henry*, pp. 116-24; *Colonial Williamsburg Journal*, Colonial Williamsburg Foundation, Winter 2002-3, p. 21ff.

'The last order of business at the convention': Wirt, p. 129.

'rape of the powder': Morpurgo, J. E., *Their Majesties' Royall Colledge.* Williamsburg: College of William and Mary, 1976, p. 171.

'he 'would issue a declaration freeing': Selby, pp. 2-3.

'For three days there was a tense standoff': Wirt, pp. 142-3; Selby, pp. 4-5.

'He issued a proclamation declaring Henry': Wirt, p. 146; proclamation reproduced in Beeman, pp. 57-58.

'Mr Purdie of the *Virginia Gazette* wrote': Selby, p. 42.

'William Tatham wrote about it in jocular fashion': Boyd, vol. 4, p. 274.

'Mrs Rathell's decision to leave Virginia': *Official Guide to Colonial Williamsburg*, Colonial Williamsburg Foundation, 2004, p. 117.

9. Mr. Wythe Goes to Congress

'According to a letter Richard Henry Lee wrote to Washington': William Clarkin, *Serene Patriot: A Life of George Wythe*, p. 96.

'He wrote a friend describing Wythe': Imogene E. Brown, *American Aristides, A Biography of George Wythe*, pp. 115-6.

'In one striking paragraph': Catherine Drinker Bowen, John Adams and the American Revolution, p. 560, Brown, p. 128.

'In complaint Wythe told Congress': Clarkin, p. 108.

'There seems no reason now to expect an accommodation': *Journals of the Continental Congress*, Library of Congress, vol. 4, pp. 401-2.

10. Independence for Virginia

'Dunmore was pleased to report to London that 'between two to three hundred': Cassandra Pybus, *Epic Journeys of Freedom*, p. 11.

'The document that Jefferson placed in Wythe's hands': *Richmond Enquirer*, 1806 June 20. This historic document was thought lost until found in Wythe's papers after his death in 1806.

'Edmund Pendleton made a suggestion': David J. Mays, *Edmund Pendleton A Biography, 1721-1803*, vol. 2, p. 122; John E. Selby, The Revolution in Virginia 1775-83, p. 108.

'Wythe, who reported back to Jefferson': Julian Boyd, ed., *The Papers of Thomas Jefferson*, vol. 1, pp. 476-7.

'Jefferson, writing from Philadelphia to his friend John Page': Boyd, p. 482.

11. Reformers and Revisors

'Make use of the house and furniture': Julian Boyd, ed., *The Papers of Thomas Jefferson*, vol. 1, p. 585.

'He immediately wrote back from Philadelphia': Boyd, vol. 1, p. 603.

'Thrown out (wrote Jefferson) would be statutes': Thomas Jefferson, *Autobiography*, p. 31.

'he had read to his men the famous opening words of a new pamphlet of Tom Paine': John Keane, *Tom Paine, a Political Life*, p. 145.

'In ten days Jefferson rewrote the entire judicial system': Daniel J. Boornstin, 'Review of Jefferson Papers', *William and Mary Quarterly*, series 3, vol. 7, p. 603.

'Washington wrote plaintively to Benjamin Harrison': Fitzpatrick, John C., ed., *The Writings of George Washington*, pp. 464, 467.

'With deep sarcasm, Richard Henry Lee pictured Jefferson': Fawn M. Brodie, *Thomas Jefferson: An Intimate History*, p. 132.

'Said Jefferson of Wythe's appointment': Jefferson, p. 29.

The bills written by the Revisors appear in Boyd, vol. 2, p. 305ff.

'I have got thro' the bill 'for proportioning crimes': Boyd, vol. 2, pp. 229-230.

'Those who labor in the earth': Thomas Jefferson, *Notes on Virginia*, pp. 290-1.

'I sincerely believe... that banking establishments are more dangerous': Andrew A. Lipscomb and Albert Berg, eds, *The Writings of Thomas Jefferson*, vol. 15, p. 23.

'To this Jefferson testily observed 'that if the eldest son': Jefferson, p. 30.

'Madison regarded the Revisors' bills as 'a mine of legislative wealth': Merill D. Peterson, *Thomas Jefferson and the New Nation: A Biography*, p. 112.

12. "Hither You Shall Go, but No Further!"

'As Jefferson once famously declared': Andrew Burstein, *Jefferson's Secrets*, p. 239.

'The spirit of skepticism which so much prevailed': 'Glimpses of Old College Life', *William and Mary Quarterly,* series 1, vol. 8., p. 159.

'Our new institution at the college has': Julian Boyd, ed., The Papers of Thomas Jefferson, vol. 3, p. 507.

'and, to the usurping branch of the legislature': *C'th v. Caton & al.*, 4 Call 8.

13. Yorktown

'In ten minutes not a white man': Cassandra Pybus, *Epic Journeys of Freedom*, p. 44.

'Johann Ewald, a Hessian officer, was troubled': *Colonial Williamsburg Interpreter*, Colonial Williamsburg Foundation, 20, p. 10.

'St George made a claim to the Office of American Claims': Public Records Office, Great Britain, A.O. 13/8-10, PRO. 247, A.O. 13/32, PRO 254; A.O. 13/33, PRO 255.

'I know not a place, at which my time would pass': Boyd, vol. 6, p. 144.

'Send me a description of the other servants': Boyd, p. 144.

'There are, in one apartment of the college': Imogene E. Brown, *American Aristides, A Biography of George Wythe*, p. 211-2.

'Wythe explained that Washington 'was very civil': Boyd, vol. 6, p. 144.

'The professor of Mathematics and Natural Philosophy': Julian P. Boyd, 'The Murder of George Wythe', *William and Mary Quarterly*, p. 515.

'Peter Carr ... with me reads Aeschylus': Boyd, vol 10, , p. 593.

'I return you a thousand thousand thanks': Boyd, vol. 12, p. 129-30.

'You did not mention the size of the plate': 'The Taliaferro Family', *William and Mary Quarterly*, vol. 20, no. 3, (1912), p. 213.

14. Constitution

'It is now too late to answer the question': Julian Boyd, ed., *The Papers of Thomas Jefferson*, vol. 12, p. 128.

'stayed away because (as he said) 'he smelt a rat': Catherine Drinker Bowen, *Miracle at Philadelphia*, p. 18.

'It is too probable that no plan we propose': Carl Van Doren, *The Great Rehearsal*, p. 19.

'they began their deliberations by so abominable a precedent': Carl Van Doren, *The Great Rehearsal*, p. 36.

'Washington, who had not spoken so far, broke his silence': Bowen, p. 98-9; Susan Dunn, *Sister Revolutions*, p. 128.

'Virginian George Mason threw up a conundrum': Carl Van Doren, *The Great Rehearsal*, p. 43.

'fifty pounds, 'to be distributed to such of his colleagues': Bowen, p. 27.

'he was most political when he was at his most philosophical': Carl Van Doren, *The Great Rehearsal*, p. 126-7; Ronald W. Clark, *Benjamin Franklin, A Biography*, p. 408-9; Max Farrand, *Records of the Federal Convention of 1787*, June 2, p. 82.

'Mrs. W's state of health is so low': Colonial Williamsburg Questions, Answers from the files, Colonial Williamsburg Foundation Williamsburg, 1991.

'The *Pennsylvania Packet* commented': Bowen, p. 185.

'he would 'sooner chop off his right hand': entry for George Mason, *American National Biography.*

15. Ratification

'However apart from advising Madison': Edmund S. Morgan, *The Genuine Article*, p. 199.

'Richard Henry Lee wrote an open letter': Carl Van Doren, *The Great Rehearsal*, Alexandra, 1981, p. 219.

'William Wirt remembered the passions unleashed': William Wirt, *Patrick Henry: Life, Correspondence and Speeches*, p. 261.

'most exhausting one for an old man,' wrote Tazewell': Imogene E. Brown, *American Aristides, A Biography of George Wythe*, p. 237.

'Mason demanded to know': Helen Hill, *George Mason Constitutionalist*, p. 226.

'according to the Virginian scholar Hugh Grigsby': Hugh Blair Grigsby, *The History of the Virginia Federal Convention of 1788*, vol. 1, p. 307.

'If I shall be in the minority': Grisby, p. 342-3; Bowen, p. 304.

'In bewilderment, he confessed': Susan Dunn, *Sister Revolutions*, p. 109.

'He told Wythe 'I know they have been': David John Mays, *The Letters and Papers of Edmund Pendleton*, (1967), p. 677.

'Wythe found little to correct': Mays (1967), p. 690-1.

16. The House on Shockoe Hill

'When you can attend to trifles, tell me': Julian Boyd, ed., *The Papers of Thomas Jefferson*, vol. 18, p. 486.

'I think the allusion to the story of Sisamnes': Boyd, vol. 19, p. 556.

'Mr Wythe has abandoned the college of Wm. & Mary': Julian Boyd, vol. 16, p. 25-6.

'I attended him every morning very early': Colonial Williamsburg Questions, Answers from the files, Colonial Williamsburg Foundation Williamsburg, 1966, p. 4.

'Munford wrote to a young friend, John Coalter', Colonial Williamsburg Questions, Answers, p.3; Imogene E. Brown, *American Aristides, A Biography of George Wythe*, p. 270.

'Records show that several years later, in 1797': Phillip P. Morgan, 'Interracial Sex in the Chesapeake', in Jan Ellen Lewis and Peter S. Onuf eds., *Sally Hemings and Thomas Jefferson*, p. 58.

'Many a time have I heard him': George William Munford, *The Two Parsons*, p. 364. In this extract he is quoting his father William Munford.

'he preferred to read it for himself': George William Munford, *The Two Parsons*, p. 417-8.

'Munford wrote of the three scholars': Munford, p. 357.

'I remember that it cost me a great deal of labor,' wrote Clay': 'B. B. Minor, of the Author', *Decision of Cases in Virginia by the High Court of Chancery*, p. xxxiii.

'Mr. Wythe's personal appearance and his personal habits': Minor, p. xxxv.

'Judge Beverly Tucker related two amusing stories': Minor, p. xxx-xxxin.

'Judge Tucker put Wythe's avoidance of conversation': William Clarkin, *Serene Patriot: A Life of George Wythe*, p. 173.

'In a thirteen-year period, appeals were taken from 150': David J. Mays, *Edmund Pendleton A Biography, 1721-1803*, vol. 2, p. 290; John T. Noonan, *Persons and Masks of the Law*, p. 32.

'British Debts Case of 1793': *Page v. Pendleton and Lyons* (1793), Wythe Rep. 127. The quotes are on pp. 127-8, 132.

'If he went wrong they all went wrong together': Mays (1952), p. 297.

'Alegebraists indeed, in resolving problems': *Hill v. Braxton*, Wythe Rep. 18.

Maze v. Hamilton: Wythe Rep. 36, 44.

'Wythe admitted that his original decree was erroneous': *Burnside v. Reid*, Wythe Rep. 51, 53.

'1. It is economical, for by it are saved the expenses': *Hylton v. Hamilton*, Wythe Rep. 88.

'John Randolph of Roanoke, once said': *Southern Literary Messenger*, vol. 12, issue 7, 1846, p. 447.

'one might read of what the ambassadors': Minor, p. xxv-xxvii.

'It concerned religion, property and the Virginia constitution': *Page v. Pendleton and Lyons* (1793), Wythe Rep. 127. The quotes are on pp. 127-8, 132.

17. Slavery

'Wythe had a victory over the Chief Justice': *Hinde v. Pendleton*, Wythe Rep. 145.

'There is yet one part of the Chancellor's decree': *Pleasants v. Peasants* (1799): 2 Call 289.

'Governor Monroe received a letter from Vice President Jefferson': Virginius Dabney, *Richmond, The Story of a City*, p. 57.

'It concerned President Jefferson': *Richmond Recorder*, September 1, 1802.

'Meantime bawdy ballads': Fawn M. Brodie, *Thomas Jefferson: An Intimate History*, p. 354-5.

'Wythe's housekeeper had accumulated considerable wealth': Andrew Nunn McKnight, 'Lydia Broadnax, Slave and Free Woman of Color', p. 19.

'lent money to Captain Tinsley': Robert B. Kirtland, *George Wythe: Lawyer, Revolutionary, Judge*, p. 150.

'the Dove Memorandum': Brock Collection, folder 4, Box 133, Henry E. Huntington Library and Art Gallery, San Marino.

'Lydia Broadnax ... understood his wants and ways': George William Munford, *The Two Parsons*, p. 417.

'in 1803, Wythe wrote a will': Minor, p. xxxvii.

18. His Last Great Case

'Wythe's most famous decision on slavery': *Hudgins v. Wrights*, 1 Hen. and M. 134.

'Elderly citizens with long memories came': Tucker-Coleman Collection, Box 71, Swem Library, College of William and Mary.

'Our constitution ... is totally repugnant to the idea': Henry. S. Commager, *Documents of American History*, p. 110.

'On the hearing, the late Chancellor perceiving': *Hudgins v. Wrights*, 1 Hen. and M. 134.

19. Murder!

'a letter Elizabeth Cabell sent to her sister': John P. Kennedy, *Memoirs of the Life of William Wirt*, vol. 1, p. 142.

Will of January 19, 1806: Minor p. xxxvii.

'The above narrative appears in the pages': George William Munford, The Two Parsons, p. 423.

'I fear I am getting old, Lyddy': George William Munford, *The Two Parsons*, p. 423.

'The next person to arrive on that Sunday': For the description of Wythe and Brown's illness and the investigation of Sweney's alleged involvement see the record of the proceedings of the Richmond Court of Hustings in W. Edwin Hemphill's 'Examination of George Wythe Swinney for Forgery and Murder', p. 551 ff and George William Munford's *The Two Parsons.*

'according to the doctor, complained of a 'great thirst': Munford, pp. 422, 424.

'Enter a neighbor, William Claiborne': Claiborne was the father of William C. C. Claiborne, the Governor of the Territory of Orleans, and later governor of Louisiana.

'The old gentleman was suffering intense agony': Munford, p. 424.

'Dr Foushee came to the door': Munford, p. 426.

'The old man 'drew a long death—and pathetically said': Julian P. Boyd, 'The Murder of George Wythe', *William and Mary Quarterly,* p. 527.

'That afternoon Randolph returned with the codicil': B.B. Minor, 'Memoir of the Author', in George Wythe, *Decision of Cases in Virginia by the High Court of Chancery,* p. xxxix.

'George Sweney was brought before Mayor Carrington and five of Richmond's aldermen': W. Edwin Hemphill's 'Examination of George Wythe Swinney for Forgery and Murder', p. 551 ff.

'DuVal decided it was time to inform President Jefferson': Exchange of letters DuVal & Jefferson: Special Collection of the International Center for Jefferson Studies, Monticello, Va. The originals are in the Jefferson Papers in the Library of Congress: 28475, 27874, 27882, 27898, 27915, 27941, 28044, 28523, 28533.

'In an emotional funeral oration': *Richmond Enquirer,* 1806, June 13.

20. A Trial and an Appeal

'a preliminary hearing by the Court of Hustings in Richmond': W. Edwin Hemphill, 'Examination of George Wythe Swinney for Forgery and Murder', *William and Mary Quarterly,* 3rd series, vol. 12, no. 4, p. 551ff.

'Dr. McClurg testified (as transcribed by the court recorder)': Hemphill, p. 560-1.

'The venerable Wythe is one who has fallen more immediately under my eye': William Browne to Joseph Prentice (letter) of Sept 24, 1804, University of Virginia, Special Collection.

'He had no wish, he wrote to a friend': Hemphill, p. 544n.

'To James Monroe he said: 'The young villain': Hemphill, p. 551n.

'Judge Nelson says I ought not to hesitate': John P. Kennedy, *Memoirs of the Life of William Wirt*, vol. 1, p. 143.

'Thus the whole legal paraphernalia of Virginia': Fawn M. Brodie, *Thomas Jefferson: An Intimate History*, pp. 92, 390-1.

'It is not my desire that this unfortunate': George William Munford, *The Two Parsons*, p. 426-7.

'article published in 1999 in the journal of Colonial Williamsburg': *Colonial Williamsburg Journal*, Colonial Williamsburg Foundation, 99, p. 11ff.

'It also made sense to the six judges': *C'lth v. Swinney* 1806 Va. 146.

'Doctor Dove in his Memorandum': Brock Collection, folder 4, Box 133, Henry E. Huntington Library and Art Gallery, San Marino.

'B. B. Minor said something similar': B.B. Minor, 'Memoir of the Author', in George Wythe, *Decision of Cases in Virginia by the High Court of Chancery*, p. xxviii.

'Yet in 1807 she wrote to Thomas Jefferson': Jack McLaughlin, *To His Excellency Thomas Jefferson*, pp. 128-9.

'In 1820 she wrote a will': Andrew Nunn McKnight, 'Lydia Broadnax, Slave and Free Woman of Color', p. 23.

"Is not that a mistake?' he said': *Hudgins v. Wrights*, 1 Hen. and M. 134.

'He promptly altered his final address': The bench notes of the appeal are held in the Tucker-Coleman Collection, Box 71, Swem Library, College of William and Mary, Va.

'The leading opinion was written by St. George Tucker': *Hudgins v. Wrights*, 1 Hen. and M. 136ff.

'Nature has stampt upon the *African'*: *Hudgins v. Wrights*, 1 Hen. and M. p. 139-40.

Epilogue

'President Jefferson wrote to Major DuVal': Exchange of letters DuVal & Jefferson: Special Collection of the International Center for Jefferson Studies, Monticello, Va. The originals are in the Jefferson Papers in the Library of Congress: 28475, 27874, 27882, 27898, 27915, 27941, 28044, 28523, 28533.

Postscript

Eugene D. Genovese, *Roll, Jordon Roll, the World the Slaves Made*, p. 616.

'a special punishment for poisoners': Julian Boyd, ed., *The Papers of Thomas Jefferson*, vol. 2, p. 494.

'Pendleton to a slave named Cupid': John T. Noonan, *Persons and Masks of the Law,* p.36; David J. Mays, *Edmund Pendleton A Biography, 1721-1803*, vol. 1, p. 43.

Select References

The best survey of George Wythe's life is Imogene E. Brown's *American Aristides: A Biography of George Wythe*. Two shorter and less academic volumes are Joyce Blackburn's *George Wythe of Williamsburg* and William Clarkin's *Serene Patriot: A Life of George Wythe*. Alonzo Thomas Dill's *George Wythe, Teacher of Liberty* conscientiously schedules the facts of Wythe but drains him and the times of life.

Two excellent volumes on Wythe which emerged from the academy are Robert Kirtland's *George Wythe: Lawyer, Revolutionary, Judge*, published as part of the Garland series of outstanding dissertations, and W. Edwin Hemphill's doctoral dissertation, which tracks the first fifty years of Wythe's life in "George Wythe, the Colonial Briton: A Biographical Study of the Pre-Revolutionary Era."

Finally, I should make mention of two well-researched essays on the murder of Wythe, which appeared in 1955 in the *William and Mary Quarterly*—namely Julian P. Boyd's "The Murder of George Wythe" and W. Edwin Hemphill's "Examination of George Wythe Swinney for Forgery and Murder." Both essays were reprinted in *The Murder of George Wythe, Two Essays*.

Manuscripts

Browne, William to Joseph Prentice, (letter): Sept 24, 1804, University of Virginia, Special Collection.

Dove Memorandum: Brock Collection, folder 4, Box 133, Henry E. Huntington Library and Art Gallery, San Marino.

Hudgins v. Wrights, Appeal Papers: Tucker-Coleman Collection, Box 71, Swem Library, College of William and Mary.

St. George's Claim: Public Records Office, Great Britain A.O. 13/8-10, PRO. 247, A.O. 13/32, PRO 254, A.O. 13/33, PRO 255.

DuVal to Jefferson re Wythe's death: copies in Special Collection of the International Center for Jefferson Studies, Monticello, Va. The originals are in the Jefferson Papers in the Library of Congress: 28475, 27874, 27882, 27898, 27915, 27941, 28044, 28523, 28533.

Articles

Anderson, D. R. "The Teacher of Jefferson and Marshall." *The South Atlantic Quarterly*, vol. xv., 1916.

_____. "Jefferson and the Virginia Constitution." *The American Historical Review*, vol. 21, no. 4, 1916.

Boornstin, Daniel J. "Review of Jefferson Papers." *William and Mary Quarterly*, series 3, vol. 7, 1950.

Boyd, Julian P. "The Murder of George Wythe." *William and Mary Quarterly*, 3rd series, vol. 12, no. 4, 1955.

Bridenbaugh, Carl. *Violence and Virtue in Virginia, 1766*, Massachusetts Historical Society, vol. lxxvi, 1964.

Carter, Landon. "Diary of Landon Carter." *William & Mary Quarterly*, vols. xv–xvi, 1907–8.

Chandler, J. A.C. "Jefferson and William and Mary." *William and Mary Quarterly*, 2nd series, vol. 14, no. 4, 1934.

Colbourn, H. Trevor. "Thomas Jefferson's Use of the Past." *William and Mary Quarterly*, 3rd series, vol. 15, no. 1, 1958.

Cullen, Charles T. "New Light on John Marshall's Legal education and Admission to the Bar." *The American Journal of Legal History*, vol. xvi, 1972.

"Descendants of John Camm." *William and Mary Quarterly*, 1st series, vol. 4, no. 1, 1895.

Dreisbach, Daniel L. "George Mason's Pursuit of Religious Liberty in Revolutionary Virginia." *The Virginia Magazine of History and Biography*, vol. 108, iss. 1, 2000.

"Francis Fauquier's Will." *William and Mary Quarterly*, vol. 8, no. 3, 1900.

Hemphill, W. Edwin. "Examination of George Wythe Swinney for Forgery and Murder." *William and Mary Quarterly*, 3rd series, vol. 12, no. 4, 1955.

Holton, Woody. "Rebel Against Rebel." *Virginian Magazine of History and Biography*, vol. 105, no. 2, 1997.

Isaac, Rhys. "Religion and Authority: Problems of the Anglican Establishment in Virginia in the Era of the Great Awakening and the Parsons' Cause." *William and Mary Quarterly*, 3rd series, vol. 30, no.1, 1973.

James, Sydney V. "The Impact of the American Revolution on Quakers' Ideas about their Sect." *William and Mary Quarterly*, 3rd series, vol. 19, no. 3, 1962.

Kirtland, Robert B. "Keep Your Eye on the Bastards: Early Virginia's attitude Towards Lawyers." *Toledo Law Review*, vol. 14, No. 3, 1983.

McKnight, Andrew Nunn. "Lydia Broadnax, Slave and Free Woman of Color." *Southern Studies*, vol. v, numbers I and II, 1994.

O'Brien, William. *"Did the Jennison Case Outlaw Slavery in Massachusetts?" William and Mary Quarterly*, 3rd series, vol. 17, No. 2, 1960.

Philyaw, L. Scott. "A Slave for Every Soldier: The Strange History of Virginia's Forgotten Recruitment Act of 1 January 1781." *Virginian Magazine of History and Biography*, vol. 109, no. 4, 2001.

Scott, Arthur P. "The Constitutional Aspects of the Parson's Cause." *Political Science Quarterly*, vol. 31, No. 4, 1916.

Shepard, E. Lee. "Lawyers Look at Themselves: Professional Consciousness and the Virginian Bar, 1770–1850." *The American Journal of Legal History*, vol. 25, No. 1, 1981.

"Sweeney Family." *William and Mary Quarterly*, vol. 16, no. 4, 1908.

"The Taliaferro Family." *William and Mary Quarterly*, vol. 20, no. 3, 1912.

Tachau, Mary K. Bonsteel, "George Washington and the Reputation of Edmund Randolph." *Journal of American History*, vol. 73, No. 1, 1982.

Tyler, Lyon G. "Ancestry of George Wythe." *The William and Mary Quarterly Historical Papers*, vol. 2, no. 1, 1893.

_____. "Virginians Voting in the Colonial Period." *William and Mary Quarterly Historical Magazine*, vol. 6, no. 1, 1897.

Wenger, Mark R. "Thomas Jefferson, the College of William and Mary, and the University of Virginia." *The Virginia Magazine of History and Biography*, vol. 103, iss. 3, 1995.

"Will of Richard Taliaferro." *William and Mary Quarterly*, vol. 12, no. 2, 1903.

Books and Dissertations

Adams, Henry. *The United States in 1800*. New York: Cornell University Press, 1955.

Alden, John R. *George Washington, a Biography*. Baton Rouge: Louisiana State University Press, 1984.

Andrews, Charles M. *The Colonial Background of the American Revolution*. New Haven: Yale University Press, 1958.

Beeman, Richard R. *Patrick Henry*. New York: McGraw-Hill, 1974.

Blackburn, Joyce. *George Wythe of Williamsburg*. New York: Harper & Row, 1975.

Blanton, Wydham B. *Medicine in Virginia in the Eighteenth Century*. Richmond: Garrett & Maddie, 1981.

Boardman, Fon W. Jr. *American and the Virginia Dynasty 1800–1825*. New York: Henry Z. Walck, 1974.

Bowden, James. *The History of the Society of Friends in America*. New York: Arno Press, 1972.

Bowen, Catherine Drinker. *Miracle at Philadelphia*. New York: The American Past, 1986.

_____. *John Adams and the American Revolution*. Boston: Little, Brown, 1950.

Bowers, Claude G. *The Young Jefferson*. Boston: Houghton Mifflin, 1945.

Boyd, Julian, ed. *The Papers of Thomas Jefferson*. Princeton: Princeton University Press, 1950 ff.

_____ and W. Edwin Hemphill. *The Murder of George Wythe, Two Essays*. Williamsburg: Institute of Early American History and Culture, 1955.

Breen, T. H. *Tobacco Culture*. Princeton: Princeton University Press, 1985.

Brodie, Fawn M. *Thomas Jefferson: An Intimate History*. New York: Norton, 1974.

Brown, Imogene E. *American Aristides, A Biography of George Wythe*. Rutherford: Fairleigh Dickinson University Press, 1981.

Burnaby, Andrew. *Travels Through the Middle Settlements in North America in the Years 1759 and 1760*. Reprint, New York: Great Seal Books, 1904.

Burstein, Andrew. *Jefferson's Secrets*. New York: Basic Books, 2005.

Burk, John Daly. *History of Virginia*. Petersburg: Dickson & Pescud, 1804–16.

Campbell, Charles. *History of the Colony and Ancient Dominion of Virginia*. Philadelphia: J. B. Lippincott, 1860.

Carson, Cary, ed. *Becoming Americans: Our Struggle to be both Free and Equal*. Williamsburg: Colonial Williamsburg Foundation, 1988.

Catterall, Helen. *Judicial Cases Concerning American Slavery*. New York: Negro Universities Press, 1968.

Chitwood, Oliver P. *Justice in Colonial Virginia*. Baltimore: John Hopkins Press, 1905.

Clark, Ronald W. *Benjamin Franklin, A Biography*. New York: Da Capo, 1983.

Clagett, Martin Richard. "William Small, 1734–75, Teacher, Mentor, Scientist," PhD thesis. Richmond: Virginia Commonwealth University, 2003.

Clarkin, William. *Serene Patriot: A Life of George Wythe*. Albany: Alan Publications, 1970.

Commager, Henry S. *Documents of American History*. New York: F. S. Crofts, 1941.

Cover, Robert. *Justice Accused*. New Haven: Yale University Press, 1976.

Cowden, Gerald Steffens. "The Randolphs of Turkey Island, A Prosopography of the First Three Generations, 1650–1806." Doctoral dissertation. Williamsburg: College of William and Mary, 1977.

Cunliffe, Marcus. *George Washington, Man and Monument*. New York: New American Library, 1958.

Dabney, Virginius. *Richmond, The Story of a City*. New York: Doubleday, 1976.

Davis, Richard Beale. *Intellectual Life in Jefferson's Virginia*. Knoxville: University Of Tennesse Press, 1978.

Davis, David Brion. *The Problem of Slavery in the Age of Revolution 1770–1823*. Ithaca: Cornell University Press, 1975.

Dewey, Frank L. *Thomas Jefferson Lawyer*. Charlottesville: University of Virginia Press, 1986.

Dill, Alonzo Thomas. *George Wythe Teacher of Liberty*. Williamsburg: Virginia Independence Bicentennial Commission, 1979.

Dos Passos, John. *The Head and Heart of Thomas Jefferson*. Garden City: Doubleday, 1954.

Dunn, Susan. *Sister Revolutions*. New York: Faber and Faber, 1999.

Egerton, Douglas R. *Gabriel's Rebellion*. Chapel Hill: University of North Carolina Press, 1993.

Elkins, Stanley M. *Slavery: A Problem in American Institutional and Intellectual Life*. New York: University of Chicago Press, 1969.

Farrand, Max, ed. *Records of the Federal Convention of 1787*. New Haven: Yale University Press, 1911.

Finkelman, Paul. *Slavery and the Founders*. New York: M. E. Sharpe, 2001.

Fitzpatrick, John C., ed. *The Writings of George Washington*. Washington: U.S. Government Printing Office, 1931.

Flexner, James Thomas. *George Washington, the Forge of Experience*. Boston: Little, Brown, 1965.

Ford, Paul L., ed. *The Writings of Thomas Jefferson*. New York: G. P. Putnam's Sons, 1898.

Freeman, Douglas Southall. *George Washington, a Biography.* New York: Charles Scribner's Sons, 1952.

Genovese, Eugene D. *Roll, Jordan Roll: The World the Slaves Made.* New York: Parthenon Books, 1974.

Glassner, Gregory K. *Adopted Son: The Life, Wit and Wisdom of William Wirt.* Madison: Kurt-Ketner Publishng, 1997.

Greene, Jack P. *Understanding the American Revolution.* Charlottesville: University Press of Virginia, 1998.

Grigsby, Hugh Blair. *The History of the Virginia Federal Convention of 1788.* Richmond: Virginia Historical Society, 1890.

Guild, Jane Purcell. *Black Laws of Virginia: A summary of the Legislative Acts of Virginia Concerning Negroes from Earliest Times to the Present.* Richmond: Afro-American Historical Association of Fauquier County, 1996.

Hatzenbuehler, Ronald L. *I Tremble for my Country: Thomas Jefferson and the Virginia Gentry.* Gainesville: University Press of Florida, 2006.

Hemphill, William E. "George Wythe, the Colonial Briton." Doctoral dissertation. Charlotesville: University of Virginia, 1937.

Hill, Helen. *George Mason, Constitutionalist.* Cambridge: Harvard University Press, 1938.

Hilldrup, Robert Leroy. *The Life and Times of Edmund Pendleton.* Chapel Hill: University of North Carolina Press, 1939.

Holmes, David L. *The Religion of the Founding Fathers.* Ash Lawn: Clements Library, 2003.

Horn, James. *A Land as God Made It.* New York: Basic Books, 2005.

Howard, George F. *Preliminaries of the Revolution 1763–75.* New York: Harper & Brothers, 1907.

Isaac, Rhys. *Landon Carter's Uneasy Kingdom.* Oxford: Oxford University Press, 2004.

_____. *The Transformation of Virginia 1740–1790.* Chapel Hill: University of North Carolina Press, 1983

Jefferson, Thomas. *Autobiography.* Online, first pub. 1821.

_____. *Notes on Virginia.* Online, first pub. 1781–2.

Jordan, Winthrop D. *White over Black: American Attitudes toward the Negro, 1550–1812.* Chapel Hill: University of North Carolina Press, 1968.

Keane, John. *Tom Paine, a Political Life.* London: Bloomsbury, 1995.

Kennedy, John P. *Memoirs of the Life of William Wirt.* Philadelphia: Lea & Blanchard, 1850.

Kirtland, Robert B. *George Wythe: Lawyer, Revolutionary, Judge.* New York: Garland, 1986.

Labaree, Leonard W., ed. *Royal Instructions to British Colonial Governors, 1670–1776.* New York: Octagon, 1935.

Lewis, Jan Ellen and Onuf, Peter S., eds. *Sally Hemings and Thomas Jefferson.* Charlottesville: University Press of Virginia, 1999.

Lipscomb, Andrew A. and Berg, Albert, eds. *The Writings of Thomas Jefferson.* Washington: Thomas Jefferson Memorial Association, 1903.

Longmore, Paul K. *The Invention of George Washington.* Charlottesville: University Press of Virginia, 1999.

Malone, Dumas. *Jefferson the Virginian.* London: Eyre and Spottiswoode, 1948.

Martin, James Kirby, ed. *Interpreting Colonial America*. New York: Harper & Row, 1978.

Mayer, Henry. *A Son of Thunder: Patrick Henry and the American Republic*. Charlottesville: University Press of Virginia, 1986.

Mayo, Bernard. *Henry Clay, Spokesman of the New West*. Boston: Houghton Mifflin, 1937.

Mays, David J. *The Letters and Papers of Edmund Pendleton*. Charlottesville: University Press of Virginia, 1967.

_____. *Edmund Pendleton: A Biography, 1721–1803*, 2 vols. Cambridge: Harvard University Press, 1952.

McColley, Robert. *Slavery and Jeffersonian Virginia*. Urbana: University of Illinois Press, 1964.

McCullough, David. *John Adams*. New York: Simon & Schuster, 2001.

McIlwaine, H.R., ed. *Journals of the House of Burgesses*. Richmond: Colonial Press, Everett Waddey Co., 1909.

McLaughlin, Jack, ed. *To His Excellency Thomas Jefferson*. New York: W. W. Norton, 1991.

Minor, B.B. "Memoir of the Author", in George Wythe's *Decision of Cases in Virginia by the High Court of Chancery*. Richmond: J. W. Randolph, 1852.

Morgan, Edmund S. *American Slavery, American Freedom: the Ordeal of Colonial Virginia*. New York: W.W. Norton, 1975.

_____. *The Genuine Article*. New York: W.W. Norton, 2004.

_____ and Morgan, Helen M. *The Stamp Act Crisis*. Chapel Hill: University of North Carolina, 1953.

Morpurgo, J.E. *Their Majesties' Royall Colledge*. Williamsburg: College of William and Mary, 1976.

Morris, Thomas D. *Southern Slavery and the Law 1619–1860*. Chapel Hill: University of North Carolina Press, 1996.

Morton, Richard L. *Colonial Virginia*. Chapel Hill: University of North Carolina Press, 1960.

Munford, George William. *The Two Parsons*. Richmond: J.D.K. Sleight, 1884.

Noonan, John T., Jr. *Persons and Masks of the Law*. New York: Farrar, Straus and Giroux, 1976.

Peterson, Norma Lois. *Littleton Waller Tazewell*. Charlottesville: University Press of Virginia, 1983.

Peterson, Merill D. *Thomas Jefferson and the New Nation: A Biography*. New York: Oxford University Press, 1970.

Pybus, Cassandra. *Epic Journeys of Freedom: Runaway Slaves of the American Revolution and their Global Quest for Liberty*. Boston: Beacon Press, 2006.

Reardon, John J. *Edmund Randolph: A Biography*. New York: Macmillan, 1975.

Reese, George, ed. *The Official Papers of Francis Fauquier*. Charlottesville, Va.: University Press of Virginia, 1980–83.

Remini, Robert V. *Henry Clay: Statesman for the Union*. New York: W. W. Norton, c. 1991.

Risjord, Norman K. *Thomas Jefferson*. Madison, Wis.: Madison House, 1994.

_____. *Forging the American Republic 1760–1815*. Reading, Mass.: Addison-Wesley, 1973.

Schurz, Carl. *Henry Clay*. New York: Houghton, Mifflin, 1899.

Selby, John E. *The Revolution in Virginia 1775–1783*. Williamsburg: Colonial Williamsburg Foundation, 2007.

_____. *Dunmore*. Williamsburg: Virginia Independence Bicentennial Commission, c. 1977.

Shewmake, Oscar L. "The Honorable George Wythe." Address delivered before the Wythe Law Club of William and Mary, December 18, 1921.

Starkey, Marion L. *The First Plantation: History of Hampton and Elizabeth City County, Virginia 1607–1887*. Hampton, Va.: Houston Printing and Publishing House, 1936.

Van Doren, Carl. *The Great Rehearsal*. Alexandra: Time-Life Books, 1981.

Wiencek, Henry. *An Imperfect God: George Washington, His Slaves and the Creation of America*. London: Macmillan, 2005.

Wilstach, Paul. *Tidewater Virginia*. New York: Tudor Publishing Company, 1945.

Wirt, William. *Sketches of the Life and Character of Patrick Henry*. Online, first pub. 1817.

INDEX

Abbott, Nelson 258, 266
Adams, John
  at Continental Congress 115, 116,
    117–8, 119, 120, 122–3, 130
  Thoughts on Government 118–20,
    130
  Vice–President and President 161,
    209–10, 211–2, 234
Adams, Samuel 84, 119, 122
Amerindians 29–30, 97–8, 157, 244–6
Andrews, Robert 157
Anglican Church: *see Church of Eng-
  land*
Arnold, Gen. Benedict
  fights for revolution 153
  fights for British 165–6

Bellini, Carlo 157, 177, 178
Ben (domestic of GW) 216, 220,
  239–40, 252
Berkeley, Norborne, Baron de Bote-
  tourt *see Botetourt*
Bland, Richard 99
Blair, John 152, 185, 198, 202
Blair, Parson 217, 258–9, 262
Boston Massacre 84–5
Boston Tea Party 93–4
Botetourt, Lord: 79–80, 81–2, 83–4,
  85 see Berkeley
Boyle, Robert 156
Braddock, Gen. Edward 29–31

Braxton Carter 130
Britain 66
  in French and Indian War 27–31,
    33–4
  Stamp Tax 55–6, 58–62, 66–9
  Import (Townshend) duties 74–5
  Boston Massacre 84–5
  Boston Tea Party 93–4
  Concord & Lexington, battles of
    105–6
  Bunker Hill, battle of 113–4
  New York, battles in 138
  Saratoga, battle of 153–4
  during revolution 159–60, 165,
    169
  Yorktown, battle of 170–2
British Debts Case 222–3
Brown, Michael 239, 252, 257, 259,
  264
Browne, William 267
Broadnax, Lydia 195, 216, 220,
  238–40, 252–5, 257, 262, 270,
  276, 282–3
  and Jefferson 275, 280
Brodie, Fawn M. 272–3
Buchanan, Parson 217, 258–9, 262
Burgesses: *see House of*
Burke, Edmund 66, 96
Burnside v Reid 224
Bunker Hill, battle of 113–4
Burnaby, Andrew, Rev. 4, 16, 18

Burr, Aaron 234–5
Burwell, Rebecca 44, 161

Cabell, William x, 220, 268
Cabell, Elizabeth 252
Callender, James 235–8, 237–8, 274
Camm, Rev. John 48–9, 155
Carr, Peter 179
Carrington, Edward 260, 265
Carrington, Paul, Judge 231–2, 276
Carter, Robert 45
Chesterville 2, 5–6, 7, 24, 89–90
    during revolution 172
    sale of 173–4
Chiswell, John 81
Church of England
    before 1776–3, 6, 8, 39–47
    after 1776 132, 145, 226
Clagett, Martin 40
Claiborne, William 257, 266
Clay, Henry 217–9, 223
Clifton, William 45
cockfights 17–8
Coles, Isaac A. 157
Committee of Safety 99
Common Hall 29, 72
Common Sense 124–5
Commonwealth v. Jennison 247–8
Concord & Lexington, battles of
    105–6
Constitution Convention, 1787–181,
    196–8
Constitution of the United States
    ratification of 208
    Bill of Rights 208–9
Continental Congress 99–100, 111ff,
    114–5, 130, 135
Cornwallis, Charles, Earl of 160, 168
C'th v. Caton & al. 162–3
Currie, Dr. James 256, 271
Cushing, William, Judge
Council, Governor's 20, 23

Dandridge, William 256, 260
Day of Fasting and Prayer 94–5
Deane, Silas 119–20
Declaration of Independence 113, 128,
    130, 134–6, 137
Declaratory Act 70
de Grasse, Admiral 169
Dewey, Stephen 6–7, 20
Dickinson, John 120, 121
Dinwiddie, Robert 21–3, 27–28, 37
Dove Memorandum 239, 275
Dunmore, John Murray, the Earl of
    Dunmore
    background 85–6
    justice of General Court 86, 88
    Indian War 97–8
    approach of revolution 95, 99,
        104, 106–7
    during revolution 128–9
    frees slaves 127–8
Dunmore's War 97
DuVal, William ix, 239, 255–6, 257,
    259, 260, 261–2, 266, 280

Eaton–Symmes Free School 4
entails, abolition 149
Eppes, Francis 20
Ethiopian Regiment 128–9
Ewald, Johann 171

Fauquier, Francis
    background 37–8
    and *partie quarree* 39, 40–2, 45,
        65
    and GW 73–4, 76–7
    political difficulties 48–9, 56,
        63–6, 67–9, 72, 76
    death & will 42, 76–8
Fleming, Judge William, Judge 276
Forbes, Gen. John 33–4
Foushee, Dr. William 255, 259, 267–8,
    284

France in French and Indian War
27–31, 33–4
role in revolution 138, 154, 160,
169–172, 176–7
Franklin, Benjamin 73,
at Continental Congress 117,
119–123, 130, 138
at Constitution Convention 188–9,
192–3
French spy 60–1

Gates, Gen. Horatio 153, 165
George II, King
George III, King 52, 59, 61, 70, 93, 97
Glebe Holding Case (Turpin v. Lock-ett) 226–7
Great Bridge, battle of 128–9
Grigsby, Hugh 206
Gwatkin, Rev. Thomas 109

Hamilton, Alexander
during revolution 171, 188
and US constitution 184, 186,
187–8, 201, 208 ·
in Washington's administration
210, 211
Harrison, Benjamin 99, 100–3
Hemings, Sally 209–10, 235–7
Henry, Patrick
studies law 50–1
as a lawyer 50–1, 53–5
and Jefferson 50–1, 168
in Parson's Cause 50–2
in House of Burgesses 56–62
and Stamp Act 58–62, 63–4
at Continental Congress 100
approach of revolution 83, 99,
100–3, 104, 106–7, 128
as revolutionary
as governor 154, 178
at Virginia Ratification x, 199,
203, 204–7

Hill v. Braxton 224
Hinde v. Pendleton 229–30
House of Burgesses 18–9, 23–4, 31
House of Delegates 134
Howell, Samuel 81
Hudgins v. Wrights 241–4, 246–7,
248–50, 276–279
Hylton v. Hamilton 224

Jay, John 120, 201
Jefferson, Thomas 1, 4, 45
and *partie quarree* 40–1, 65
student of GW 42–5
and Rebecca Burwell 44
as lawyer 80–1
and Patrick Henry 50, 58, 61
in House of Burgesses 80, 83
slavery reform attempt 80–1
*Summary View of the Rights of
British America* 95–7
at Continental Congress 119,
122–3
approach of revolution 83, 98–9,
100–3
in as revolutionary 130
and Virginia Constitution 130–4
Declaration of Independence 130,
134–6
as law reformer 139–140, 141–52,
283
as governor 154–7, 166, 168
Monticello 91, 92, 95, 167, 173,
209, 211, 221, 236–7
Martha (wife) 91, 176
Notes on the State of Virginia 5,
97–8, 147, 174–6, 183–4
and slavery 80–1, 145–8, 173
and GW 42–5, 91, 173, 212, 213,
252, 261, 262–4, 280
and government 183, 200
and Sally Hemings 209–10,
235–7

in Washington's administration 209, 210
Vice–President and President 211–2, 233, 234–5
Reaction to GW's death ix, x
Jennison, Nathaniel 247

Keith, George 3, 4
Kemp's Landing, battle of 128
Knowledge, Bill for a More General Diffusion of 144–5
Knox, Henry 210

Lafayette, Marquis de 167, 170, 182
Law in Virginia 6, 7–8, 43, 223–5, 247–8, 277–8
the practice of 7, 8–11, 20, 221–3
Lee, Francis L. 94
Lee, Light–horse Harry 200
Lee, Richard Henry 83, 94, 99, 100–3, 129–30, 200
Lee, Thomas Ludwell 140, 141–2
Lewis, Ann 11
Lewis, Zachary 9–10, 13
Lewis, Charles 202
Livingston Robert 130
Logan, Chief 97–8
Longsworth, Polly 273

Madison, James 131, 151–2,
at Constitutional Convention ix, 184, 185–6, 191, 192, 198
at Virginia ratification 200–205
Madison, Rev. James 156, 157–8, 177
Marbury v. Madison 161
Marsh, James 270–1
Marshall, John 152, 160–2, 200, 206, 231
Mason, George
approach of revolution 83, 100–3
and Virginia Bill of Rights 132–3
as law reformer 140, 141–2, 152

at Constitutional Convention 185, 191, 198, 200
at Virginia Ratification ix, 199, 203–4, 205
Maury, Rev. James 51–3
Maze v. Hamilton 223
McClurg, Dr. James 157, 185, 198, 256, 258, 261, 267, 284
McCraw, Dr. Samuel 257–8, 266
McCraw, Dr. James 255–6, 258, 261, 267, 284
Mercer, George 67–8
Minor, B.B. 32, 219, 275
Monroe, James ix, 203, 206, 232, 269
Monticello 91, 92, 95, 167, 173, 209, 211, 221, 236–7
Morris, Gouverneur 186
Munford, George Wythe 217, 220, 239, 262–4, 273
Munford, William Green
as GW's student x, 215
funeral oration for GW
Murray, John: *see Dunmore*

Nelson, Gen. Thomas Jr. 168
Nelson, Thomas 106
New York, battles in 138
Nicholas George 200, 205, 206
Nicholas, Phillip. N. 268. 270
Nicholas, Robert Carter 73, 106, 126, 128, 133
North, Lord Frederick 85, 107, 154
Notes on the State of Virginia 5, 97–8, 147, 174–6, 183–4

Olive Branch Petition 121

Page v. Pendleton and Lyons see British Debts Case
Paine, Tom 124–5, 141
Parson's Cause 47–8
Pendleton, Edmund ix,

as a lawyer 86–9, 212, 229–30
and slave raffle 88–9
approach of revolution 100–3
in revolution 99
and Virginia Bill of Rights 133
as law reformer 140, 141–2, 143,
    150, 152
as judge 154, 223–4, 226–7, 232,
    283
at Virginia ratification 200, 203,
    207
death of 227
Philadelphia 116–7, 153
Pinckney, Charles 184, 186, 234
Pistole dispute 22–3
Pitt, William, the Elder 33, 66
Pleasant (a slave) 257, 270
Pleasants v. Pleasants 230–2
Prentis, Joseph, Judge 268
Primogeniture 4–5, 7, 149
Prosser, Gabriel 232–3

Quakers 3–4,

Raleigh Tavern 83, 98,
Randolph, Edmund 162
    at Constitutional Convention
        185–6, 190, 198
    and Virginia ratification 200, 204,
        205
    in Washington's administration
        210, 242–4
    lawyer 231, 242–4, 246–7, 250,
        276–9
    and GW's will, death 259, 266–7,
        268, 273
Randolph, John 51, 73
Randolph, John of Roanoke 225
Randolph, Peter 61
Randolph, Peyton 22, 51, 60, 63, 83,
    99, 101–3, 109, 112, 115
Rathell, Mrs. 110

Revere, Paul 84, 105
Richmond 100, 160, 203, 216–7
Roane, Spencer, Judge 231, 276
Robinson, John 57–8, 63, 70–2, 229
Rochambeau, General 169
Rose, William 257–8, 266
Rush, Benjamin x
Rutledge, Edward 122

Saratoga, battle of 153–4
Seixis, Rabbi 217
Shays, Daniel 182–3
Sherman, Roger 120, 130
Skelton, Martha Wayles 92
slavery
    of Africans 5–6, 42, 80–1, 127–8,
        149, 171, 173, 233, 245,
        277–8
    freed slaves 195, 233
    of Amerindians 244–6
    law of 81, 197–8
    Somerset's Case 90–1
    Jefferson's reform attempt 81–2
    Gabriel Prosser's revolt
Small, William 39–40, 42, 65
Somerset's Case 90–1
Sons of Liberty 67, 69, 75
Stamp Act 55–6, 58–62, 66–9
St. George, Hamilton Usher 90, 172–3
*Summary View of the Rights of British
    America* 95–7
Sweney, George Wythe
    in GW's house 251–2
    suspicion of murders 257–8
    imprisonment & trials 257, 260–1,
        265–270, 274–5
    theories of GW's murder 270–4,
        282–4
    later life 275

Taliaferro, Elizabeth (wife of GW) see
    Wythe, Elizabeth

Taliaferro, Richard 25, 179. 194
Thoughts on Government 118–20, 130
Taylor, George 243–5, 277
Tazewell, Littleton Waller x, 202, 214
Tinsley, Peter 239–40, 256–7, 260
tobacco 5, 16, 47–8, 158, 180
Townshend duties 74–5
Trenton, battle of 141
Tucker, Beverly, Judge 219–20
Tucker, St. George, Judge 276,
   277–8
Turpin v. Lockett *see Glebe Holding*
   Case
Two Penny Act: *see Parson's Cause*
Tyler, John, Judge 268

Virginia Bill of Rights 131–2, 248–9
Virginia Constitution 130–3
Virginia Conventions 83, 98, 100,
Virginia, ratification of US Constitu-
   tion 199–208
Virginia, seal of 136
Virginia, society of 12–3, 16–7, 20–1,
   84

Walker, Anne 3
Walker, George 3–4
Walker, Quock 247–8
Waller, Benjamin 18–9,
Warrington, Thomas 49–50
Ward, Artemas, Gen. 112
Washington, George
   in French and Indian War 27–31,
      33–4
   in House of Burgesses 33–5
   and slave raffle 88–9
   client of GW 35–6, 88
   approach of revolution 83, 94, 99,
      100–3, 128
   as commander in chief 112–3,
      138–9, 141, 143, 153, 159,
      169–72, 179–80

   at Constitutional Convention
      184–5, 186–7, 189–90, 193
   President 208–10, 242–4
   death 233–4
Wayles, John 92
Webb, Tarlton 257, 265
West, Benjamin 213
William and Mary College 4, 33
   before revolution 39–40
   during revolution 155–8
   after revolution 176–8
   Wythe as professor: *see Wythe*
Williamsburg 15–6, 160, 168, 216
Wirt, William 53, 54, 87, 201, 268–9,
   274
Wright, Jackey 242–5, 246–7, 276–7
Wythe, Ann (wife of GW) 12, 13
Wythe, Anne (sister of GW) 5, 7
Wythe, Elizabeth (wife of GW) 25, 92,
   111, 192, 193–4
Wythe County 154
Wythe, Margaret (mother of GW) 3,4,
   5
   death 7
   relations with son 4
Wythe, George
   forebears 1,
   birth 1
   parent's death 4, 7
   at school 4
   appearance 21
   studies law 6–7
   marriage to Ann Lewis 12, 13
   marriage to Elizabeth Taliaferro
      25, 193–4
   religion of 42, 152, 217, 258
   and slavery 5, 42, 149, 195
   a lawyer 7–8
   as magistrate 24, 32–3, 49–50
   in Williamsburg
   as a lawyer 17, 35–72, 80, 86
      at Common Hall 19, 20–1

and Jefferson 42–5, 91, 212
in House of Burgesses
  member 33, 56, 63, 65
  attorney General 23, 73
  clerk of committees 18–9, 20
  clerk of House 74, 76, 80, 82–3,
    95
and Townshend duties 75
and Fauquier 73–4, 76–7
and *partie quarree* 39–41, 65
approach of revolution 56, 83, 94,
  100–3, 108–9
at Continental Congress 111ff,
  119–122, 135, 137
during American Revolution 109,
  169
and Virginia Constitution 130–4
designs seal of Virginia 136
signs Declaration of Independence
  137
and House of Delegates 143–4
as law reformer 139–140, 141–52
at Constitution Convention 181,
  183, 185, 187, 189, 190
at Virginia ratification 200, 201–2,
  206, 207–8
as an educator
private students 179, 214, 215

professor at William and Mary
  157–8, 176–7, 214
as judge 154, 215, 221–4, 225–7,
  229–32, 241–4
seal of court 213–4
decision of Cases in Virginia
  223–5, 230
in Richmond 215–7, 238–40
death of Wythe
sickness 253–5, 257–8
death and funeral 262–4, 280
trial of Sweney: *see Sweney*
theories of GW's murder: *see
  Sweney*
Wythe, Thomas (great grandfather of
  GW) 2
Wythe, Thomas (grandfather of GW)
  2
Wythe, Thomas (father of GW) 2–3, 4
Wythe, Thomas (brother of GW) 5,
  19, 24
Wythe, Anne (sister) 5
  marriage of

Yorktown, battle of 170–2